Sisters, Secrets
and Sacrifice

Sisters, Secrets and Sacrifice

A True Story

Susan Ottaway

HARPER

An imprint of HarperCollins*Publishers*
77–85 Fulham Palace Road,
Hammersmith, London W6 8JB

www.harpercollins.co.uk

First published by HarperCollins*Publishers* 2013

1 3 5 7 9 10 8 6 4 2

A catalogue record of this book is
available from the British Library

ISBN 978-0-00-749305-0

Printed and bound in Great Britain by
Clays Ltd, St Ives plc

MIX
Paper from
responsible sources
FSC™ C007454

Photographic credits
All images courtesy of Odile Nearne,
unless otherwise stated

In loving memory of
Muriel Ottaway, my wonderful mother
1922–2012

Contents

Acknowledgements

A book of this kind could not have been written without the help of many people, and I am very grateful for all the kindnesses shown to me during the writing of *Sisters, Secrets and Sacrifice*.

I would like to thank Odile Nearne for sharing her memories of her aunts, Didi and Jacqueline Nearne, for allowing me to use her family photos, for sending me copies of family letters and documents, for her patience in answering my questions and for her encouragement in writing the book in the first place. She is justifiably proud of her aunts and did not want the stories of their modesty, bravery and sacrifice to die with them.

I am also very grateful to the following people: Mrs Debbie Alexander, RAF Headquarters Air Command, for the information about Frederick Nearne's RAF career; Mr and Mrs Murray Anderson, for permission to use the photograph of pilot Murray 'Andy' Anderson who flew the Lysander in which Didi went to France at the start of her SOE mission; Ian M. Arrow, HM Coroner for Torbay and South Devon District; Jenny Campbell-Davys, Didi's friend, for sharing some of her stories about her friend with me; Laurie Davidson for translating numerous French documents and letters for me, and Laurie's friend Tony for managing to decipher some of the handwriting in letters written during the Second World War; Sharon Davidson, for her legal advice; Iain Douglas of Lisburne Crescent in Torquay; Sue Fox, excellent New York researcher, for her patience in examining files at the United Nations Archive and locating documents and information about Jacqueline Nearne's career at the organization; Elaine Harrison at Torbay and District Funeral Service; David Haviland for his help and advice; Pat Hobrough of the Torbay and South Devon District Coroner's office; Paul Jordan at Brighton History Centre; Bob Large, a pilot who flew SOE agents in and out of France with the 'Moon Squadrons'; Messieurs P. Landais and Jean-Louis Landais, and Jessica Fortin who wrote to me on behalf of Mme S. Landais, all in answer to my queries about Didi's friend Yvette Landais; Monsieur Hugues Landais, the nephew of Yvette Landais; Monsieur Pierre Landais, Yvette's brother, for his letters and his kindness in sending me the information about his sister and her photos, and for suggesting other sources of information; Ian Ottaway, for allowing me to use his photo of the Westland Lysander; John Pentreath, Devon County Royal British Legion; Noreen Riols, a former member of the SOE, for her help; Solange Roussier, at the Archives Nationales, Paris; Susan Taylor, at the Mitchell Library, Glasgow; and Captain Rollo Young, the Army officer who helped Didi get back to England after securing her release from American custody at the end of the war.

My thanks also to my agent, Andrew Lownie, without whose help, encouragement and advice I would not have written the book at all; to Anna Valentine at HarperCollins for her enthusiasm, patience and kindness; to Anne Askwith for editing the book; and to my family for their constant support and encouragement, especially Nick, who has always been there for me, more than ever throughout this particularly difficult year.

Prologue

At the end of August 2010, after several weeks of sunshine and fine weather, a strong wind began blowing in from the sea. The hitherto blue sky disappeared to be replaced by low cloud, and the Devon resort of Torquay was subjected to an unseasonable downpour, which continued for several days.

High above the town's harbour, in a small flat in Lisburne Crescent, an elegant Victorian Grade II listed building, lived an elderly lady, Eileen Nearne. Although 89 years old, Eileen was still quite sprightly and, despite the steep slopes of Torquay's roads, could often be seen walking into town with her large shopping bags to fetch her groceries. Sometimes when the weather was fine she sat on a bench in the communal gardens in front of the flats, reading a newspaper and occasionally exchanging pleasantries with one or other of her neighbours. But the people who lived in the flats at Lisburne Crescent knew only two things about their neighbour: the first was that she spoke English with a foreign accent and the second, that she loved cats. They knew about her fondness for cats because she had rescued, and looked after, a ginger stray. The little animal was the only thing she ever spoke about to her neighbours and was the reason they called her, when she was out of earshot, Eileen the cat lady.

Although as the rain fell her immediate neighbours remarked to each other that they had not seen the cat lady for a few days, they were not unduly worried, reasoning that she was simply staying indoors to avoid the worst of the weather. But when the sun came out again and Eileen had still not appeared, they began to grow concerned. She had always guarded her privacy closely, so they knew that if one of them were to knock on her door to check that she was all right, she would not answer. They were uncertain what to do. Most of the neighbours thought of Eileen as a rather sad old spinster who never had visitors and did not have any family or friends. But although during the many years that she had lived at Lisburne Crescent no one had ever managed to get close to her or discover anything about her life, she was a harmless old soul and no one liked to think that she might be ill or have had a fall.

September came and Eileen was still in hiding. It was obvious by now that something had happened to her and, having no contact details or name for anyone who might be interested, one of the neighbours called the police. When they arrived they had to break into her small flat and there, on her bedroom floor, they found her body. A doctor was summoned and declared that she had been dead for several days – perhaps even a week. He ordered a post mortem and the pathologist reported to the Torquay coroner that the death was due to natural causes: Eileen had died of a heart attack brought about by heart disease and hardening of the arteries. An inquest was not necessary, so the local funeral home was contacted and preparations were set in motion for a publicly funded funeral.

The police, meanwhile, were sorting through the contents of Eileen's tiny flat in an effort to find some evidence of family or friends. It was a difficult task. The flat was very small and filled with furniture – far too much for a home of that size. There were also cupboards filled with beautiful but rather old-fashioned dresses, ornaments, books, religious pamphlets, letters and photos. The police did not have time to read more than a few of the letters, which seemed to be old, and found nothing to suggest that she was important to anyone. The neighbours to whom they spoke could only confirm that they were not aware of any family.

Satisfied that they had done their best and that there was nothing to give any clues about her next of kin, the police were on the point of giving up the search when they came across some French coins, old French newspaper cuttings and medals. These included the British 1939–1945 Defence Medal and the War Medal 1939–1945, which were awarded to many people during the Second World War. The police took more notice when they came across the France and Germany Star, which was awarded only to those who had done one or more days' service in France, Belgium, Luxembourg, Netherlands or Germany between 6 June 1944 and 8 May 1945 – D-Day and VE Day. They were even more surprised when they discovered an MBE and the French Croix de Guerre. Eileen Nearne in her later years may have been a rather solitary, eccentric figure but in her youth she had clearly done something special. With the clue of the medals, it didn't take long for them to find out that she had worked for the Special Operations Executive, the secret organization that had sent agents to occupied countries during the Second World War and which had been tasked by Prime Minister Winston Churchill with 'setting Europe ablaze'.

Her neighbours were flabbergasted. Damian Warren said that he recalled seeing a letter addressed to Eileen Nearne MBE. He said that he had asked Eileen about it and that she had dismissed it as being a mistake.[1] Another of the residents, Iain Douglas, who lived at the opposite end of the crescent, said of her:

> She was indeed a very strange lady, and quite reclusive. She would walk around all day with some large bags in tow and I used to wonder if she could only go into her flat at a certain time. I did wonder if she was part vagrant sometimes. She would sit outside waiting for ages. She had long, grey, unkempt hair. She would scurry away from anyone who approached her and on the sole occasion I said hello to her, she looked so shocked and horrified that I never attempted [to] again. It was a huge surprise to us when her past surfaced following her death.[2]

Yet another neighbour, Steven Cook, declared: 'We thought she may have been in the French Resistance from rumours and hearsay over the years. I was very surprised at the extent of her heroism. You would never have thought it, as she never spoke of it.'[3]

Soon the story reached the local and then the national newspapers. Some articles said that she had been a spy; others claimed that she was just like Charlotte Gray, the eponymous heroine of Sebastian Faulks's novel. Neither claim was true. She had in fact been a wireless operator, sending and receiving messages for the leader of a

Resistance circuit in Paris, and so was clearly neither a spy nor anything like the fictional Charlotte Gray. Similar reports were given on national radio and on the television news bulletins, but still no relatives appeared.

John Pentreath, the Royal British Legion's manager for Devon, was reported as saying: 'We will certainly be there at her funeral. We will do her as proud as we can ... She sounds like a hugely remarkable lady and we are sorry she kept such a low profile, and that we only discovered the details after her death.'[4]

By the time the international newspapers had taken up the story of the death of the courageous old lady, genealogists and probate researchers Fraser & Fraser had begun searching for any heirs. They soon discovered that Eileen was one of four children and that she had never married. Her sister was deceased and had also remained single, but her two brothers, who had both died in their early 50s, had married and each had had a child. The elder brother had had a son who had died in 1975 but the younger of the two brothers had had a daughter, and Fraser & Fraser believed that she was still alive.

One of the company's researchers managed to find Eileen Nearne's niece, Odile, in Italy. She had married an Italian and was living in Verona. A telephone call was made to her and she was informed that her aunt had died. Since everyone believed Eileen was alone and unloved, her niece's reaction to the news was, perhaps, not quite what they had expected: Odile was distraught.

Over the years Odile had regularly come to England with her family to visit Eileen and had last seen her aunt six months before her death. Eileen Nearne was a very important figure in her niece's life and Odile was devoted to her. She was not only inconsolable when she learnt the details of her lonely death but also horrified to discover that her aunt had been destined to have a pauper's funeral, with no one to mourn her loss, and quickly made plans to come to England. After her arrival she took over the funeral arrangements and was able to answer many of the questions about her aunt's life that had been puzzling the people of Torquay and reporters from around the world. And as she answered them, it soon became clear that almost everything that had been believed about Eileen Nearne was incorrect, and the true story of her amazing life, along with that of her elder sister Jacqueline, who was also an SOE agent, began to unfold.

CHAPTER I

Exile

Eileen Nearne was born at 6 Fulham Road, west London, on 15 March 1921, the youngest of the four children of John and Mariquita Nearne. When her father registered her birth two days later, he gave her name as Eileen Marie. It seems to have been the only time in her life that her middle name was spelt this way, as all other documents refer to her as Eileen Mary – a strange choice, as Mary was also one of her sister's names. In any case, Eileen was known to all, friends and family alike, as Didi. The name stuck and those who knew her well called her Didi for the rest of her life.

John Francis Nearne, Didi's father, was the son of a doctor also named John[1] and so, to avoid confusion, was known as Jack. He was a 23-year-old medical student when he married French-born Mariquita Carmen de Plazaola at Marylebone Register Office on 6 November 1913. Mariquita, then 26 years old, was the daughter of Spanish Count Mariano de Plazaola and his French wife, the Marquise of La Roche de Kerandraon.[2] By the time Jack and Mariquita's first child, a boy they named Francis, was born on 16 July 1914, the couple had moved from their London address, 70 Margaret Street, Marylebone, to Brighton.

With the onset of the First World War in 1914, Jack became a private in the Royal Army Medical Corps. Mariquita remained at the family home, 32 West Hill Street, a neat Victorian terraced house just a short walk from the beach. It was here that on 27 May 1916, their second child, Jacqueline Françoise Mary Josephine, was born.

After Jack's military service ended he gave up being a doctor and became a dispensing chemist. The family left the seaside and returned to London, setting up home at 58 Perham Road in Fulham, another Victorian terraced building, and, on 20 January 1920, their second son, Frederick John, was born. The family was completed the following spring with the arrival of Didi. As the baby of the family Didi was rather spoilt and, according to her own account, she was a very naughty child.[3]

In 1923, with Europe still in turmoil as a result of the war, Jack and Mariquita decided to leave England and move to France. Mariquita's parents owned several houses and apartments there, and offered the family an apartment in Paris, to which they moved with their young family.

Of all the children Francis, the eldest, was the one who had the most difficulties in adjusting to the move. He was nine years old and had already completed nearly four years of schooling in England. He couldn't speak French but was sent to a French school in the rue Raynouard, on the right bank of the river Seine, in the hope that he would soon settle down there and learn both his lessons and the language. The school was close to his mother's birthplace at Auteuil in the capital's wealthy 16th *arrondissement*, a pleasant area his mother knew well. But Francis was not happy at school. He found the lessons complicated and

difficult and, despite his mother speaking to him in French
in an effort to help him, could understand only a few
words. It was a good school but Francis did not do at all
well and was very disheartened by his lack of progress. A
shy, sensitive boy, he found it difficult to make the friends
who might have made his assimilation into the French
education system a little easier. He had to endure this
unhappy situation for a year before his parents took him
away. They looked for another school that might suit him
better and enrolled him in one in Le Vésinet in the north-
west of Paris where, for six months, he received intensive
coaching to bring him up to the standard required for a
boy of his age. It was an unfortunate start for the poor
little lad, and his lack of early success damaged his self-
confidence to such an extent that he never really recovered.
The feeling of failure was exacerbated when his younger
siblings managed to fit in at school with far fewer difficulties than he had had and he was too young to understand
that it was because they had been brought to France at an
earlier age than he, so their transition to the French way of
life was much easier.

Jacqueline, who was seven years old when she arrived in
France, had a much more straightforward time at the
exclusive Convent of Les Oiseaux at Verneuil to the north-
west of Paris, being only a few months behind her French
classmates, who didn't start school until they were six
years old. She also found it less of a problem to speak
French and quickly settled in to her new life.

The two youngest members of the family, Frederick and
Didi, had not attended an English school at all, as neither
was old enough, and by the time they went to French
schools they were both able to speak the language as well

as French children, so they didn't have to make the adjustments their elder siblings had; their education was completely French, from beginning to end.

Mariquita was determined that all her children should be brought up in the Roman Catholic faith. She herself had been educated at a Catholic convent and she intended that both her daughters should have a similar start in life. Didi enjoyed the rituals of the Catholic Church and at a very early age she found a strong faith in God, which stayed with her all her life. Her mother never had to insist that Didi attend church services, as she went willingly without any prompting. Jacqueline once remarked that Didi was the most religious member of the entire family, although they were all believers.

Didi was never far away from her sister. She hero-worshipped Jacqueline, and wanted to be like her and do whatever she did. It must sometimes have been irritating for Jacqueline to have her little sister trying to tag along wherever she and her friends went, but she was very fond of Didi and didn't like to turn the little girl away unless she really had to.

After two years in the French capital the family was on the move again, this time to a terraced house that had been given to Mariquita by her parents, 260 boulevard Saint-Beuve on the seafront at Boulogne-sur-Mer. Francis and Frederick attended the Institution Haffreingue, a Catholic school, while Jacqueline was enrolled at the Ursuline convent in the town, where before long Didi joined her. Didi loved her new home. It was the first time she had lived on the coast and the beginning of her lifelong love of the sea.

The house in Boulogne was a happy home and the family felt very comfortable there. Jack Nearne had attempted to learn and improve his French but had had little success. The language didn't come naturally to him and he was not confident about speaking it. Despite living in France for the rest of his life, he couldn't ever be described as being fluent in either spoken or written French. This rather hampered his employment prospects but, as he was part of a wealthy family following his marriage to Mariquita, it did not seem to be a major problem. His ineptitude with the language gave his children an advantage, as well as amusing them greatly, because it meant that in order to communicate with their father they had to speak fluent English as well as French, a skill that would serve them all well in their future lives.

Both parents encouraged the children to work hard at school and to read or listen to music when at home. Jacqueline and Didi were avid readers. Jacqueline liked books such as *Vanity Fair*, Sherlock Holmes stories and *The Forsyte Saga*. Didi preferred religious books and didn't like novels at all. They both enjoyed the music of Strauss, Chopin and Beethoven and later, when they were older, that of Glenn Miller, Frank Sinatra, Dean Martin and Jean Sablon.

During the school holidays Jacqueline liked taking part in all kinds of outdoor activities. She loved sport and played for a girls' hockey team called the Gulls, along with her friends Claire Turl, Marie, Jeanne and Madeleine Louchet, Anne and Marie Louise Cailliez and Nelly Pincedé. She also loved the countryside around Boulogne and cycled to local beauty spots or went for long walks with her friends. When they all got together at the home of one of the group they played cards, told each other jokes and laughed a lot. Jacqueline also liked

Jacqueline's membership card for her
local hockey team, the Gulls.

to knit, and she made lots of colourful socks for herself
and her friends.[4]

When she was old enough Didi also played hockey, and
she and her friends laughed a lot too. They all enjoyed fooling around, no one more so than Didi, but she also had a
serious side. She liked being with other people, but was
also able to keep busy and was quite content when she was
alone. She was good at art, and liked to paint and make
little clay models; and, of course, she had her belief in God.

In 1928 Mariquita's mother died and left her house in
Nice to her daughter. By 1931 the family had packed up
their belongings, closed up the house in Boulogne-sur-Mer
and moved to Nice, to 60 bis, avenue des Arènes de Cimiez.
Situated in the old part of Nice, in the gentle hills behind
the coastline, the house was only a short distance from the
seafront and the elegant promenade des Anglais, playground of the rich and famous. The family would live there
very happily until the Germans invaded France in 1940.

Francis left school in 1930 when he was 16 and went on to a commercial college, where he took a business course and, having passed it, became a representative for a confectionery company. Over the next few years he had a variety of sales jobs that never seemed to last long, so, tiring of sales, he tried working as a barman. Then in 1938, against an increasingly difficult economic backdrop, he lost yet another job and, despite applying for different positions, remained unemployed for the next two years.[5]

Frederick left school just before the start of the war and also found it difficult to obtain work. He considered going back to England to see if it would be any easier to get a job there and was still weighing up his options when the Germans marched into Poland in September 1939. Didi had not even begun to look for work by then, as she had only just left school at the age of 18. She wanted to be a beautician, but with the political unrest that was making itself felt more and more each day, and the ever-present question of what the immediate future might bring, her parents convinced her to stay at home with them until what was happening became clearer. When the war started she gave up the idea, pushing it to the back of her mind in the belief that she would be able pursue her chosen career once the war was over.

Of all the children, Jacqueline was the only one who found a secure job. When she left school she too became a sales representative, working for an office equipment company, and, although based in Nice, she travelled all over the country. In those days such an occupation was considered to be quite an unusual one for a girl but she enjoyed the work, and the travel, which allowed her to see a lot of the countryside. Although she didn't know it at the time, it would be a foretaste of what was in store for her a few years later.

For the first few months of the war nothing really changed for the Nearne family. The sun was still shining over their home in Nice; Jacqueline was doing well in her job; Francis, who had recently married a young Frenchwoman, Thérèse Poulet, was continuing to look for work; Frederick was thinking about going to England to join the Royal Air Force; and Didi remained at home with her mother and father.

Then, on 10 May 1940, German troops swept into Belgium, Luxembourg and Holland, and all three countries capitulated. Two weeks later Calais and Boulogne were attacked, and the British Expeditionary Force, pinned down by the Germans in the coastal town of Dunkirk, was evacuated, along with several thousand French troops, in what was known as Operation Dynamo. By the middle of June Paris had fallen to the Germans and, on 22 June, the French signed an armistice in the forest of Compiègne, north of Paris, in the same railway carriage in which the Germans had surrendered at the end of the First World War. The threatened war had suddenly become real.

Some months earlier Jacqueline had gone to Boulogne to make sure that the family home on the boulevard Saint-Beuve was secure. The furniture was covered with dust sheets, the curtains drawn, and all the windows and doors locked, but there was little else that she could do to ensure its safety in the event of the German invasion they had all prayed would not take place. Now that had happened, and the family began to wonder what would become of them if enemy troops reached them in the south of France. They didn't have long to wait for their answer.

Following the French surrender, the country was divided into two parts. The northern part was occupied by the Germans, while the southern sector remained in French hands, with the whole country nominally under the government of Marshal Philippe Pétain, hero of the Battle of Verdun of 1916, who had taken over when Prime Minister Paul Reynaud resigned days before the armistice. Pétain, no longer showing any heroic qualities, based his regime in the city of Vichy, from where he and the puppet administration did nothing for the French people, bowing completely to the will of the Germans. It was an enormous betrayal. Three days after the French surrender Pétain's betrayal was compounded by the signing of another armistice, this time with Italy, and the formation of a demilitarized zone within France, which included the cities of Nice and Grenoble and which was administered by occupying Italian forces.

Foreign nationals were being forced to move from the coastal areas of France and the Nearne family was no exception. Even French-born Mariquita was regarded as being foreign, as she was married to an Englishman. The Nearnes were given just eight days to pack up and leave their home in Nice and find somewhere else to live.[6] The edict that forced them to move was known as '*residence forcée*' – enforced residence in an area, where residents were kept under police surveillance and life was often made very difficult for no apparent reason, other than that they were not French. The seaside house in Boulogne was obviously not an option as a place to relocate to and they doubted that they would be able to return to the Paris apartment even if they had wanted to, because the capital was swarming with Germans. After a hurried discussion,

Jack and Mariquita elected to go to the Grenoble area which, although in Italian-occupied France, was where Francis and his wife had settled. Thérèse was expecting the couple's first baby later that summer and they wanted to remain close for the arrival of their first grandchild.[7]

The family home at avenue des Arènes de Cimiez was leased to a Frenchwoman at an inexpensive rent and the Nearnes left Nice, taking as many of their personal belongings as they could carry to a hotel in Grenoble, where they remained while searching for a new home. Eventually in rue Adolphe Muguet, Saint-Egrève, in the mountains north-west of the city, they found a large, rambling old villa that needed restoring and they were able to purchase it. It was nothing like the comfortable home they had had in Nice, although the views of the mountains were beautiful. But at least they had their own house again and their enforced move meant that they were closer to the newest member of the family, a boy born on 24 August, whom Thérèse and Francis named Jack, after his paternal grandfather.[8]

Gradually the Nearnes managed to introduce some degree of comfort to the draughty old house, but Jack and Mariquita, their two daughters and younger son never really regarded the villa as a home. For them it was just somewhere to stay until the Nazis had been defeated, when they could reclaim the house in Nice and find out what had become of their other home in Boulogne and their Paris apartment.

By the late autumn of 1940 Frederick, along with so many other young men, had decided that, with no job and the ever-present threat of being sent for forced labour to Germany, he could no longer remain in France and would therefore go to England. It must have been a time of great anxiety for his parents, but they knew better than to try to persuade him to remain with them in Grenoble, believing that Britain would be a safer place for him than German-occupied France. Upon arrival in England he volunteered for the RAF, was sent to the recruits' centre at RAF Station Uxbridge in Middlesex, and as Aircraftman 2nd Class Frederick John Nearne (1270875) began his service career on 1 November 1940. A month later he was posted to Ford in Sussex and six days later started his training at HQ Number 17 (Training) Group, part of Coastal Command. He remained there for a year before being posted, on 5 January 1942, to the Middle East Command, where he served at the RAF station in Amman, Jordan; the Middle East Torpedo (Training) school; Lydda (now in Israel); and various maintenance and operational training units in the Levant. He eventually returned to England and received his discharge on 23 October 1946.[9]

No longer seen as the well-to-do French family that they had previously appeared to be, the members of the Nearne family who remained in France were now regarded, at least by the authorities, as foreigners – citizens of an enemy state – and had to get on with their lives as best they could. Since they were unable to find any of the domestic help that they had formerly relied upon, Jacqueline and Didi had to help Mariquita run the house. One of their tasks was to collect and chop firewood, which was always in short supply but which they needed both for warmth and as fuel for cooking, and they helped with the shopping, cleaning, washing, ironing and cooking. Neither girl minded having to help with these chores – Didi even began to enjoy cooking – but they both minded very much about the reason they had had to move to the house in the first place.

Although they were British nationals, they had almost no memories of the country of their birth and spoke English with French accents. France was their home and they loved their life there. But as time went by and they saw how Britain was standing alone in the fight against the Germans, they began to think that perhaps they too should be doing something for the war effort. The war had made Jacqueline realize how patriotic she felt towards this small country, even though it was so unfamiliar to her. From that moment she knew that she would not be able to remain in France, subjected to the will of the Nazis and the weak-minded French appeasers who had formed some sort of a collaborative government. Slowly over the next few months, perhaps inspired by her younger brother's decision to leave home, she came to the conclusion that she too would have to go to England and do something to help Britain fight the Germans, although she didn't have any idea how she was going to do it. She discussed the situation with Didi, who immediately said that she wanted to go with her. Jacqueline was nervous about this, as Didi was still very young and quite naive. But once Didi had an idea in her head, nothing would stop her. If her sister was going off to fight, then so was she.

Meanwhile time passed slowly. The girls had made friends in Saint-Egrève but there was no possibility of employment for either of them. At an age when they should have had lots to do, they were stuck in their mountain hideaway, bored with their enforced inactivity and frustrated that what should have been the most exciting years of their lives were passing them by. For Didi at least, there was a glimpse of that excitement when she met her first boyfriend.[10] Andy was a pleasant young man, with a cheeky grin that showed off his slightly protruding front teeth. He was smitten by Didi, but although she was fond of him, the excitement of her first romance couldn't prevent her from thinking about escaping to England.

Jacqueline was eager to leave for England as soon as possible and, as they were both still British citizens, she and Didi contacted the British consulate in Lyons and obtained British passports. Jack and Mariquita, understandably, did not want them to go but knew that, as with Fred, it would be wrong to try to stop them. So at the beginning of 1942, not knowing if they would ever see their daughters again, they reluctantly said goodbye to Jacqueline and Didi and waved them off on a train bound for Marseilles, at the start of what would undoubtedly be a difficult and dangerous journey.

Once there the girls hoped to find a boat to take them out of the country but they were unaware of what conditions were now like outside their own sheltered world. Although both in their 20s – Jacqueline was by then 26 and Didi 21 – they were, after all, convent girls and had had protected lives thus far, being cosseted by their wealthy family. Although Jacqueline had travelled for her work before the war, she had had no experience of how everyday life in France had been affected after the German invasion. Neither girl had realized that because Marseilles was a port there were very rigorous checks, and they were distressed when they were refused permission to continue on their journey and were sent straight back to Grenoble.

Undaunted, they again contacted the British consulate to ask, this time, for advice on the best way to get to Britain, and were told to stay away from the coastline and try to get to Portugal via Spain. Portugal was officially neutral but had strong sympathies for the Allied cause. Spain, also officially neutral, favoured the Axis powers and there were German spies all over the country, but the sisters were sure that they would be able to reach England. The journey would still be dangerous, but they were determined to succeed and knew that they were better prepared than on their first attempt. Although it was a difficult time to be leaving their home and their parents, they had each other and each girl knew that she could rely on her sister completely.

In April they again said goodbye to their parents and this time they reached the Spanish border by train, managed to cross the country without problems and entered Portugal, where they were given transit visas enabling them to travel onwards to another country. Making their way to Lisbon, they went directly to the British consulate there and asked for more help. The consul told them that he would try to find them a ship to take them out of Portugal, so they booked into a small hotel, where they stayed for nearly three weeks, contacting the consulate at regular intervals to see if there was any information for them. Eventually the consul had news and it was good. He told them that he had found a ship that would soon be leaving for Gibraltar and the captain would be willing to take them on board. He gave them the name of the vessel and of the captain, and advised them to contact him as soon as possible.

The sisters immediately hurried down to the docks to meet the man, who was a jovial Englishman. He told them that although he had never carried passengers before he would be willing to take them, and so the arrangement was made. Jacqueline and Didi went back to their hotel, collected their bags and paid the bill. They returned to the ship and found that the captain had moved out of his cabin so that they could share it and have some privacy from the all-male crew on the voyage. When they reached their new quarters they could hardly believe what they found. The captain had filled the cabin with flowers for them and decorated other parts of the vessel with more flowers. It was such a kind gesture and they were very touched by his thoughtfulness. They reached Gibraltar without any problems and, after docking, had only three days to wait before continuing on the next stage of their journey. This time they were bound for Glasgow.

The entire expedition had taken around five weeks and had been very tiring but, in May 1942, as the ship made its way up the west coast of Scotland and into the river Clyde, Jacqueline and Didi were elated to have finally reached Britain. As they presented their passports they saw that some people were being directed to what seemed to be a holding area and discovered that they were refugees who had nowhere to go. Although the girls intended to stay with family friends in London, they were nervous that they too might be regarded as refugees, so they gave the name and address of a distant cousin, Mrs Plunkett of Heaton House, Cheshunt, Hertfordshire,[11] thinking that they might stand a better chance of going through the formalities successfully if it was believed that they were going to be living with family. Whether or not they were actually in danger of being classified as refugees is doubtful. But they had had enough of bureaucracy and didn't want to take any chances, now that they were so close to their destination. They needn't have worried. Handing back their passports, the official waved them through the barrier and they were free.

The train journey to London took hours and left them feeling exhausted. They eventually arrived and, looking for somewhere to get a drink and something to eat, they came across a Lyons Corner House and decided to order afternoon tea to celebrate reaching the capital. They sat down and looked around them at the other customers. Everything seemed so much better than it had been in France. They even spotted someone eating a piece of cake and could hardly believe their eyes; they had not seen such luxury for a long time. When the waitress came to take their order they asked for tea and then, rather hesitantly, enquired if there was any chocolate cake. The waitress, noticing their foreign accents, stood and glared at them, her hands on her hips, and then snorted in disgust and enquired sarcastically, 'I suppose you have not heard there is a war on?'[12] They didn't get their cake that day but, remembering what they had just endured in order to reach the relative freedom of London, they laughed at the waitress's reaction. Refreshed by cups of tea, they found their way to the home of their family friends, Odile and George, at 97 Darenth Road, Stamford Hill, N16. Now all they had to do was find some war work.

CHAPTER 2

Secrets and Lies

It had not occurred to either sister that they might have problems finding suitable work on arriving in England and as they began to receive rejection after rejection they started to become despondent. Surely there must be something suitable for two intelligent girls who were fluent in English and French?

Jacqueline applied to the Women's Royal Naval Services – the WRNS – whose advertising slogan at that time was 'Join the Wrens and free a man for the fleet' and was called for an interview. She set off with high hopes, but these were dashed when she was told that they needed drivers. Her disappointment was compounded when she was rejected for the post of driver after admitting that she had never driven in the blackout. Didi fared no better. She almost obtained a position as a barrage-balloon operator but was deemed unsuitable for the role. The sisters were beginning to think that they had wasted their time and effort in coming to England. In desperation, they contacted the Ministry of Labour, stressing their language abilities.

Life in England wasn't all a disappointment. Although Jacqueline and Didi stuck closely together there were times when they went their own ways and met new people. Soon after arriving in London Jacqueline met a young army cadet called Jimmie and they went out together a few times before he was posted. He extracted a promise from her to write to him and said that he would like to see her again when he came back to London on leave. He even told her that he had seen a brooch that he wanted to buy for her.[1] It was flattering, as he was obviously quite keen on her, but soon all thoughts of the new friendship were forgotten when Jacqueline received a letter, sent to Mrs Plunkett's address in Cheshunt, from a Captain Jepson at the War Office. Dated 5 June 1942, it said:

> Dear Miss Nearne,
>   Your name has been passed to me as that of someone possessing qualifications which may be of value in a phase of the war effort. If you are available for interview I would be glad to see you at the above address at 3.30 p.m. on Thursday 25th June, 1942.
>   I would be glad if you would let me know whether you can come or not.
>   Yours truly,
>   Selwyn Jepson
>   Captain.

The address that Captain Jepson gave was Room 055a, War Office, SW1. Jacqueline wrote back immediately, saying that she would be pleased to meet him on 25 June. She told Didi about it but asked her not to say anything to anyone else, as the letter was vague enough either to be something very important or to mean nothing at all; she was also beginning to feel embarrassed about her difficulties in obtaining employment. Jacqueline was eager to

Room 055a,
War Office,
S.W.1.

SJ/1322.   5th June, 1942.

Miss J. Nearne,
        Heaton House,
            Cheshunt, Herts.

Dear Miss Nearne,

        Your name has been passed to me
as that of someone possessing
qualifications which may be of value
in a phase of the war effort. If you
are available for interview I would
be glad to see you at the above address
at 3.30 p.m. on Thursday 25th June, 1942.

        I would be glad if you would
let me know whether you can come or not.

                    Yours truly,

                    Selwyn Jepson

                    Captain.

know what this 'phase of the war effort' meant, but she
had nearly three weeks to wait until the appointed date
and the time passed slowly. Didi was also impatient to
receive her own letter inviting her for an interview, which
she was convinced would soon arrive. It didn't and, as the

time got closer for Jacqueline's interview, Didi kept remind-
ing her to ask why she hadn't been invited too. Jacqueline
had to promise her several times that she would make a
point of asking before her sister was satisfied.

Thursday, 25 June arrived and Jacqueline, dressed in a
smart but understated outfit, left Stamford Hill to travel to
the War Office. There she was met by Selwyn Jepson
himself and ushered into a small room. Jepson was a
quietly spoken man, nothing like how Jacqueline had
imagined a military officer would be, and the room, apart
from two hard chairs and a small table, was empty. There
were no personal touches, no books or manuals, no charts
or maps, no telephone or framed photo on a desk.
Jacqueline was confused by the surroundings and by now
rather worried about the interview, but when Jepson began
to speak to her, asking her questions about her previous
employment, her family background and her reasons for
coming to England, his calm manner put her at her ease.
She found herself telling him about her family and what
had happened to them after the fall of France, how her
brother was already in England in the Royal Air Force and
how she desperately wanted to do something that would
make a difference in winning the war.

Jepson considered everything she had said and then
asked her how she would feel about going back to France.
She immediately wondered if it would be as a spy and
asked him if that was what he meant. He told her that it
would not exactly be as a spy but that it would be in an
undercover role and that there were risks involved. He
explained that if she were selected – and at that stage this
was by no means certain – she would be enrolled in the
First Aid Nursing Yeomanry (FANY), which would give

her a cover story for her friends and family, as the work he was suggesting was so secret that she mustn't tell anyone at all what they had discussed. He advised her to go home and think hard about what he had said, and told her that he would write to her again to let her know whether or not he thought she would be suitable.

With the interview at an end Jacqueline suddenly remembered her promise to Didi, and told Jepson that she had a younger sister who had come to England with her and who was also keen to find useful war work. He thanked her for the information and for attending the interview, and repeated that he would be in touch very soon. Shaking her by the hand, he pointed her towards the exit and was gone.

Jacqueline emerged from the War Office feeling dazed and confused. She was relieved that there was a possibility of employment for her but she hadn't dreamt that it would be anything like this. Although she had been keen to use her French language skills, she thought the role might possibly have been as an interpreter or a translator. She hadn't considered going back to France as a secret agent and, after all the problems that she and Didi had had getting out of France, felt that it was ironic that if all went well she would soon be back where she had started.

In the short time that it had taken to attend the interview her entire world had turned upside down. She was elated yet scared, and she couldn't wait to get home so that she could tell Didi what had happened. But as she walked along the road she suddenly realized that she couldn't tell Didi, as she had been told that she mustn't tell anyone. Her mind turned to ways of concealing what she now knew about the job. She knew that, try as she might, it would be almost impossible to fool her sister; they were so close that she felt Didi would know immediately if she lied to her. She didn't want to lie but neither did she want to disclose what she had been told. She also realized with an uncomfortable jolt that if Didi discovered what the job really was, she too would want to return to France; and, while she was quite prepared to be put in such a perilous position herself, she was horrified by the thought of her young, unworldly sister being subjected to the same danger. Her dilemma occupied her thoughts throughout her journey home.

When she reached Stamford Hill an anxious Didi was waiting for her. Wanting to know everything that had happened, she began firing questions at her sister. Who had interviewed her? What sort of a job was it? Had she been successful? Her final question was the one that Jacqueline had been dreading: was there a possibility that there might be another vacancy that she could fill?

Taking a deep breath, Jacqueline told Didi that she had been interviewed by the man who had written the letter to her, Captain Selwyn Jepson, and that the job was as a driver for the First Aid Nursing Yeomanry. She said that she would soon hear if her interview had been successful but she thought it had. Jacqueline assured Didi that she had told Jepson about her and he had said that he would contact her if he felt there was also a suitable position for her with the FANY.

Didi was puzzled and slightly disappointed. She was curious to know why Jacqueline had not, it seemed, emphasized her desire to use her language skills. Surely her ability to speak, read and write fluent French could have been used to better advantage than by merely becoming a driver. Knowing her sister so well, she began to suspect that

Jacqueline was hiding something from her. Perhaps she wasn't even going to work for the FANY. Had she just told Didi that to make her believe that it was important war work she would be doing when really it was just a way of making ends meet?

Jacqueline herself could not stop thinking about the interview, and what it would mean to her if she was offered the position and accepted it. Jepson had told her to think very hard about what it involved and advised her not to rush into a decision, but she already knew what she was going to do. Although the role was not what she had imagined and she knew that it would be hazardous, she felt that she would be doing something that was really worthwhile, which was why she had come to England in the first place.

Didi's suspicion that her sister had been keeping something from her continued to trouble her. Then Jacqueline received the news that the interview had been successful, and within two weeks of her interview had passed a medical and completed the application form to join the FANY. In order to be accepted she needed sponsorship in the form of recommendations by two people; one had to be a woman, and both had to have known her for at least two years. Her sponsors were Lieutenant Prudence Macfie of the FANY and Captain Selwyn Jepson, neither of whom had known Jacqueline for more than two weeks.

When Jacqueline appeared wearing the uniform of the FANY, Didi realized that her main worry hadn't really been about Jacqueline joining the FANY. It was the driving job that had given her the nagging doubts and she was now sure that it was this that was the lie. She had wondered why the FANY would have picked her sister for a job that any English girl could have done, and she hadn't been able

M.O. 1. (S.P.),
War Office,
Whitehall,
London,
S.W.1.

9th July, 1942.

Officer in Charge,
    Headquarters Women's Transport Service, (F.A.N.Y.)
        Room 98, Horseguards,
            Whitehall.

Madam,

<u>Miss Jacqueline Nearne.</u>

In reply to your BP/9.1.41. in respect of the
above, I have known this applicant socially, for a
considerable period and I have no hesitation at all
in saying that she is, in my opinion, fully qualified
to be a member of the F.A.N.Y. To the best of my belief
she has never belonged to or had any connection with an
organisation of a subversive character, and is morally
of good name.

In reply to para. 6 of your letter this lady will
do excellent work in connection with the special
employment in which it is proposed that she should serve.

Yours truly,

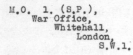

Captain.

to understand why even though the WRNS was unwilling to accept a driver who had no experience of the blackout, the FANY didn't seem to have considered that at all.

Despite Jepson's instruction not to discuss her interview with anyone, Jacqueline knew that she would have to disclose some details to Didi. So, impressing upon her that she mustn't tell a single soul, she admitted that she had been selected to work for a new organization called the Special Operations Executive (SOE) in the French Section. Enrolling in the FANY was a cover for what she would actually be doing. Didi, of course, wanted to know what that work was, but Jacqueline said that she had already told her too much and really couldn't tell her anything else.

While she waited to hear when she would be starting her SOE training, Jacqueline kept in touch with her friend Jimmie, mostly by post, as he had been sent on a training course, although they spent a day together in July, after which Jimmie wrote to Jacqueline expressing the hope that 'you managed to get back safely on Monday and that your sister etc had not telephoned all the Police in order to discover the wandering one'. He later wrote to ask Jacqueline to

tell me more about your life and your thoughts. I am very interested in your life and want to hear all about it, if you will tell me. How do you really like your new life?

It is a pity your location appears to be a closely guarded secret – why I don't exactly know – yours is certainly the first training centre that has not had a proper address ... I hope that you will not forget me now that you are making lots of new friends. The F.A.N.Y.s had the reputation at the beginning of the war of being rather select and snobbish. It never pays to be like that and I hope very much that you won't get that way – always remember that old friends are the best.[2]

This letter appears to have been the last one that Jacqueline received from Jimmie. It may, of course, just have been the last one that she kept but, by the time she read it, she had already started her SOE training and she was determined not to let anything interfere with that.

Frustrated that she was still unemployed and beginning to believe that she knew what Jacqueline was going to be doing, Didi was delighted when she too received a letter asking her to attend an interview at the War Office with Captain Jepson, a month after her sister's.

Jepson was a 43-year-old Army captain. A well-known playwright in peacetime, he was also the author of several books. When he joined the SOE as a recruiting officer in early 1942, he was found to be very good at picking the right sort of person for undercover roles within the organization. Calm and efficient, he managed to put prospective recruits at ease while asking questions that would reveal whether or not the person concerned would be good at the job. A report from the SOE to Military Intelligence placed on his file in March 1942 described him as being 'far ahead of anyone as [a] talent spotter'³ and he himself said of his role: 'I was responsible for recruiting women for the work, in the face of a good deal of opposition, I may say, from the powers that be. In my view, women were very much better than men for the work. Women, as you must know, have a far greater capacity for cool and lonely courage than men.'⁴

When Didi attended her interview it didn't take her long to realize that her suspicions about her sister's new job were correct and she told Jepson that she wanted to do the same as Jacqueline. He felt that she was, perhaps, a little young to be sent to France as an agent but asked her to tell him about herself. She told him that she had been born in England but had lived in France since she was a baby. She talked about her parents and brothers and sister, and described how she and Jacqueline had escaped from occupied France to come to England and obtain war work. She said that she knew several areas of France quite well, and was fluent in spoken and written French. She also stressed that although she liked people and generally got along well with them, she also liked her own company and was sure that she would be able to work completely alone should the need arise. She simply wanted to do something worthwhile for the war effort.

Jepson could see that Didi, although lively and enthusiastic, had a serious side as well. She was obviously intelligent and sincere, but he was still concerned that she might be too young. Being the baby of the family and having had a convent education, she had obviously led a sheltered life and he worried that she might not stand up to life in occupied France, alone and with no family support. He did, however, feel that there was about her a hint of the cool and lonely courage he was seeking. He told her that the SOE needed to recruit wireless operators who would send and receive messages to and from agents in France. There was also a requirement for decoders to interpret the messages, all of which had been encoded before transmission. He believed that Didi would be effective in either role and asked her which she would prefer.

Although disappointed that she would be staying in England, Didi decided that of the two positions offered, she would rather be a wireless operator and Jepson recruited her as such. She also decided that she would continue to press for a job as an agent whenever an opportunity arose. It had occurred to her when making her decision that the training she would need to be a wireless operator would be more beneficial to her than becoming a decoder, should she manage to persuade Jepson at a later date to send her to France.

Satisfied that she wouldn't be remaining in England for long, Didi was also enrolled in the FANY, joining what was known as Bingham's Unit. This unit had been established

by a member of the FANY, Phyllis Bingham, at the behest
of her friend Major-General Colin Gubbins, Vice-Chief of
the SOE Council, because of the necessity for absolute
secrecy in the SOE; those who joined Bingham's Unit were
the SOE women selected to serve as wireless operators and
decoders in the United Kingdom. One of the sponsors who
recommended Didi to the FANY was Mrs Bingham herself.
This was done, of course, as with Jacqueline's sponsors, to
keep the paperwork straight and believable, and the undercover roles secret; Mrs Bingham did not know Didi personally and at the time she recommended her to the FANY
they had not even met.

Didi then went off to learn how to receive and send
Morse code. She proved to be quite a good student and
passed the course satisfactorily.[5] She then settled down to
life in the listening station.[6] Although she had a flair for the
work, she found it tedious and longed for the day when she
would be able to do something more exciting. With the
impatience of youth, Didi began to send in requests to be
transferred to the French Section of the SOE so that she
could train to become an agent like her sister.

When she had told Jacqueline that she had guessed what
her real role with the SOE was to be and that she intended
to join her as soon as possible, Jacqueline had responded
with a lie, saying that Didi wouldn't be allowed to go to
France until she was 25 years old. Didi was still only 21,
and Jacqueline hoped that the war would be over by the
time Didi reached this fictional minimum age. But knowing
Didi so well, she also knew that the small detail of an age
limit would not stop her from asking to be sent overseas.
She worried that Didi might discover her lie and, worse
still, manage to persuade someone to allow her to go to

France, so she asked to see Colonel Maurice Buckmaster, head of the French Section of the SOE.

A meeting was arranged that was also attended by Buckmaster's assistant, Vera Atkins. Jacqueline explained to them that she was worried that her sister Didi wanted to go to France as an agent and that she had told her she was too young. She asked if there was some way that her lie could be kept up so that when Didi applied she would be told that she was too young. As well as explaining that Didi had led quite a sheltered life, she wanted them to know that Didi was unworldly but very strong-minded, impetuous and stubborn, so they could expect several more requests from her if her first request was denied. It was obvious to Buckmaster and Atkins that Jacqueline was very worried about Didi, and since she was in the middle of the training herself they agreed to go along with the story so that she could concentrate on her work and not worry about her sister.

Just as Jacqueline had predicted, Didi began to put in requests to be transferred as an agent to France. Each time she did so her request was refused. Buckmaster kept his promise to Jacqueline but Didi had no intention of giving up; determined to follow in her sister's footsteps, she repeated her requests at regular intervals.

Although some individual female agents had been sent to France before, Jacqueline was one of the first to be trained with a group of other women. This group was known as training party 27.OB.6⁷, and Jacqueline's fellow students were Odette Sansom (code name *Lise*), Lise de Baissac (*Odile*) and Mary Herbert (*Claudine*). It was fairly clear that the whole training programme for this women's group had been rather rushed and haphazard. Although

the men being sent to France were given a strenuous paramilitary course in the wilds of Scotland, these women were
simply sent on a parachute course at Ringway near
Manchester, and then on a finishing course in the New
Forest. There seemed to be a misconception that, as women,
they were not in the same danger as the men and that if
caught, the Germans would treat them in a better, more
gentlemanly way; training them in subjects such as unarmed
combat and silent killing would not, therefore, be required.
It took the SOE only a short time to realize that it was
mistaken, and courses in these skills were soon made available to both male and female agents.

Jacqueline proved to be a good shot and had no trouble
at all with a pistol. But parachuting was another matter.
Wearing protective clothing, which included overalls and
a large, round, padded hat, the students were attached to
ropes as if on an enormous playground swing so that they
could become used to the motion of a parachute descent
before making an actual jump. This didn't give Jacqueline
any problems, but she was less than enthusiastic about
her first parachute jump, which was made from the
specially adapted basket of a hot-air balloon. She was
frightened by it and felt very insecure, as the basket had a
hole, large enough for an adult to pass through, in its
base. It was also very quiet, which she and her fellow
students found disconcerting. When she finally made a
jump from an aircraft she declared it to be much better,
even quite exciting, attributing this to the sound of the
aircraft's engines, but parachuting wasn't something she
ever really enjoyed and she wished that there was some
other way to get to France so that she didn't have to use
a parachute at all.

It was while undertaking their parachute training that Jacqueline and Lise de Baissac became friends. Lise was 37 years old when she joined the SOE. She had lived in France since the age of 14 but came from a Mauritian family and had been born in Curepipe so, as the island of Mauritius was a British possession, she was British. Like Jacqueline she had escaped from France and, as an intensely loyal British subject, come to England looking for war work. Her brother Claude, two years her junior, had also escaped to England and had preceded her into the SOE, becoming the head of the Scientist circuit in south-west France. Maurice Buckmaster described Claude as being 'the most difficult of all my officers without any exception'[8] and it seems that this was a family trait, as Lise herself was thought to be 'difficult but dedicated'.[9] But despite this, and their 11-year age difference, Lise and Jacqueline became firm friends. It was a friendship that would last for the rest of their lives.

When they had successfully completed the parachute training the four women went on to the finishing school at Brockenhurst. Hastily set up in January 1941, this was housed in several requisitioned large homes built amongst the trees of the New Forest on the isolated Beaulieu estate of Lord Montagu. The section to which the women were sent was known as STS 31, which comprised two houses, the Rings and the House in the Wood. These facilities soon proved to be too small for the large number of administration staff, lecturers and students, and the students were moved to other buildings in the complex, while a third house was also requisitioned. The chief instructor at this time was 50-year-old Lieutenant Colonel Stanley Woolrych, a First World War veteran, who was soon promoted to commandant of the school, a post he held until the end of the war. Subjects taught included evasion techniques, recognition of German military uniforms, escape techniques in the event of an agent being apprehended by the enemy, coding and decoding of messages, wood craft, living off the land, shooting with a pistol, and security and propaganda warfare. The instructors were a varied bunch and included convicted criminals, a former gamekeeper from the royal estate at Sandringham and a man who would later be disgraced for his spying activities, Kim Philby.

When the course was over, the four women parted company. Lise was the first to leave England, parachuting into France at the end of September 1942 with another agent, a Frenchwoman named Andrée Borrel (*Denise*). They were the first two female agents to arrive in France this way. Lise went on to Poitiers, where she was tasked with setting up a new circuit to be called Artist, and with finding safe houses for agents. She was known in the area as Irene Brisse. Borrel's destination was Paris, where she was to be the courier for the Physician circuit and its leader Francis Suttill.

Mary Herbert and Odette Sansom managed to reach France without the use of parachutes but theirs was a difficult and lengthy journey, undertaken at the beginning of November. They were originally due to be taken by flying boat, but their flight was cancelled at the last minute and they were transferred to a submarine for a very uncomfortable trip to Gibraltar, from where they continued their journey by felucca to Port Miou near Cassis, south-east of Marseilles. Mary was to become the courier for Claude de Baissac (*David*), Lise's brother, in the Scientist circuit, while Odette headed for Cannes, where she met Peter Churchill

(*Michel*), head of the Spindle circuit. Although it was intended that she would eventually work for a circuit in Auxerre, Churchill persuaded the SOE in London to let him keep Odette with the Spindle circuit as its courier.

Although Jacqueline had done everything that was asked of her on the course to the best of her ability, her final training report, written and signed by Lieutenant Colonel Woolrych on 25 August 1942, said of her:

> Mentally slow and not very intelligent. Has a certain amount of determination but is inclined to waver in the face of problems.
>
> A reserved personality and somewhat shy. Little depth of character – in fact, she is a very simple person.
>
> She is lacking in self-confidence, which might be entirely due to inexperience.
>
> She might very well develop after long and careful training, but at present she could not be recommended.[10]

After all her good intentions and hard work, it seemed that Jacqueline had failed. She was inconsolable, knowing that she would never have a chance like this again.

CHAPTER 3

A Shaky Start

What Jacqueline did not know, when she learnt of Lieutenant Colonel Woolrych's damning report, was that the final decision about her suitability as an agent was left to Colonel Buckmaster in his role as head of F Section.

Maurice James Buckmaster, born in 1902, had been too young for military service in the First World War, and by the time the Second World War started he was almost too old. The son of a wealthy businessman, he had been educated at Eton and awarded an exhibition at Oxford to study Classics. He was on the point of taking it up when his father was declared bankrupt and there was no longer any money to spare for a full-time education. Abandoning Oxford, he decided to go instead to France, where he remained for several years, first working as a reporter in Paris for *Le Matin* and eventually becoming a manager for the Ford Motor Company, promoting the company's image to French car buyers. He returned to England in 1936 and two years later joined the Army Officers' Emergency Reserve. He received his call-up papers in the first month of the Second World War, serving with the 50th Division as an intelligence officer. He was soon back in France as part of the British Expeditionary Force and remained there until he was evacuated from Dunkirk during the last few days of Operation Dynamo. When he learnt sometime later that his division was going to be posted to North Africa, he contacted his divisional commander and asked him to intervene on his behalf and obtain a position for him where his knowledge of France, French business practice and the French language would be of use. In the spring of 1941, at the age of 39, he found himself in Baker Street, working as an information officer for the SOE.

In July 1941 Buckmaster was made the temporary head of T Section, looking after the agents operating in Belgium, and later that year was appointed head of F Section, in which position he remained for the rest of the war. His appointment was surprising given that his real forte was public relations, but times were hard and people with his knowledge of France were in short supply. He was not, however, agent material. Although he was not frightened of hard work, his personality was not suited to the life of an agent. Whereas public relations was not a profession in which one kept quiet about what was happening, the work of an agent relied almost entirely on secrecy. In addition, Buckmaster could be short-tempered and irritable at times, was too trusting of people and disliked difficult situations, finding them hard to handle. There were many who believed he was offered the job as F Section head not because he possessed any particular talent for the work but simply because there was no one else.

Buckmaster tackled his new role with gusto, however, and worked very long hours, often going home at the end of a working day and then returning to the office after dinner. Many of those with whom he worked in London and those he sent to France thought of him as an avuncular figure, the guardian of those who faced danger every day in Nazi-occupied territory. They liked him tremendously – one of the staff members at SOE headquarters declared him to be 'an absolute sweetie' – and many referred to him affectionately as 'Buck'.[1] But not everyone shared this opinion. There were those who thought of him as an antisocial, unapproachable man in an ivory tower.[2] They believed him to be a well-meaning but ineffectual man whose understanding of his agents, and the lives they led in France after the German occupation, was unsound and, in some cases, badly flawed. He could be stubborn and often dismissed the opinions of others, preferring to rely on his own instincts about people and situations. Sometimes these instincts served him well but he made some serious errors of judgement that he failed to acknowledge.

Vera Atkins, who helped Buckmaster, was an intelligence officer who had been with the SOE since April 1941, when she had been employed as a secretary to Major Bourne-Paterson, Head of Planning. She pushed for Buckmaster's appointment as F Section head when his predecessor was sacked for ineptitude and no one could think of anyone suitable to replace him. At face value it was difficult to see Atkins's motivation for promoting Buckmaster for this role but there were at least two reasons for her support. Extremely intelligent and capable, much more so than Buckmaster, she would herself have been a highly effective head but, as a woman, would never have been given the chance to show her enormous talent in this role. He, on the other hand, had far less aptitude but was grateful for the support she had given him in obtaining the position he coveted and never forgot that he was in her debt. Having made herself indispensable to him, she was able to exert her influence in many ways that would not have been open to her had she not ensured his appointment.[3]

However, perhaps the most significant reason for her championing of Buckmaster was that she needed someone on whose loyalty she could rely, as she should not have been working for the SOE at all. The organization's regulations stated that its London headquarters' staff should be British by birth. Vera was not British-born; nor did she have British nationality. She was Romanian, having been born in Galatz, Romania, in 1908, the daughter of Max Rosenberg, a German Jew, and his British-born wife, Hilda Atkins. Vera had not even lived in Britain until her arrival with her mother in the autumn of 1937, when she adopted the latter's maiden name and obtained an Aliens Registration Certificate. After the Allies declared war on Romania in 1941, she was regarded as an enemy alien and, as such, could have been sent to an aliens' internment camp, but somehow she managed to avoid this indignity. She applied for naturalization the following year but was refused, and she didn't manage to secure her British nationality until 24 March 1944.[4] Her success in obtaining the Certificate of Naturalization was due, in no small part, to the lengthy letter supporting her application that was written on her behalf by Maurice Buckmaster. Whilst there was never a suggestion that Vera Atkins was anything but loyal to her adopted homeland, her appointment to the SOE in contravention of its own security regulations, and the support she received from the head of F Section, show a worrying disregard for security in the organization, a situation that became a trend rather than an exception as the war dragged on.

Buckmaster revelled in the power his position gave him and, although he had no knowledge or experience of the training that agents undertook, countermanded the recommendations made by the instructors about prospective agents on several occasions.

When Jacqueline Nearne's finishing school report arrived on his desk, Buckmaster gave it a cursory glance and then took a pencil and scribbled in the margin, 'OK. I think her one of the best we have had.'⁵ He gave no further explanation of why he believed her to be so good but it is likely that his decision was based on Jacqueline's appearance alone, as he hardly knew her. She was a beautiful young woman and Buckmaster admired beauty. He had a particular fascination with bone structure and, in *Specially Employed*, a book he wrote after the war, said of her: 'Jacqueline is the sort of girl whom most people would describe as typically Parisian. She has the dark hair and eyes, the slim figure and the delicate bone of that type of Frenchwoman, of whose chic the French themselves are most proud.' In the same book he waxed lyrical about another recruit, Violette Szabo, who had also been given a less than satisfactory finishing report, declaring her to be 'really beautiful, dark-haired and olive-skinned, with that kind of porcelain clarity of face and purity of bone that one finds occasionally in the women of the south-west of France'.⁶

Jacqueline had no idea about Buckmaster's admiration for her 'delicate bone'; she was just delighted that she had been given a second chance. She promised herself that she would work as hard as she possibly could and prove to everyone that Lieutenant Colonel Woolrych's comments on her finishing report had been completely wrong.

Preparations now began for her departure for France. She was given a new name, Josette Norville, and told that her cover story would be that she was a sales representative of a pharmaceutical company, Pharmacie Bienfait of Lyons,[7] travelling extensively around a large area of France in the course of her work. Her cover had similarities to her own life. The new name gave her the same initials as her own and the fake occupation was virtually the same as her real employment had been, although she would be selling different commodities. She had two code names, one of which was *Designer*. The choice of the other was bizarre: she was to be known as *Jacqueline*. This was the same name as that adopted by Yvonne Rudellat, one of the first female agents to be sent to France in July 1942. (She too had received a bad training report and, at a time when political correctness would have been regarded as an alien concept, her instructor referred to her as 'the little old lady'.[8] She was 45 years old.) Jacqueline's code name was not only already allocated to someone else but was also her real name, thus rendering it useless as a security measure. Not wanting to make a fuss, she accepted this absurdity without comment, assuming that Buckmaster knew what he was doing. Before long she was introduced to a man called Maurice, for whom she would be working in France as a courier.

Maurice Southgate (*Hector*) was born in Paris. It was said that his British parents had spent their honeymoon in the French capital and had liked it so much that they decided to stay, although they and their son remained British citizens. Southgate grew up in France and, like Jacqueline, spoke the language fluently without a trace of an English accent. Three years older than his new courier, he was married to a Frenchwoman, Marie Josette Lecolier – known as Josette – and, until coming to England to join the Royal Air Force, had lived in Paris, where he ran his own successful business, designing and manufacturing furniture. When he arrived in England his main desire was to become a pilot, but the Air Ministry declared him to be too old and had other ideas for his employment. Because of his language skills he, now Sergeant Southgate, was sent back to France as an interpreter for the RAF members of the British Expeditionary Force. He was still in France when, at the beginning of June 1940, Operation Dynamo ended its mission to rescue the BEF from the clutches of the Germans and Operation Ariel, a mopping-up exercise and the follow-on to Operation Dynamo, began.

Southgate, along with several thousand troops and British civilians, boarded HMT *Lancastria*, one of the ships at anchor in the Charpentier Roads, around 10 nautical miles from St Nazaire, on 17 June. Brought out from St Nazaire in smaller boats, the passengers were desperate to get away from the advancing German troops and back to Britain, but the master of the *Lancastria*, Captain Rudolph Sharp, wanted to sail across the Channel in convoy with the other ships. While they waited for these to be boarded, the *Lancastria* took on more and more passengers herself. Originally built to carry 2,200 people, by the time she was ready to sail on that June day she was seriously overloaded. Estimates of the actual passenger numbers varied from 4,000 to 9,000, with many being forced to travel in the ship's holds, well below the waterline.

Just before 4 p.m. that afternoon several German bombers – Junkers 88s – appeared overhead and dropped bombs on the waiting ships. The *Lancastria* was hit four times and

within 20 minutes she sank. Of all the thousands who had
wearily climbed on board that day, there were only 2,477
survivors. Maurice Southgate was one of them. He spent
hours trying to keep afloat in water that was covered with
wreckage, dismembered bodies and burning fuel oil.
Eventually he was rescued and, exhausted, was brought to
England, landing at the Cornish port of Falmouth two days
after his ordeal. He recorded what had happened to him in
a diary:

> I disembarked in Falmouth 19th June 1940, covered in a
> blanket and shoeless. I was taken by ambulance to a
> nearby camp, where I was able to take a shower and lose
> my watch. Then came a coach journey, a magnificent trip
> in the English countryside, to Plymouth RAF Station
> where I met with several of my squadron companions in
> the Sergeant's mess. I was met with open arms, cries and
> lots of beer.
>
> Next morning, in ill-fitting uniform, I left for London
> and arrived at my parents on the evening of 20th June
> 1940, my birthday. Both parents crying, as they had no
> news for several days, whilst the evacuation was taking
> place. I was listed missing and have had a lot of trouble
> establishing my credentials at the finance department of
> the ministry.[9]

The sinking of HMT *Lancastria* was, and remains to this
day, the worst ever British maritime disaster. The total
number of lives lost in the debacle was more than the
combined number of deaths in both the *Titanic* and the
Lusitania, yet the full circumstances of the tragedy were
never properly reported, as Prime Minister Churchill was

concerned that it was one catastrophe too many for the British public to bear and ordered a ban on the reporting of the ship's demise. The news was eventually broken in America, with a few subsequent reports in British newspapers several weeks later.

Despite his narrow escape from death, Southgate was anxious to return to France as soon as he could. By now resigned to the fact that he would never become an RAF pilot, he was determined to do something to help defeat the Nazis, but it took him nearly two more years before he was able to join the SOE. Once he had been identified as a possible agent, however, things began to move fast. He was given an RAF commission and attended training courses, from which he emerged with glowing reports.

When he and Jacqueline Nearne were introduced to each other in the early autumn of 1942 it was the beginning of what would become a close and highly efficient working relationship. The pair had a huge task in front of them. They would be building a circuit that stretched from Châteauroux, capital of the *département* of Indre in central France, to Tarbes in the south-western *département* of Hautes-Pyrénées, only 100 kilometres away from the Spanish border. Their circuit, named Stationer, would cover almost half the entire area of France and for a time Jacqueline would be its only courier.

With their departure for France imminent, Jacqueline and Southgate were given clothes made in the French style and bearing French labels. Jacqueline had two suits, two blouses and skirts, two pairs of pyjamas and two pairs of shoes. The pyjamas were almost useless after the first wash, as the material was of a very inferior quality and they shrank badly. But since this was all that was available in

France at that time, it was what the agents had to have. Jacqueline was given a few days' leave and used the time to say goodbye to Didi.

Undaunted by the lack of a positive response to her pleas to be sent to France, Didi had continued to press for a transfer. Still unaware of the pact her sister had made with Maurice Buckmaster and Vera Atkins, when she met Jacqueline she cheerfully relayed the details of her latest application to Jacqueline and, in turn, received the news that her sister was leaving her. Although she had known that their parting would eventually come, it still gave her a jolt to know that Jacqueline would soon be gone. The girls had been together for all Didi's life and now they would be in different countries, but they would always be close to each other in spirit and both looked forward to the time when they would be together again; Didi hoped it would be in France while Jacqueline fervently prayed that it would be in England. She was still frightened for her sister but had done everything she could to ensure she remained at her listening station in relative safety for the rest of the war.

Back at SOE headquarters Jacqueline was told that she and Maurice Southgate would be leaving at the end of October, and was instructed to be ready. Two days before departure Buckmaster came to see them both and gave Jacqueline a necklace and a watch, as well as 100,000 French francs. It was his habit to give female agents some item of jewellery, not only as a parting gift but, believing that they might be able to sell it, as a source of money should they find themselves without funds. Jacqueline was touched by this thoughtfulness and felt that Buckmaster was someone she could trust, declaring him to be 'sympathetic and very capable'.[10]

She and Southgate were taken to the aerodrome in Bedfordshire from where they would be leaving and, on the appointed day, boarded a Royal Air Force Halifax and took off for France. Arriving over the dropping zone, the pilot saw no lights from the reception committee and so the pair were returned to England. Eight days later there was a new moon and another flight was organized, but as the plane approached the dropping zone a thick fog swirled up and covered all sight of the ground. Again they were forced to return to England. It is likely that they returned home after this abortive trip, as the next attempt to reach France, their third, was not made until 30 December, with the same result. Jacqueline was beginning to believe that she would never get to France. This belief became more entrenched when, on the fourth attempt, the aircraft developed a technical problem before it had even left the runway and the flight was cancelled.

Eventually on the evening of 25 January, three months after their first attempt, Jacqueline and Southgate boarded another Halifax of 161 Squadron and were flown by Flight Lieutenant Prior to a dropping zone near the small town of Brioude in the Haute-Loire *département* of the Auvergne. This time everything went as planned and they made a blind drop on the landing ground. Although most drops were made to reception committees, some were not and these were known as blind drops. It was usually preferable for agents to be received by other agents, who could help them bury their parachutes and quickly take them away from the landing ground to ensure that if there were German patrols around they wouldn't find them. The reception committees often took arriving agents on to a safe house, where they could rest before making their own way to the circuits they were joining. Sometimes, however, it was not practical to provide a reception committee, and it is possible that after the many problems that Southgate and Jacqueline had had in reaching France it was thought best to let them drop blind in case there were any more problems and the reception committee wasted more time in waiting for agents who didn't arrive. Since both Southgate and Jacqueline had lived for most of their lives in France they should, in theory, have had fewer difficulties in coping with a blind drop than agents who were unused to the country.

Jacqueline jumped first and landed safely, quickly collecting up her billowing parachute in order to bury it as soon as possible and hide all traces of her arrival. As she stood up, she saw in the dim light of the French countryside the figure of a man holding a gun, which was pointed at her. On either side of the man were more figures. Jacqueline said later that she 'felt it was very unfair to be caught so quickly'[11] and that she didn't know what to do. She walked back and forth for a moment, trying to gather her thoughts, and then heard a male voice whispering her name. She suddenly realized that the man with the gun was Southgate and that in the dark he had been unable to identify her. His companions turned out to be tree stumps.

Filled with relief that they were not about to be arrested, they quickly buried their parachutes and gathered up their bags to walk to the station in Brioude, from where they intended to take a train to Clermont-Ferrand. Although they had not been in any danger, they were both shaken by the experience, and when they came across a woman on a bike along the road, Southgate asked her for directions to the station in English. Jacqueline was horrified but quickly retrieved the situation by asking the woman the same question in French. As she did so the look of bewilderment on the woman's face vanished, and Jacqueline realized that she had not understood what was being said to her and obviously thought that they were Germans.

They made their way to the station, a walk of nearly 32 kilometres, through the night. It should not have been so far, but in the dark they became lost and found themselves going round in circles for a time. After the encounter with the cyclist they preferred to find their own way to the station rather than ask for any more directions. On arrival, they took the first train leaving for Clermont-Ferrand. As they sank on to their seats, a German soldier came into the carriage and sat down opposite them. Jacqueline had a feeling of revulsion at having to share the carriage with him, and one of fear that he was there at all; to her it seemed as if her heart had jumped into her mouth, but she quickly recovered and opened the French newspaper that she had bought at the station and began to read it. Southgate did the same and the journey passed with no more drama.

For security reasons the details of contacts in France were given to only one person, and it was Jacqueline who had the information about where they would be able to find accommodation in Clermont-Ferrand. Leaving Southgate at a café near the station, she went to the address she had been given. A boy answered her knock on the door and she told him, 'Je suis la fiancée d'André' (I am André's fiancée). The boy called back into the apartment, 'A woman wants to speak to you,' and André Vasseur, who was in reality George Jones (*Lime*) and who was known to Jacqueline from the SOE office in London, appeared. He was the wireless operator for the Headmaster circuit and would be one of those who would transmit messages for Stationer until its own wireless operator was sent from London.

The apartment at which Jacqueline had arrived, 37 rue Blatin, was the home of a family called Nerault and the boy who had answered the door was Jean Nerault. Jacqueline was welcomed into the family's home, where she explained that she had left her circuit chief at the station and that they needed somewhere to stay for a while. She was told that they could stay there, so she went to find Southgate. He was relieved to see her, as although she hadn't been gone for very long, it had felt like a lifetime to him and he was beginning to think that something had happened to her.[12] She assured him that she was fine, although she couldn't get used to seeing so many Germans in the streets. During the time she had been on her training courses and afterwards waiting to reach France she had had an idea of how it would be to be back in her homeland, but the reality was nothing like she had imagined. France had changed after the German invasion and she hated it, as it made her realize that she had placed herself in a very dangerous position. She also knew, though, that whatever she now felt, she would just have to cope with it: there could be no going back.

CHAPTER 4

Escape

Since the area to be covered by the Stationer circuit, from central France to the far south, was vast, nearly half of the entire country, Southgate and Jacqueline's remit to unite the various groups in this area into efficient fighting forces, so that they would be ready when the longed-for Allied invasion of western Europe eventually began, presented a challenge. It was rather unrealistic, therefore, to have sent a new circuit leader on his first mission with an equally inexperienced courier and no wireless operator, and expect them to work miracles. Yet London could not have picked a better pair for the task.

Southgate had passed his training courses with flying colours and was highly thought of by F Section. He in turn had full confidence in his courier and was not to be disappointed when they began to work together in earnest. He was soon reporting, 'Jacqueline is grand, and is rendering great service to my organisation and to England. I could not have done half what I have without her.'[1] But although they got along very well and were soon beginning to achieve a lot of what they had come to France to do, Southgate regarded Jacqueline as a bit of an enigma. She was pleasant, polite, always did her job to the best of her ability and had a good sense of humour, but he felt that there was more to her than met the eye and that behind her pleasant façade was a woman who did not want to give away too much of her real self.

During their first few weeks in France Jacqueline and Southgate travelled tirelessly all over the large area that constituted the Stationer circuit, meeting when possible about three times each week to bring each other up to date with their progress. They soon began to establish some order among the disparate groups of resisters, and arranged training and supplies for them. Part of Jacqueline's work as a courier was to take and fetch messages from the other groups. Before Stationer received its own wireless operator, she also had to take messages to a wireless operator of another circuit to be sent. This was a security risk for both her and the Stationer circuit as a whole, but it was nearly three months before the news reached them that the arrival of their own wireless operator was imminent.

Then, in mid-April, Amédée Maingard (*Samuel*) parachuted from an RAF Halifax on to a dropping zone 6 kilometres from Tarbes. Southgate met him and the two men made their way to Châteauroux, where Maingard, a Mauritian, made his base at a safe house organized for him by Jacqueline. He and Jacqueline began to meet regularly, usually at least three times a week, and his arrival made a huge difference to the efficiency of the circuit and lessened the security risk to Jacqueline, as she now only had to pass messages to one person. She always carried the messages by hand and was prepared to either destroy them or swallow them if there was any danger of her being caught. She sometimes had to carry what she referred to as 'compromising objects' in her bag:

If I feared an inspection at a station exit I would call a porter and get him to take my bags to the left luggage where I would collect them later. If my cases had been opened I always had enough time to disappear.

Sometimes the Germans helped me as I got off a train and gallantly carried my luggage. That helped me get through the checks without any problems.[2]

Southgate's cover story for his role in the circuit was that he was an inspector and engineer for a company manufacturing gasogene,[3] the gas substitute used for powering cars in France during the war. This gave him a good reason for all the travelling he undertook and sometimes gained him access to factories, which allowed him to assess the practicalities of sabotage. As a security precaution he always carried literature about his supposed employer and could speak with some authority about gasogene. Jacqueline's cover as a saleswoman for a pharmaceutical company[4] also gave her a very plausible reason for being on the move and, since the story was so close to her actual employment before leaving France to come to England, she too had few problems in maintaining the deception. But despite this the work was very dangerous.

Because of the distances she travelled, Jacqueline sometimes had to stay in hotels. This was not as easy as she had imagined. Not only did she have to avoid German soldiers without overtly appearing to do so; she also had to be on the lookout for those in plain clothes and for checks carried out by the Milice, the Vichy French volunteer paramilitary organization whose members subscribed to the abhorrent Nazi ethos. Although in her previous career she had been used to staying in hotels, she had done so as a legitimate sales representative, with genuine papers. Those she had carried when she first arrived, although excellent, were fake and one of her first tasks had been to obtain French-made documents. The day after she received her new cards she had to use them when the hotel in which she was staying in Châteauroux was subjected to a police raid.

She was washing her underwear in the basin in her room when there was a knock at the door. Believing it to be an expected visit from a member of the Resistance, Jacqueline hurriedly opened the door to be confronted by a plain-clothes policeman. Genuinely dismayed about being caught with her wet undergarments still in her hand, she began to blush and stammer her apologies for coming to the door in such a state. The young policeman was also flustered, and their mutual confusion diffused the situation. He asked for her papers, she produced them, and he gave them a cursory look before handing them back and fleeing in embarrassment.

Jacqueline's ID card in the name of her alias, Josette Norville.

Later that evening there was another raid and this time Jacqueline was prepared. When the knock on her door came she opened the door but pretended to have been asleep and, rubbing her eyes and yawning, asked what the policeman wanted. He mentioned Southgate, using the name under which he was known in the area – M. Philippe. Jacqueline yawned some more, and tried to look drowsy and confused. Her acting fooled him and, seeing that he would get no sensible answers from her in that state, he apologized for disturbing her and went away. She didn't get much sleep that night. The police knew Southgate's alias and that he was somehow linked to her. She couldn't understand who could have told them and knew that she had to get away as quickly as possible. Not wanting to attract attention in the hotel by leaving in the middle of the night, and afraid that, if she did take that chance, the police might be keeping a watch outside, she decided to stay until the morning. As soon as it was light she took her small bag and checked out of the hotel. Later she learnt from a member of the Resistance group in the area that the police had returned just after she left, no doubt hoping to question her again when she was wide awake.

The incident proved to Jacqueline that it was not safe to stay in hotels too often and thereafter she tried to avoid them as much as possible, preferring tried and tested safe houses. But sometimes there was no other choice. On another occasion she was again disturbed twice, by two different police officers knocking at her door. She did not panic; she just showed her papers and answered their questions, and later she discovered that they hadn't been interested in her at all. There had been a robbery in the area and every hotel room was being checked in the hope of finding the thieves.

When not taking a chance by staying in a hotel Jacqueline frequently slept during her long train journeys. More often she could only cat nap, and spent much of her time knitting socks for herself and her colleagues. On the rare occasions when she had to stay in Paris, she used her own family home there. The apartment that had belonged to her grandparents and in which the Nearne family had lived when they first came to France was empty, so Jacqueline made it available as a safe house for Southgate and other agents, although, ever cautious, she stipulated that it was not to be used very frequently. An empty apartment that had different people coming and going regularly was bound to arouse suspicion, and she wanted to avoid the possibility of it being the target of a raid.

Jacqueline's frequent trips away from her base in Clermont-Ferrand gave her an opportunity to contact her brother Francis. He had remained in the Grenoble area, living with his wife, Thérèse, and son, Jack, at the Villa Picard in Saint Egrève, a few kilometres from the city. When, in May 1943, he heard from Jacqueline that she was back in France and would like to meet up with him, he jumped at the chance. Francis knew only that both his sisters had gone to England to look for a way to help the Allies, but when he and Jacqueline met she swore him to secrecy and told him something of what her work in France entailed. She described how difficult it was for her entire group because of the vastness of the area they covered and asked him if he would be willing to undertake ad hoc courier missions for the circuit.

Francis was still a rather nervous young man. He believed that the difficulties he had faced after arriving in France as a child, and the fact that the education he had received had been rather poor, had resulted in him being unable to secure a good job that would allow him to look after his wife and child properly. Because of his nervous disposition he had been unable to hold down any job for very long but had been getting along quite well in his last position as a salesman for a stationery company, Maison Marassi, until it had closed soon after the start of the war because the manager was Jewish. Francis, like the rest of his family, had remained British and, as a foreigner, had also been made to live in a *residence forcée*, but he had been allowed to go into Grenoble every day, where the company for which he had worked was located. The closure of the business had created problems for him, as he had barely been able to support himself and his family on the meagre wages he had received, even with the help of 2,600 francs that he received from the Swiss consulate in Lyons,[5] and without the wages, his life and the lives of his wife and child had had to change drastically. He was also acutely aware that he was the only one of the four siblings not to be doing anything for the war effort. He decided that the time had come for him to join the fight against the Nazis and agreed to Jacqueline's proposal. She reassured him that if he did become a courier he would be looked after and that she would be the one to allocate the work he undertook. She would be his contact in the circuit and would arrange all the meetings that he had with members of the group so that no one would have to know his true identity, nor he theirs, and the safety of his family would not be compromised.

Because of Maurice Southgate's complete confidence and trust in Jacqueline he had no problem with her brother becoming a part-time courier for the Stationer circuit. So Francis was given the name Jacques Perrier, was issued with a fake French identity card and began his new work. Using the code name *Jacques*, he passed messages between members of the circuit, carried equipment for wireless operators of the sub-circuits all over the area when they moved to new addresses, and collected explosives which he delivered to the saboteurs in the group for their attacks on factories and railway yards. He worked mainly in the southern part of the country, in the area between Grenoble, Vichy and Clermont-Ferrand, and usually travelled by train. Sometimes he took Thérèse and Jack with him, having observed that families were far less likely to be caught up in police raids on trains than adults travelling alone. It was not difficult work but it was extremely dangerous, and Francis was always very careful about covering his tracks. In case of police raids, when he had a parcel to carry he would put it in an overhead rack and then stand in the corridor of the train or take a seat in another compartment so that should a raid take place he could walk away from the offending package. When it came to leaving a station building, he would deposit his baggage in the corner of the buffet or ticket hall and then check what controls there were at the exit gate. If there was no control, he would return to his luggage and bring it through the gate; if there was even a hint of a check being made at the station exit, his plan was to leave the package where he had deposited it and walk through the gate empty handed. He was fortunate in never having to do this and attributed it to sheer good luck, as he had often seen these checks taking place before becoming a courier himself.[6]

Francis was only once the subject of an investigation while working for the Stationer circuit. This was on a train when the German authorities came through the carriages asking passengers for their papers. Francis had both British and French identity cards, and carried a letter of safe conduct that identified him as a foreigner living in France. It was this he showed the Germans and that made them suspicious, and when the train pulled into the station at Lyons they handed Francis over to the French police. He had been able to hide his forged French card from the Germans by placing it in between the pages of the newspaper he had been reading, and he managed to retrieve it and hand it over to the policeman. Francis believed it to be an excellent forgery and it obviously was, as the French officer could find no fault with it and immediately released him.

Jacqueline had made arrangements for her brother to stay with the Nerault family at 37 rue Blatin in Clermont-Ferrand that evening. The Neraults' home was a large apartment in an elegant building five storeys high, with shuttered windows and fancy wrought-iron balconies, close to a busy crossroads. She herself had lived there for some months after her arrival from England. She had told him that she would meet his train and take him to rue Blatin herself, so after his release he went back to the station and hopped on another train for Clermont-Ferrand. He had no more problems during the journey and Jacqueline was waiting for him at the station. As they always were with agents seeking refuge, the Neraults were very welcoming and gave Francis a comfortable bed and a feeling of security at being in a family home once more.

By September he was gaining confidence in his ability and felt that he was, at last, doing something worthwhile – something of which he could be proud; he felt better about himself than he had done for a long while. After having completed another successful mission late one afternoon he was looking forward to meeting up with Jacqueline the following evening. When he went to bed, he slept very well. So well, in fact, that it was ten o'clock the next morning before a loud noise woke him. When he realized what it was, he was terrified but he managed to slip noiselessly out of his bed, creep across the floor and lock the bedroom door. The sound that had interrupted his slumber was of a Gestapo raid. If caught, he knew he would not be able to escape.[7]

On the other side of his bedroom door he could hear several loud voices barking out orders in German. Doors were banging, and drawers and cupboards were being opened, followed by the sound of things being flung on the floor. In between the strident, guttural tones of the Germans were the quieter voices of his hosts. He didn't understand the Germans and couldn't hear what the Neraults were saying, but he knew he had to get out immediately. But how? He couldn't think how to do it without giving away his presence in the apartment. He dressed quickly and put what few belongings he had into his small bag, all the while trying to calm himself and consider what would be his best course of action. The room had a window but there was no way he could make his escape through it. He quickly had to admit to himself that the only way he would survive would be by going through the apartment's front door and out into the street below. It was a terrifying thought but he had no other choice. So, hardly daring to breathe, he waited until he sensed that the Germans had moved into another room across the hall. Then he carefully turned the key in the lock of his bedroom door and, pushing it open a fraction, peered into the hallway. It was empty. Before his courage failed him, he crept across the floor, opened the outer front door, and made his way down the stairs as quickly and quietly as he could, praying that he wouldn't meet any Germans on the stairway or outside on the street. He reached the courtyard at the back of the apartment block, and then cautiously made his way through the arch and into the street, only pausing for breath when he was well away from the building.

He had never been so frightened in his entire life and couldn't stop shaking. Over and over again he thought about the kind family who had offered hospitality to so many people without a thought for their own safety, in the knowledge that they could soon be taken away by their German captors and might never be seen again. He wondered if the Neraults' teenage daughter, Colette, had been at home at the time, or the couple's small son, Jean. Thoughts of the boy made him shake anew, for he realized that if he had been caught the Germans might have arrested his wife, Thérèse, and two-year-old son, Jack, as well. He loved them both dearly but didn't think that he would be able to withstand German interrogation or torture, and suffered agonies thinking that his actions could have condemned them.

Then he remembered that he was supposed to meet his sister at the apartment that evening and he began to panic once more. He didn't know where she was and couldn't warn her not to come. In fact, in his panic, he couldn't think of anyone that he could contact to tell what had happened. Finally, he resolved to return to rue Blatin and wait for Jacqueline to arrive so that he could warn her.

Retracing his steps, Francis eventually found himself outside the apartment building again. He watched it from a discreet distance, and from the comings and goings of other residents concluded that the Gestapo had left. By nightfall he had steeled himself enough to enter the building and search the flat to see if anything important had been left behind. He found nothing except the wreckage of the family's home and belongings, and hoped that they had managed to destroy anything incriminating before the Gestapo had broken into the apartment. He met the concierge and had a few words with her. She confirmed that there had been five Gestapo men in the raiding party, and that M. and Mme Nerault and their daughter had all been at home and had been arrested and taken away. She did not know where they were being kept or what had happened to the boy.

Francis left and again positioned himself outside so as to be able to see Jacqueline before she entered the building. Twelve hours after the raid had begun he was horrified to see the Germans arrive yet again and go back into the apartment. They remained there for four agonizing hours while Francis kept watch for his sister's arrival.[8] She didn't turn up and by the time the Germans left again at two o'clock the next morning he realized that she must have found out about the raid. Exhausted, he hid in an outhouse, where he remained for the rest of the night. In the morning, having had a little rest and feeling slightly calmer, he managed to contact Jacqueline.

CHAPTER 5

Broken Promises

With the terror of the Gestapo raid haunting him, Francis began once more to suffer badly from his nerves. The self-confidence that had been growing with every mission he had successfully completed vanished and he shrank inside himself all over again. Then came the news via Maria, the concierge of the Nerault family's apartment block, that she had received a letter, written in German supposedly by a family friend, to say that M. Nerault was in Germany, and that he was well and able to receive food parcels. Soon afterwards a card arrived from Mme Nerault and Colette, also saying that they were in a camp in Germany but giving no actual location. Whether or not these were genuinely from the family was unknown, but Maria chose to believe that they were and consoled herself with the thought that at least they had not been shot. This proved to be of no comfort to Francis, who still tortured himself with thoughts of what had happened to them, and what might have happened to his wife and son if he too had been caught. He was sure that Thérèse and Jack would have been targeted because his wife knew about his undercover role.

Despite Jacqueline's best efforts she could not help her brother. He was so tense and worried that he couldn't function effectively and, much as he wanted to, was no longer able to undertake any courier missions. Jacqueline was so concerned that she enlisted the help of Maurice Southgate. He was sympathetic towards Francis and did not want to lose his services as, until this setback, he had been a most reliable and trustworthy courier. He contacted Baker Street with a request that Francis be sent to London for training and to enable him to receive some medical help for his bad nerves. He stressed that he was sure that, given the right treatment, Francis would regain his self-confidence and be able to resume his courier work. Then he, Jacqueline and Francis waited to hear what London would decide.

Back in England, Didi was unaware of her siblings' problems and was delighted with the news she received in the autumn of 1943. After her countless attempts to persuade her bosses to release her from her listening station, she was told at last that she was going to be sent for training as an agent. Buckmaster had broken his promise to Jacqueline and decided to send Didi to France where, he hoped, she would be as effective in the field as her sister.

Quite why he had chosen this moment to release Didi from her mundane work is not recorded. Jacqueline had made it quite clear to both him and Vera Atkins that she was strongly opposed to Didi going to France; and she, after all, knew her sister better than anyone. She had stressed her sister's naivety, and her lack of experience in many aspects of life. She had never doubted Didi's courage, but she felt that she had perhaps looked at the role of an agent through rose-coloured glasses and that when faced with the reality of the situation, she might find herself out of her depth – and by then it would be too late.

The pragmatic view might be that here was a young woman, fluent in French and English, completely used to the French way of life and eager to return to her homeland to do her bit. Was it not ridiculous for Buckmaster to waste this valuable resource simply because of a promise made to the girl's sister? Perhaps so, but if Jacqueline was right and her sister wasn't up to the task, Buckmaster would have to answer not only for his deception but also his own bad judgement. With Jacqueline preoccupied by her own heavy workload and her concern for the welfare of Francis, he perhaps hoped to have Didi well into her training course before her sister got wind of what was happening back in England.

The whole situation was becoming a tangled web of deceit, as Didi was still not aware that her sister had extracted the promise from Buckmaster to keep her in England; nor did she know that the age restriction that Jacqueline had told her about was a lie. She was just very excited that she would soon be in France, like her sister, and was impatient to start the training course.

Before long she was released from Bingham's Unit and transferred to the SOE French section of the FANY. Having already learnt Morse code and worked in the listening station it was felt that all she now needed was a finishing course, and for this she was sent to a house called the Drokes on the Beaulieu estate in the New Forest, in a party numbered 27.OB.[1] Unlike the finishing courses for couriers, this one, for wireless operators, not only concentrated on the security aspects of the role but also allowed time for the students to study and practise the technicalities of transmitting and receiving messages every day, to ensure that the transmissions were sent swiftly and efficiently and that the messages being received could be quickly understood. Speed was of the essence for a wireless operator.

A new syllabus had come into being a month before Didi's course began. It was not extensive but it highlighted one or two things that might not have occurred to a novice wireless operator. It said of a wireless operator, for example, that 'Other agents should not go to his residence or place of operation. It is even better if they do not contact him direct.' Since most people crave the company of others, especially when they are feeling frightened or stressed, it would seem natural to seek out other agents who would understand the pressures of the job, but it would be unsafe for all concerned. The syllabus went on to decree that a wireless operator 'Should live with friends as key-taps [are] audible'. This, of course, made a difficult task even trickier. On the one hand the agent was rightly being told that he or she should not have much contact at all with other members of the circuit and on the other that they should live with friends to reduce the risk of the tapping of Morse code being heard by strangers. Where they were supposed to find these friends if they were not to have much contact with their colleagues appears not to have been considered. It was certainly dangerous to assume that friends from outside the Resistance groups, even if they had been known to the operator for many years, could be relied upon in dangerous situations. The Germans had ways of turning the most patriotic French citizens into collaborators, and the most devoted friends into enemies. They only had to threaten the friend or his family with torture or a horrible death to make the friendship untenable. Like many ideas that look good on paper, in practice it didn't work, and many wireless operators found themselves living solitary and boring existences while in France.

The part of the syllabus that told each operator about their own specific plan to which he or she must adhere was also flawed. This plan, or 'sked', as it was known, meant that even if there were an urgent message to be sent, the operator could only transmit it at one of two scheduled times each day. For London this made sense. It ensured that Baker Street could keep a check on its agents and, when messages were sent hurriedly and sometimes came through garbled, it enabled those decoding the transmission to sort out what was actually being said by applying their own knowledge of who it was that had sent it and what the general situation in the circuit concerned had been. On the downside the regular broadcast and reception times gave the enemy, who used fairly sophisticated direction-finding equipment, the knowledge of when to expect an operator to be transmitting. This made it far easier for them to locate the place from which the broadcast was being sent. To circumvent this danger, agents were told to 'constantly move set and/or aerial'. This again seemed sensible until one realized quite how difficult it was to find a safe house from which to transmit. Having several places was an almost unheard of luxury. Didi, who worked hard on her course, was yet to discover the anomalies of the security training she was receiving.

Having completed the course at the end of January 1944, she was confident that she had done her very best. She felt that she had benefited from the training and she had enjoyed the company of her fellow students. She knew that her ability with Morse code was good, and she was in no doubt that her final report would be fine and that she would soon be leaving for her new life in France. She wondered what part of the country she would be sent to, with whom she would be working and what her new life would be like. But when Colonel Buckmaster received her final report, he was not pleased by what it said.

The report, dated 26 January 1944, was written by 36-year-old Major John H. Wedgwood (the great-great-great-grandson of Josiah Wedgwood, the master potter), who said:

> She is not very intelligent or practical and is lacking in shrewdness and cunning. She has a bad memory, is inaccurate and scatterbrained. She seems keen but her work was handicapped by lack of the power to concentrate.
>
> In character she is very 'feminine' and immature; she seems to lack all experience of the world and would probably be easily influenced by others.
>
> She is lively and amusing and has considerable charm and social gifts. She talks a lot and is anxious to draw attention to herself, but was generally liked by the other students.
>
> It is doubtful whether this student is suitable for employment in any capacity on account of her lack of experience.

Had any of Didi's friends been able to read this report, they would have been puzzled. It was simply not a true reflection of the caring friend they knew and loved. Her family would not have recognized what had been written about Didi either. Jacqueline thought of her sister as being the odd one out in the family but not because she was frivolous, attention seeking or unintelligent: quite the opposite.

She was sometimes playful and light-hearted but she also had a serious side, she was very intelligent and her whole life was directed by her religious beliefs. The report was so scornful that it was difficult not to think that Major Wedgwood either had a personal dislike of Didi or perhaps had mistaken her for someone else, as unlikely as that seemed. A second reading of the offending document, however, would have revealed that he understood some aspects of her character. He, like Jacqueline and Captain Jepson, who had conducted Didi's initial interview for the SOE, had recognized her immaturity and her inexperience; those close to her would also have acknowledged that she was lively and amusing. But not only was Wedgwood completely off the mark when he said that she was anxious to draw attention to herself but his opinion that Didi would probably be easily influenced by others was just that – an opinion – and had no real basis in fact. Perhaps the only person who would have been able to influence Didi to any extent was her sister and, despite being in France, Jacqueline would not be working with her.

The report gave Buckmaster a problem. Should he accept it and, if Wedgwood's views were wrong, lose a good agent, or should he take a chance, as he had with Jacqueline? His belief in Jacqueline had been correct. She was one of the best agents that the SOE had. Why should Didi not be the same? He himself had observed her during one of the training exercises, in which she had undergone an interrogation designed to show how forceful the Germans could be when endeavouring to obtain information from a captured agent. The students had been taught never to be afraid or dominated, but when some of them came up against the interrogation tactics that they might have to endure, they cracked. Didi did not. She sailed through this part of the course and Buckmaster commented, after he had observed her, that he really couldn't tell when, or even if, she had lied, so convincing was she. With this talent, her experience of day-to-day life in France and her language skills, he would have been foolish to reject her.

What was left unsaid, but what Buckmaster undoubtedly knew, was the reputation of Major Wedgwood. He was an extremely capable, intelligent instructor but one who was well known to the other instructors, and the secretaries in Beaulieu, as being 'absent minded', 'vague, dreamy and eccentric', 'delightful but vague', 'a very engaging, whimsical character', 'pale and wide-eyed' and someone who 'would break long silences by unexpected and devastating sallies'. The final two comments were made by Kim Philby, a man of dubious character and loyalty, as his post-war activities would show, but whose remarks nonetheless, along with those of the others at Beaulieu, gave the impression of Wedgwood being an absent-minded professor who would sometimes make strange pronouncements about those in his charge.[2] Buckmaster thought carefully about this predicament and announced his verdict: Didi was accepted.

Unaware of the dilemmas behind the scenes, Didi was looking forward to leaving for France. Expecting to be leaving sometime in February, she still had much to do to be ready and was measured for her French clothing, which duly arrived from the SOE tailors. She was given a new identity: Jacqueline du Tertre, a dizzy shop girl from the south of France. In line with the complicated identification processes of the SOE she also had another name: Marie Louise Tournier, which was shown on her personal file as being her 'documentary name'. Then there was her code name, *Rose*, the name by which she would be known to her colleagues in France. Finally she had two wireless code names: *Petticoat* and *Pioneer*. What her personal file did not show was any evidence of her having taken parachute training. It would soon become clear why she did not need it.

CHAPTER 6

Betrayal

Francis had gone back to Grenoble to await the result of Maurice Southgate's request for him to be sent to London. Still terrified by his experiences in Clermont-Ferrand, he was delighted to be with Thérèse and Jack again but knew that he would soon have to leave them. He could easily have stayed with his wife and son, picking up work as and when it became available until the war was over and life got back to normal, and it was a tempting proposition; but, at that stage of the war, it was by no means certain that the Allies would be the victors and, much as he wanted to stay, he knew that if he didn't try to conquer his fears and do something to make France a better place for his son to grow up in, he would have failed as a father.

By the end of September, the paperwork for Francis's arrival had been completed to ensure he could begin his training and his medical treatment immediately. He was told that his flight had been arranged and that he would be leaving France in late October and was instructed to go to Paris, where he would meet the man organizing his departure.

Feeling sick at the thought of saying goodbye to his family, Francis bid an emotional farewell to Thérèse, Jack and his parents, knowing that he was going for a very good reason. He set off for the capital, hopeful that he would be able to make them all proud of him by the work he was going to do. On 20 October he met Henri Déricourt, the SOE F Section air operations officer, a short, stout man with wiry, light-brown hair, who, Francis said, answered to two code names, *Gilbert* and *Claude*. Déricourt told Francis to take a train to Angers, 300 kilometres south-west of Paris, where he and the other passengers would meet to have dinner before cycling to the aircraft landing zone, which was between Angers and the village of Soucelles.

The train journey was without incident, but once they all reached the restaurant an argument started between Déricourt and one of the passengers. This man was known to Francis by his code name *Louba*, but his real identity was Henri Jacques Paul Frager, the head of the Donkeyman circuit, which operated in a large area approximately 200 kilometres to the south-east of Paris. A tall, grey-haired, bespectacled man, he was accompanied by his second-in-command, a man called Roger Bardet, whom Déricourt had believed would be travelling with Frager that night. Bardet, however, had no intention of leaving France but had merely provided company for Frager during the journey. Déricourt was furious, saying that this was a major breach of security, and tried to insist that they both leave on the flight. One of the other passengers, Alexandre Levy, Chief Engineer of the Bridges and Roads (Ponts et Chausées) section of the Public Works Department of Paris, tried to bring a calming influence to the proceedings, with some success.[1] The remaining passengers, a Giraudist agent by the name of Leprince, and Francis, took no part in the disagreement. The latter tried hard not to listen but until

Levy intervened it was impossible to ignore it, so fierce was the confrontation. Although Francis did not understood much of what he had heard, the altercation did nothing to settle his nerves.

Frager had been wrong to quarrel about Bardet's presence – it was a security risk – but Frager had never liked Déricourt and whenever they met there was always friction between them. Despite the fact that only those who would be taking the aircraft to England that night should have been present at the landing zone, he was convinced that the real risk was not Bardet but Déricourt himself, and Frager's purpose in flying to England that night was to report his belief that Déricourt was actually a double agent who had been working for the Germans for some time. It was not the first time that Frager had tried to tell those in Baker Street of his concerns about the air operations officer. He had previously provided what he thought was damning evidence of his belief, but despite this the staff at SOE headquarters, including Maurice Buckmaster, who had employed him in the first place, refused to believe that Déricourt was anything but a patriotic Frenchman.[2] What was unknown to Frager at the time was that Bardet was just as much of a risk as Déricourt, as he was later found to be spying for the Germans too.[3]

When the meal was finished, Déricourt took the four men to fetch the bicycles he had brought for them to ride to the landing zone and wait for the aircraft to arrive. Bardet went along with them, and Déricourt still believed that he might be able to get him to board the departing aircraft too, but it was not to be.

Soon after reaching the landing zone the argument broke out again, but it didn't last long as their voices were silenced by the sound of the arrival of a twin-engined Lockheed Hudson, piloted by Flying Officer J. Affleck of the RAF's 161 Squadron. Four inbound passengers quickly disembarked. They included two SOE agents, Albert Browne-Bartroli (*Tiburce*) and Robert Benoist (*Lionel*), a former French racing driver. As they made their way to the reception committee sent to fetch them, Francis and his companions passed them in the opposite direction and quickly boarded the Hudson. Within a minute or two they had taken off for England. Dericourt had not been able to get Bardet on to the aircraft, despite strenuous efforts, and the second-in-command of the Donkeyman circuit returned to look after it during Frager's absence.

It was a very nervous Francis who emerged from the Hudson when it landed in England. He had not been there since he was nine years old and, to him, it felt like a foreign country. His paperwork described him as being of medium height, with dark-brown hair, brown eyes and, curiously, a shapeless nose. His photo showed a young man who looked typically French. Despite several errors in the records, not least the one that took two years from his age, Francis was soon able to go about his business in England without hindrance. He was taken to a hotel and given a few days to settle in before being called to SOE headquarters. Whoever it was who conducted the interview, which was a standard procedure for agents coming in from the field, noted that Francis 'seemed nervous and rather scared'. He was certainly not comfortable with what he was being asked, but answered to the best of his ability and acquitted himself quite well.

Having passed that hurdle he was sent to an SAB – a Student Assessment Board – prior to attending a paramilitary course in Scotland. The SAB report did not show him in a good light. His instructor was not impressed with him and made the following comments about him: 'A man of exceptionally low intelligence. Rescued rather than recruited in the field. He gives no history of any sustained work and his performance here fully confirms this impression. He shows many signs of an unstable personality and should on no account be sent into the field.' Despite this uncomplimentary account of his ability, Francis was not immediately rejected.[4]

Instead he was sent to see the SOE doctor, Isaac Jones, who, after a thorough examination, sent a memo to Maurice Buckmaster telling him that: 'Mr Nearne has an intercurrent para-nasal infection which should subside fairly soon. He is not an easy mind.'[5] Buckmaster scribbled a pencilled note at the bottom of the report which said, 'Does this mean he has a runny nose?' To those who knew Buckmaster well this was just an example of his sense of humour,[6] but it seemed rather derisive, especially since he ignored the part about Francis not having 'an easy mind'. Nevertheless he made an effort to help the young man and the day after he received the medical report he sent a memo to several high-ranking SOE officials, including the Director of Operations for North-West Europe, Brigadier Eric Edward Mockler-Ferryman, to try to secure a place for Francis on a paramilitary course in Scotland. He explained that Francis was

a brother of our first class couriers, DESIGNER [Jacqueline Nearne], and another sister is shortly proceeding to the field as a W/T operator. DESIGNER was especially anxious that her brother should proceed here for training. We were most disappointed in his appearance and level of intelligence, and do not quarrel with the S.A.B. rating, although we think that this may have been in part caused by nervous reaction after the strain of continuous work in the field.

We believe that this man may improve mentally and physically during training, and we stress the bad effect that his rejection and consequent disillusionment would have on (a) DESIGNER (who we hope will be here on a visit next month, and our good impression of whom has been more than confirmed by STATIONER [Maurice Southgate] whose judgment is so particularly reliable), and (b) on Eileen Nairn [sic], who is just about to proceed to the field.

I agree that one should not occupy a valuable training space out of compassion, but would be extremely grateful if you would agree exceptionally to F. Nairn's [sic] going to SCOTLAND at least to see whether the Scotch air produces a change in his mental activity. In no case would we propose to send him out to the field until immediately before D-Day.[7]

Buckmaster's plea had the desired effect and Francis was allocated a place at STS23a, the special training school at Meoble Lodge in Morar, Inverness-shire. He left London almost immediately and made his way to the isolated school in the Highlands, determined to work hard and prove that he had the ability to be as good an agent as his sisters. But despite his good intentions he was not allowed to complete the course. In fact, he stayed in Scotland for only one week before being told that he was being sent back to London on medical grounds. His instructor, Acting

Lieutenant Gordon, had great sympathy for Francis and, in a report written on Christmas Eve, said of him:

> Born of English parents [*sic*], but lived almost entire life in France, educated there, but considers his education insufficient, probably right. Worked as a commercial traveller or representative of Paris firm. Knows Boulogne s/mer, Grenoble, Paris, Nice. Married to a Frenchwoman, 1 child aged 3.
>
> Has left us today 23rd. This is our unhappy case and he has all my sympathy. He has two sisters who are our people and well thought of, one over here now, both graduates of STS. He is a nervous man, lacking in self confidence and power of concentration. He is more than anxious to go on, and feels it very much that his sisters have succeeded where he has apparently failed. He failed SAB but came here on family consideration. He is clearly a man who has not succeeded very well in life, and with the responsibility of a wife and child, life was probably difficult. His nervousness etc. were already much better after only 5 days here, he tried very hard and to everybody's satisfaction, and I think encouragement and sympathy plus the life and training here would have done him a world of good. He has the inestimable advantage of speaking perfect French and has done a little work in France, and although obviously not of organiser calibre, I should have thought him a better investment than most of our candidates here. He was, I think, liked by the others and no one found [him] strange. He left, I understand, for medical reasons, and buoyed up with false hopes supplied by myself, as he was so very distressed when I told him that he was returning to London.[8]

Thoroughly mortified and despondent, Francis came back to London and was again accommodated in a hotel, with nothing to do, while a decision was made about his future. It was a humiliating end to the poor man's SOE career and a devastating blow to his already low self-esteem. He was alone and almost penniless, stuck in an England he barely recognized, amongst people he did not know. His nervous state became worse. He worried constantly about what was happening to Thérèse and Jack. Did they have enough money to survive? Were they well and happy? In his misery he bitterly regretted the patriotic impulse that had brought him to this uncaring place, full of hard-hearted people, and he longed to return to the warmth and comfort of his little family, where he knew that despite all his shortcomings, he was loved and appreciated. Under the terms of the National Service (Armed Forces) Act of 1939 British subjects living abroad at the outbreak of war were not liable for service with the military and only became liable once they returned to Britain. But no one had told him this and now, because of his patriotic gesture in coming to England and his desire to help, Francis was no longer going to be able to return home.

CHAPTER 7

Buckmaster Passes the Buck

Throughout 1943 and into 1944 Jacqueline's workload became increasingly heavy. The Stationer circuit's vast area meant that she was constantly on the move, taking and receiving messages, and coping with the ever-increasing number of members joining the Resistance groups.

At the start of the war the BBC had played a large part in keeping up the morale of the people of France with its French-language transmissions; but as the conflict staggered into its fourth year, the population was beginning to tire of the broadcasts, especially those concerning the *maquisards*, the French Resistance fighters. Every day the BBC would urge young Frenchmen to join the Resistance to avoid being sent to Germany for forced labour, the Service du Travail Obligatoire instituted by Chief Minister of Vichy France, Pierre Laval. The BBC message was, no doubt, well intentioned, but many men had already joined the Resistance and the message was creating as many problems as it solved. The circuits that were already in existence had been operating for a long time, and the fighters were trained and knew what they had to do. The sudden influx of so many young men, answering the calls that were put out on the BBC French service, was causing chaos in some areas. The resources of the established circuits were being ever more stretched and discipline was being eroded, as many of the new recruits were really only offering their services to escape being rounded up, and a good many of them had no interest in working for the Resistance at all, simply seeing it as the BBC had depicted it: a way of avoiding forced labour.

The Stationer circuit was fortunate in having Maurice Southgate at its helm. He would stand no nonsense from these latter-day patriots and soon began to knock some sense into them. Jacqueline too was rather good at dealing with them. Most young men would not have taken any notice of a hardworking but rather shy young woman, but there was something about Jacqueline that was different from most young women and she too was able to bring some sense of discipline to these rowdy groups. She was friendly towards them without being familiar and always behaved professionally, putting off any would-be suitors with a smile and a kind word. She let them know that if they had problems and needed her help she could be called on for assistance, but if she felt that they were trying to take advantage she knew how to deal with them without bruising egos or making herself unpopular. It didn't take her long to gain their respect and very soon they regarded her with affection. Should the need arise, they would even take orders from her – something almost unique in a country that didn't give women the right to vote until 1944[1] and wouldn't even allow them to open a bank account or take a job without their husbands' permission for a further 21 years.[2] But although Jacqueline won these men's trust, their presence in the circuit and its sub-circuits caused much extra work for her. Some of the old hands were disgruntled by the arrival of these young tearaways, believing that they threatened the circuit's security. Fearing that the situation might get out of hand, Jacqueline did all she could to help Southgate with the headstrong young volunteers and, at the same time, calm the situation and ensure that the morale of those who had already been working for Stationer for some time was not damaged.

Jacqueline was not altogether surprised when she discovered that Amédée Maingard, the circuit's wireless operator, needed cheering up. He lived and worked from a small room in Châteauroux which, for security reasons, was in a fairly isolated part of the town, and he hardly ever left it. A quiet, thoughtful young man, he was completely reliable and would never have done anything to compromise the circuit, but his devotion to the cause was seriously affecting his mood and he told Jacqueline that he was feeling really fed up. He had his two regular times each day to send and receive messages, but apart from that he had nothing else to occupy him and the inactivity was driving him mad. He was seriously thinking of asking to be returned to London so that he could become a paratrooper and see some real action. Jacqueline tried her best to keep up his spirits. Ironically her own role meant that she hardly ever had time to herself and sometimes longed for some breathing space so that she could read a book or listen to some music. She told Southgate that Maingard was suffering and he agreed that the wireless operator should be given something else to do before he became really depressed.

Southgate valued Jacqueline's opinions on a number of issues, and knew that he could always rely on her insights and common sense. When he was away, he was quite happy to leave her to get on with her work and keep an eye on the

various sections of the circuit as well. In his absence
Auguste Chantraine (*Octave*) and Charles Rechenmann
(*Julien*), the leaders of two of the large sub-circuits, took
their orders from her and, both to give him something else
to do and as a support to her, she involved Maingard in the
decisions she made.

Chantraine's men were almost all Communists and operated in the northern part of Stationer around the area of
Châteauroux where Maingard had his base. Chantraine
could call on the services of approximately 500 men there,
although he always had problems arming that many men,
as supplies were short and when they did arrive were not
always what had been requested. Rechenmann had a
smaller group of men, between 50 and 100, most of whom
were escaped prisoners of war. The area in which they
operated stretched from the south of Châteauroux to
Tarbes and Pau, 600 kilometres away.

Although it was not strictly part of the work of a courier
or a wireless operator, Jacqueline and Maingard were
co-opted into a group of ten of Southgate's most trusted
agents who helped him organize and carry out several
sabotage operations.[3] For Maingard it was a relief to be
able to leave his room and see some action, however
sporadic, and he was pleased that Southgate had named
him as his assistant.

The operations were varied and widespread. By the
middle of 1943 the group had made several daring raids.
They had blown up the generators at the Gnôme et Rhône
aircraft engine factory in Limoges, putting it out of action
for three days and denying the Luftwaffe replacement
engines. In Bersac they destroyed an electricity sub-station
and set fire to 27 new trucks that had been bound for

Germany. Two pylons at Dun-le-Palestel were blown up, and many more destroyed between Vierzon and Pau. Three transformers were wrecked at the Hispano-Suiza works, a former luxury-car maker in Tarbes which by then had been forced to make engines for German aircraft, and the arsenals at both Tarbes and Tulle were bombed. The group also targeted the railway, damaging the rails and signals at various places on the network, and wrecking loading cranes at Brive and Tulle. Southgate, with the help of only two men, cut off the electricity to the aluminium works at Lannemezan, causing all the aluminium to solidify, and there was a raid on a large aircraft factory in Marignane, near Marseilles, in which abrasive substances were put into engines on the test beds, rendering them useless. The sabotage spree of 1943 ended in December with the destruction of pumps at the steelworks in Ancizes, which disrupted production for three months, and with the theft of 30,000 litres of German petrol in Saignes.

Taking part in some of these raids had certainly lifted Maingard's depression, and although she was becoming very tired, Jacqueline had enjoyed the variety that her participation had brought to her day-to-day work too.

In addition to her sabotage work Jacqueline sometimes formed part of the reception committees that received agents and supplies. These could be just as dangerous as sabotage missions and were certainly not helped by having the wrong details of supplies being sent. She often found that the number of packages expected was wrong, and she and the others spent valuable time looking for things that had not been on the aircraft in the first place. This put them all in danger of being discovered and arrested by the Germans, who sometimes saw the containers descending on their little parachutes and immediately sent out search parties to look for those who were receiving them. There were times when the number of packages was correct but the contents were wrong. On the odd occasion when some little luxuries were included they caused more problems, as with so many people in the various sections of the circuit, a few bars of chocolate or some other little treat could not be divided properly. The arrival of new agents usually went much more smoothly, although these too were subject to the moon, the weather conditions and the skill of the pilot.

One of the agents who arrived on 22 September 1943 was a new courier for Stationer, Pearl Witherington (*Marie*), who had been one of Southgate's school friends and who parachuted from an RAF Handley Page Halifax piloted by Flight Sergeant Cole of 138 Squadron to a dropping zone near Châteauroux. Southgate had arranged her reception committee and was there to meet his old friend himself. He also alerted Pearl's fiancé, Henri Cornioley, to her arrival and the following day took her to meet him. It was the first time they had seen each other in three years and according to Pearl, Cornioley was 'shaking like a jelly'.[4]

When she met Jacqueline, Pearl began to wonder why she was there at all, as she could see that Jacqueline was most efficient and evidently invaluable to Southgate. She soon realized, however, that even with two couriers, there was still too much for them both to do. They were so busy that they barely saw each other and mostly worked in different areas of the huge circuit.

Three weeks after Pearl's arrival, Southgate was recalled to London and left Stationer in the capable hands of Jacqueline and Maingard. They, along with Chantraine and Rechenmann, continued to undertake sabotage missions, and the reception and distribution of material, which they spread around the entire circuit among Resistance members, telling them to keep everything safe for when it was needed. They were stockpiling as much as they could for D-Day, which they were sure could not be far off, not realizing at that stage just how far distant that day still was.

By the end of 1943 Jacqueline was desperately tired and longing for some rest, but she refused to take even one day off. The responsibilities she was shouldering and the tireless work she continued to undertake were inevitably having a bad effect on her health. She found that she didn't have the strength to walk very far or carry anything heavy; every movement was a huge effort for her. But still she hung on, refusing to admit how ill she was feeling.

Then disaster struck. Just before Christmas there had been a failed attempt to free captured Resistance members from the prison in Châteauroux and, although he had not been involved, for some inexplicable reason Auguste Chantraine was suspected by the Germans of being one of the rescue party. He was arrested and deported to Germany. Later he was moved to the concentration camp of Mauthausen near the Austrian city of Linz where, in March 1945, he was executed. The arrest of Chantraine was a huge blow to Jacqueline and Maingard, who felt that they had lost a friend and a trusted colleague. To the Resistance fighters whom he had led it was a calamity. It was something they all felt personally, as Chantraine had been a major part of their lives, and was a valuable and respected leader. His arrest also meant that his land, which had long been a dropping zone for agents and supplies, could no longer be used. When Jacqueline and Maingard learnt of

Chantraine's capture they knew that they would have to act quickly to ensure that Southgate wasn't dropped in this area, as had been the plan for his arrival from England. There was a further problem, as Chantraine knew Maingard's address in the avenue de la Gare in Châteauroux and the two men had been seen together, so the address was no longer a safe place for anyone from the circuit.

At the end of 1943, as Southgate was preparing to return to France, unaware of the tragedy that had befallen Stationer, Buckmaster sent him a note, telling him:

> I once said to you that yours was the ideal circuit, and I would like you to have that as my New Year's message to you and all who are working with you. I know that you are inspired by the same spirit as we all are and I would like to congratulate you on the discreet but force-ful way in which you have given expression to it in your work.
>
> … If Jacqueline would like a rest for a week or 10 days in a country house in Sussex – nothing to do but eat eggs for breakfast and play with a puppy – I shall be very glad to arrange it chez some friends of ours, who will not ask any indiscreet questions, and who are absolutely trust-worthy from the security angle.[5]

Before Southgate left London, he received a message from Maingard telling him not to go to his address in Châteauroux because of Chantraine's arrest. He flew back to France at the end of January 1944 in a 138 Squadron Halifax piloted by Flight Sergeant Hayman and parachuted on to a dropping zone near Lubbon in south-west France. The drop had been hastily arranged with the leader of the

Wheelwright circuit, George Starr (*Hilaire*), and went without a hitch. Southgate immediately caught a bus to Toulouse and then went on to Tarbes, where he saw members of Rechenmann's sub-circuit before heading for Montluçon to meet Maingard and Pearl.

In the first week after his return he received word from London of a drop of 20 agents, for which he had to arrange a dropping zone and a reception committee. Soon afterwards he was part of a reception committee for another three agents arriving from England. While speaking to the aircraft captain on one of the new S-Phones (a two-way wireless system), Southgate was also asked to arrange a drop for a Major Antelme and his wireless operator and courier. He suggested a zone near Poitiers and this information was passed back to London.

When he eventually caught up with Jacqueline, whom he had not seen for over three months, Southgate was profoundly shocked by her appearance. She had lost a lot of weight and was obviously exhausted. Finding a moment to talk to her alone, he told her about the offer Buckmaster had made and said that he was going to get Maingard to send a message to the Colonel, asking him to arrange for a flight to take her back to London for a good rest. She told him that she was fine and that she wasn't going anywhere, as she didn't need a rest. It was the first time that Southgate had sensed any sort of defiance in Jacqueline's manner. She didn't want to leave him in the lurch with D-Day coming up, and she was determined to be there herself to greet the Allies when they finally arrived. Southgate allowed himself to be talked out of sending a message for the time being, but resolved to keep an eye on her and see how she was in a week or so. Despite his time in London he, too, was worn out but also desperate to be in France when the longed-for Allied invasion began. He could fully understand why Jacqueline wanted to be there too, but he had to think about the safety of the other members of his circuit. After all the backbreaking work they had both done, he knew that it would seem like failure to Jacqueline to go home before the final push was under way and the liberation of the country they both loved was beyond doubt. But he worried that unless her health improved very soon Jacqueline might slip up, simply because she was so weary.

After a very short time Southgate knew that whatever Jacqueline said to the contrary, she would have to return to England; she was not getting any better. He asked Maingard to send a message to Buckmaster with a request for transport for her. In February an aircraft arrived to take her back to England. The pilot had been instructed to make sure that Jacqueline, who had been told to be ready to leave, was on board the return flight. She, however, had decided not to take any notice of Buckmaster's order and gave her seat to a French politician who needed to get to London in a hurry. It was probably the only time in her SOE career that she disobeyed an order. Buckmaster was not pleased but he soon forgave her; after all, she was still one of his favourites and he was annoyed mainly because he was worried about her.

Back in England Francis was still staying in a bed-and-breakfast hotel, with very little money and no idea of what was going to happen to him. His case had been referred to Captain Jepson by Vera Atkins after she had consulted Colonel Buckmaster. They had agreed that the kindest way of explaining his removal from the SOE was to say that they couldn't use him operationally because the Gestapo knew too much about him. Atkins told Jepson that until Francis found employment or was called up for the Army, the SOE would pay him £1 per day but they would not provide him with any accommodation, the rationale being that it would 'leave him quite free to go and do as he pleases until he is fixed up'.[6]

Jepson acted promptly. Two days after being given the task of removing Francis from SOE's employ, he contacted Military Intelligence to say that Francis was 'to be disposed of' and returned to civilian life, where he would have to take his chance of being called up for military service. Jepson wanted to know if this course of action would amount to a security risk, since Francis had already completed some of what was a top-secret course. By the end of February 1944 it had been decided that he did not present a threat and two weeks later he was told that he was to be 'landed'. Because he had entered Britain on a secret flight and had been in the charge of the SOE since his arrival, the British authorities had no idea that he was in England. The purpose of his 'landing' was to bring him into the country officially and to this end he was taken to the Immigration Office at Ibex House in the City by a member of SOE's Security Section, who told an immigration official that Francis was a British subject and had arrived that day, 14 March 1944, from France via Gibraltar. He was issued with British documents, and told he would have to have a medical for the Ministry of Labour and that, if found to be fit, he would be classified for military service.

Two days later Francis was 'sworn out' of the SOE by signing a declaration that he would not disclose anything he knew about the establishment's work or special training schools. Having given his signature he was, in effect, cast adrift from the organization that had taken him from his home and family, and had brought him to England five months earlier.

Confident that Jacqueline would not dare to disobey orders again and would, therefore, be back in England soon, Buckmaster decided to make one more attempt to resolve what had become an impossible situation. He did not want her to return and, after giving such wonderful service to his section, discover that he had abandoned her brother. In March he wrote a note to the Director of Finance, telling him:

> This man is a brother of one of our very good women couriers. She has been in the Field since January 1943 and at the beginning of November 1943 she sent over her brother for training in this country and return to the Field.
>
> Unfortunately he has completely failed to pass the medical standard required and we have been compelled to return him to civilian life. He is in a very nervous and weak condition and it will prove exceptionally difficult to find him suitable employment and to make things more difficult, his English is far from perfect ...
>
> In view of the special circumstances surrounding this case and the very good services being given by his two sisters, I am afraid we shall have to support this man until his health is sufficiently recovered or until his sister [Jacqueline] arrives: she may be able to help. At present he is still receiving pay at trainees' rates and we are paying his hotel for bed and breakfast. I think it would be more satisfactory to pay him say £10 per week and let

him look after himself. In view of the fact that he is an ill man and has neither friends nor family in this country, I do not think he will be able to keep himself on less.

Buckmaster ended his note by asking the director, 'Will you please let me have your views?' Yet again, the fate of poor Francis had been passed on to someone else.

CHAPTER 8

Coming Home

With her departure for France now imminent, Didi could hardly contain her excitement. She knew that she had a lot to live up to; she had heard rumours about how well Jacqueline was doing in her circuit and was determined to do as well herself. Despite her eagerness, she knew that what she was going to be doing in France would be neither easy nor safe. Everyone, from her instructors to Buckmaster himself, had impressed upon her what a difficult task she was taking on and she was aware that her life would depend upon how she adapted to the conditions she found on her arrival. Buckmaster had done her a favour when he commented that she was a good liar: the remark had given her confidence in her ability to become someone she was not, which was what she had to do if she were to be believable and stay secure. She spent a lot of time rehearsing her cover story, convincing herself that she really was a not-too-bright shop girl called Jacqueline du Tertre, until the story became so familiar to her that she could almost have repeated it in her sleep.

She was told that she would be leaving for France at the end of February 1944 and would be travelling with her new boss, William Jean Savy, known usually as Jean, who was to be the head of a new circuit called Wizard, based to the south-west of Paris in the *département* of Seine et Oise. When she met him, she knew that the reason she would not need to use a parachute was that he had a physical disability, a withered arm, which prevented him from controlling a parachute. Instead they would be flown to France onboard one of the tiny, black-painted Westland Lysanders, which could take off and land quickly on a very short runway or in a small field, a vital attribute in ensuring that they avoided German patrols in the area of the landing zones.

Didi liked Savy. She sensed that he was a solid, dependable type. He in turn realized that his wireless operator had a strong love of France and felt that she was a serious young woman who would help him in the great task he had been set.

Savy had been brought into SOE by France Antelme, a former businessman from Mauritius and now a British Army major, who had begun his own SOE career in Madagascar during the British invasion of the island in 1942. Antelme's work there had been so successful that he was picked for undercover work in France where, when he arrived in November 1942, his task had been to contact prominent bankers, businessmen and politicians, and to arrange provisions and finance for the Allied invasion of mainland Europe which, they all hoped, would herald the end of the war. He met Savy while in France and arranged for him to be trained by SOE, accompanying him to England in July 1943.

A well-respected Paris lawyer, Savy remained in England for the next seven and a half months, assisting F Section in the preparation of false documentation in advance of the

Allied invasion. It was then arranged that he should return to his homeland and, having many influential contacts himself, extend the work that had already been done and would continue to be done when Antelme himself returned to France. Savy was given the code names *Regis* and *Alcide*, and the alias Capitaine Jean Millet of the French Army.

In many ways an ideal candidate for the SOE, 37-year-old Savy was well travelled, with a variety of skills including the ability to cycle, drive, ride horses, swim, sail and shoot. He also possessed a pilot's licence. He had, however, two major flaws which, should the Germans suspect him of clandestine activity, would make him easy to identify: his disabled right arm and the fact that he was a well-known figure in Paris. He was so well known that he saw no point in disguising himself in the capital and, when there, worked from his own office at 6 rue d'Alger, happy to disregard his own safety in order to serve his country.

As the departure date for Didi and Savy drew near, Didi felt a slight twinge of unease as well as the excitement that had sustained her since finishing her training, but she brushed it aside. Her suspense was to last a little longer, as bad weather in late February delayed their departure for several days, but they eventually arrived at a landing zone near Vatan in the *département* of Indre, north of Châteauroux, on the night of 2/3 March, having flown from RAF Tempsford in Bedfordshire in a Lysander piloted by Flight Lieutenant Murray 'Andy' Anderson of 161 Squadron.

Recalling the flight, Didi said: 'I well remember how I felt when, from the aeroplane, we saw the red lights of the reception committee. We had a good landing and when the Lysander came to a stop we were met by two men with

strong Parisian accents, asking us "Are you OK? We have
to be very quick or we'll all be caught."' The men were
from the Greyhound circuit and, hearing their voices, Didi
felt that she had come home. As she and Savy moved away
from the tiny aircraft, they came face to face with two
agents who were returning to England on the Lysander,
Georges Lovinfosse and Maurice Durieux. When they saw
Didi they were worried that she was much too young for
the work that she had come to do. They told her that
France was too dangerous for someone so young and urged
her to return to England immediately. She ignored their
advice, telling them that she had no intention of going
anywhere, except to where she was being sent. Lovinfosse,
a Belgian businessman, had a country house near
Châteauroux and was head of the Greyhound circuit to
which the reception committee was attached, while
Durieux was an agent of the Political Warfare Executive
(PWE), whose task had been to destroy German labour
records to impede the conscription of labour from France
to Germany. Giving a final glance to the man and the very
young woman who had just arrived, they boarded the
aeroplane and were soon on their way to England.

   Didi's recollection continued: 'The reception committee
had organized a cart which was waiting for us and our
baggage. Then, carrying our revolvers in our hands, we
were taken across the field in it, to a barn where we spent
the rest of the night. The next morning my *chef* and I
parted.'' Didi's first night in France, after so long in
England, was not what she had expected. She had never
slept in a barn before. It was dirty, uncomfortable and full
of spiders. It was also bitterly cold. She was not sorry when
it became light and the two men from the reception

committee told her that it was time to go to the station. Savy was left to make his own way and went off to find France Antelme, who had returned two days earlier.

With her two companions, Didi set off for the station, the young men having told her that they would go with her as far as Orléans and take her to a safe house where she could stay the night. As they left the isolation of the farm and the barn and headed towards the town, they passed very few people. It was still early in the morning and, apart from a few farm workers, there was hardly anyone around. They reached the station, found the train for Orléans and climbed aboard.

So far everything was going well, but when they reached Orléans and Didi saw German soldiers at the station, she was horrified. Her dismay increased as they walked through the town, as there were more soldiers in the streets. She couldn't help staring at them, frightening the life out of her companions, one of whom hissed at her, 'For God's sake, don't do that. Don't ever stare at them like that.' She quickly realized that she had done a stupid thing and she averted her eyes, managing to ignore the Germans for the remainder of the journey. Although she hadn't attracted any unwanted attention from the soldiers she realized that it was not enough to have adopted a new identity; she had to show that she was at ease in any situation or else her cover would be blown. Her companions took her to the safe house, where she would spend the remainder of that day and one night before leaving the following morning for Paris. They then wished her good luck and went back to the station for their return journey to their Greyhound circuit, very relieved that their charge's indiscretion had not caused any unwanted encounters with the Germans.

The following day Didi set off alone for Orléans station. Remembering her mistake of the previous day, she ignored the soldiers she passed on the way. At the station itself there were many more Germans but, gritting her teeth and trying to ignore the revulsion she felt at the sight of them, she bought a ticket for the train to Paris and went to the platform to wait for it.

Once on board the train Didi mentally went through everything she needed to do on her arrival. Her instructions had been to get in touch with a young woman called Louise as soon as possible after arriving. She would be Didi's contact in Paris and would help her find somewhere to live. As soon as the train arrived at the Gare d'Austerlitz – the station named after the Battle of Austerlitz of 1805, which, according to Napoleon, was the finest he had fought – Didi set off for the Pont-Neuf to find Louise. She walked along the quai Saint-Bernard, past the Jardin des Plantes, the main botanical garden of France, on her left and the Pont-de-Sully on her right, and then continued along the quai de la Tournelle until on her right she saw the magnificent cathedral of Notre-Dame on the Île de la Cité. The Pont Neuf led from the left bank – the Rive Gauche along which she had walked – across the Seine to the Île de la Cité and then on again over the part of the river on the other side of the island. She had been told that Louise would be waiting for her on the bridge.

It was still bitterly cold and was snowing heavily. Didi began walking across the bridge looking for a woman she knew to be about her own age but saw no one who could have been her contact. Then, as she reached the part of the bridge that crossed the island, she stopped for a moment to admire the bronze statue of Henry IV astride his horse and saw a girl who was just standing in the snow, while all around her hurried past. Didi knew she had found Louise.

The two women walked towards each other and Louise greeted Didi as if she were an old friend. Then, taking her arm and tucking it into her own, she turned and led the way back across the bridge. She told Didi as they walked that she was taking her to her own home, since it was her first day in the capital. Once they arrived at the apartment in the Place Saint-Michel, Louise began to explain what she could do for Didi and how they would be able to contact each other in the future. She told her that although she could come to the house to pick up and deliver messages, she could not stay there, so it was imperative that she find a room as soon as possible. Louise explained that she shared the apartment with her mother and her sisters, and she couldn't allow anyone to stay there long term because of the danger to her family. But she told Didi that she could stay that night, and in the morning she would help her find somewhere to live and another room from where she could make her wireless transmissions.

Now that she had safely arrived in Paris, Didi began to feel more relaxed about the work she had come to do. Even if she couldn't stay with Louise she knew that she would have a place where she could occasionally see a friendly face, even if only for a few minutes, and she felt that her faith in God would help her whenever she felt lonely. She wasn't worried about being alone; she was comfortable with her own company and in her heart she was sure that she would be safe. Now all she had to do was find somewhere to live and begin her work.

CHAPTER 9

Monumental Errors

By 1944 accommodation in Paris had become scarce. Many of the rooms that had been available earlier in the war had now been taken by people coming into the capital in search of work; the Germans had commandeered others. Although it might be tolerable for a wireless operator to live in a building close to where Germans lived, it would be impossible to send messages from such an address, so Didi's requirement for two places made her task very difficult. After staying in a safe house for a few days, with Louise's help she managed to find a room in Porte Champerret, an area in the north-west of Paris named after one of the gates in the nineteenth-century Thiers Wall, the last of the seven defensive walls of Paris. For Didi it was a very convenient place in which to live, as it was close to the city and had its own Metro station. However, it proved to be much more difficult to secure a place for her wireless set.

Remembering what she had learnt on her training course, Didi knew that the place from which she would make her transmissions had to be away from neighbours' prying eyes, yet somewhere where she would not look suspicious if she were seen entering and leaving it regularly. She also recalled being told that suburbs were the safest places from which to broadcast, as the Germans had most of their direction-finding equipment in cities and towns. Eventually, again with the help of Louise and her contacts, she found a house in Bourg-la-Reine, a suburb south-west of Paris about 8 kilometres from the centre of the city. It belonged to a M. and Mme Dubois, who were agreeable to the young wireless operator using it for her transmissions. The Dubois house was, therefore, as close to being ideal as it could be.

Didi's next task was to take the wireless set to its new home. She wasn't looking forward to this, as she would have to travel across Paris carrying the equipment, which weighed around 18 kilos and was the size of a small suitcase. She could take the train and hope that she got a seat in an empty compartment. It would certainly be quicker than walking, but would not give her a good chance of escape should things not go as planned. On the other hand, carrying a case of that weight through the streets of Paris, while it might allow her a better chance of flight should she be suspected of anything, would be very tiring, possibly dangerous, and could take her a long time.

When the Germans had first come to Paris they had behaved reasonably well for an invading force. Although the local people hated them being in their capital city, they had been left alone in most cases. Four years on, however, many of the occupying forces had lost their manners and life had become much more difficult for the locals. Even walking along the same street as a German soldier could be risky. The troops often stopped and searched people whose faces they didn't like. It was not unusual for a soldier to hit or kick a Frenchman or woman, and there was also the danger of being knocked over on the street by one of their vehicles. Didi still had to send a message to London to tell the SOE that she and her circuit leader had arrived safely and, although she needed to be ready to transmit whenever Savy contacted her, she hadn't yet found out if he had returned from his trip to visit Major Antelme. Whenever she called on Louise to find out what was happening, she was always disappointed to discover that Savy had not been in touch. Then one day, Louise told her that the circuit leader was back in Paris.

Jean Savy had been having problems of his own. When he and Didi had parted the morning after their arrival, Savy had gone directly to the area where he knew France Antelme had planned to be. He was keen to start the work that they were going to be doing together as soon as possible, as there was still much to be done, and many more people to contact and persuade to donate money and goods for the Allied invasion army. When Antelme had arrived on the night of 28/29 February, as head of the Bricklayer circuit, his wireless operator Lionel Lee and his courier Madeleine Damerment had gone with him. Since this was only two days before Savy had arrived, he had assumed that finding Antelme would be relatively easy. Then he received some devastating news.

The trio had landed at Sainville, approximately 30 kilometres east of Chartres, parachuting from a 161 Squadron Halifax, piloted by Flight Lieutenant Caldwell, London having ignored Maurice Southgate's advice to use the dropping zone near Poitiers. Antelme had asked that they be dropped to a reception committee and was pleased to find people there to meet them. After landing they gathered up their parachutes and quickly made their way towards their reception committee. Too late they realized that the waiting group of men was not the team they had expected but Gestapo officers. All three of the new arrivals were arrested and taken to the offices of the Sicherheitsdienst in Paris at 84 avenue Foch, where Sturmbannführer Hans Josef Kieffer, senior German counter-intelligence officer, interrogated them.

Antelme was in a rage and refused to disclose any details of who he was or what he had been sent to do. When Kieffer let him know that his identity was already known he admitted that he was France Antelme but refused to give any other details, claiming instead that he was to receive orders on his arrival in France. Lionel Lee and Madeleine Damerment also refused to disclose information about their roles.

When Antelme had asked to be dropped to a reception committee, it was decided that it should come from Cinema/Phono, a sub-circuit of the famous Physician/Prosper circuit operating just south of Paris. Before leaving for France, Antelme himself had expressed confidence in this circuit, although there were a few officers in London who had suspicions that all was not well and that there was a possibility that the circuit had been penetrated. As a precaution Antelme was told that after his arrival he was to cut all contacts with Cinema/Phono.

A few days after the arrests, F section, believing that the Bricklayer team had arrived safely, received a message that told them that Antelme had hit his head on a container of supplies when he landed on 29 February and that he had been severely injured. The message came from the wireless operator of the Cinema/Phono circuit, Noor Inayat Khan – or so they thought. In reality she had been captured in October 1943, four months before.

When she was arrested, Noor used a special security measure given to her by code master Leo Marks, who had told her, during an extended briefing in London before she left for France, that she should never use an 18-letter key phrase in any of her transmissions. If a message arrived from her containing such a key phrase, he said he would know that she had been arrested.[1] The very first message sent by Noor under duress contained just such a key phrase and Marks knew that she was in trouble. He immediately contacted Buckmaster and told him what had happened, but the Colonel refused to believe him and announced his intention of continuing to send messages to Noor. When she was next made to send a message she omitted one of her two regular security checks to alert London but this did not work either. Although she had never left out the codes in any of her previous messages, it was assumed that she had simply forgotten them and, unbelievably, this 'oversight' was ignored.

For the next few months the wireless messages purporting to be sent by her had in fact been sent by Kieffer's subordinate, Dr Josef Goetz, a teacher and language expert in civilian life, or by one of his signals officers. Every one of them had been sent with only one security check, as told to them by Noor, yet no one in London, including Buckmaster, seemed to be concerned. Since there were those, albeit a small number, who had doubted the veracity of the messages sent by this circuit anyway, one has to wonder why the decision to send the three agents to a reception committee from Cinema/Phono had been made. Whatever the reason – sloppiness? arrogance? complacency? – this gross lack of judgement ensured that three valuable agents were lost.

On 24 March, nearly a month after Antelme, Lee and Damerment had been captured, Lee was instructed to make a broadcast to London confirming the details about Antelme's injury. He gave the Germans false details about where his security checks should be placed and another message was sent, reporting this time that Antelme's health was deteriorating. Soon yet another message was sent, again with the security checks in the wrong place, which told London that Antelme had died of his injuries. Despite Lee's efforts to let them know that his messages were not safe, officers in the Signals Directorate had marked 'Special check present' on the transcripts of the broadcasts and the paperwork had simply been filed. Three weeks after Lee's transmission, Gerry Morel, F Section's Operations Officer, who was one of the few who doubted the reliability of the messages, was still feeling very uneasy about them and asked for the transcripts to be re-examined. They were all pulled out of the files and each one was scrutinized. Finally it was admitted that the checks had been put in the wrong place. F Section accepted that the Germans had been work-ing the wireless sets, and that it was therefore safe to assume that Noor Inayat Khan, France Antelme, Lionel Lee and Madeleine Damerment were all in the hands of the enemy.

In Paris, after their interrogation in the avenue Foch, Antelme and Lee were taken to the Gestapo torture cham-bers in rue des Saussaies in a final attempt to make them talk. Believing that London would know by the wrongly placed checks that they had been arrested and would be able to alert all their contacts in France, so that they could disperse and save themselves and the circuit, they bravely endured the torture and remained silent. After a few days the Germans assumed that the people expecting the three agents to arrive would have realized that they had been captured and would have disappeared. The torture was stopped, as any information they might have gained by continuing it would, by now, be out of date. Antelme and Lee were no longer of any use to them and were sent on to the concentration camp at Gross-Rosen in Lower Silesia (now Rogoznica, Poland), where they were both executed, Antelme on 19 May and Lee on 27 June 1944. Madeleine Damerment was taken to the civilian prison in Karlsruhe, where she was kept for some months before being transported to Dachau concentration camp near Munich. Noor Inayat Khan, who had been behind bars in the prison of Pforzheim, was brought to Dachau to join Madeleine in late summer and on 13 September 1944 both women were executed by shots in the back of the neck.

Had these been the only errors made by F section regarding the transmission of messages and missing security checks that led to the deaths of agents, it would have been bad. But there is strong evidence that this was only one of several occasions on which similar mistakes had been made, yet London had learnt nothing from the blunders.

In June the previous year Gilbert Norman, the wireless operator for the Physician/Prosper circuit in Paris, had been arrested, along with courier Andrée Borrel and the circuit leader Francis Suttill, whose code name *Prosper* gave Physician its alternative name. Norman, an excellent wireless operator who rarely sent a message with any errors, transmitted one in which one of his checks was missing. Because it was so unlike him to do this, Leo Marks was convinced that he had done so to inform London of his arrest; this, after all, was what the checks were for.

Others in London were also convinced that he was no longer free and was sending the messages under duress. But Buckmaster, ignoring the obvious proof of his arrest, immediately sent off a reply, reprimanding him for his serious breach of security and warning him not to do it again.[2] This reply told the Germans that Norman had lied to them about the way he transmitted to London and sealed the wireless operator's fate. Gilbert Norman was taken to Mauthausen concentration camp, where he was hanged in September 1944. Francis Suttill, the circuit leader, died in the concentration camp of Sachsenhausen near Berlin and courier Andrée Borrel was executed in the only Nazi concentration camp built in France, Natzweiler-Struthof, south-west of Strasbourg.

If more proof of London's ineptitude were needed, Maurice Southgate knew of similar situations and, in a report written on his return to England, made the following accusation:

> Several times I have had proof of agents from SOE being dropped on grounds held by the Germans themselves. The Germans then used the wireless sets, codes and crystals of the new arrivals, but for a long time they did not realise that there were two checks on outgoing telegrams (from the field to England), one the true check, the other the bluff check. These telegrams were sent out with one check only and most obviously should have been phoney to London HQ. Time after time, for different men, London sent back messages saying: 'My dear fellow, you only left us a week ago. On your first messages you go and forget to put your true check.' (Squadron Leader Southgate would very much like to know what the hell

the check was meant for if not for that very special occasion.) You may now realise what happened to our agents
who did *not* give the true check to the Germans, thus
making them send out a message that was obviously
phoney, and after being put through the worst degrees of
torture these Germans managed, sometimes a week later,
to get hold of the true check, and then sent a further
message to London with the proper check in the telegram, and London saying: 'Now you are a good boy,
now you have remembered to give both of them.'

   This happened not once, but several times. I consider
that the officer responsible for such neglect of his duties
should be severely court martialled, because he is responsible for the death and capture of many agents, including
Major Antelme for one, who was arrested the minute he
put his foot on French soil.[3]

Colonel Buckmaster still could not admit that some dread-
ful errors of judgment had been made. Commenting on
Southgate's report he said: 'The attached is clearly the
report of an extremely tired man. Its lack of continuity and
its abrupt switching of subjects bear eloquent testimony to
the sufferings of the author.'[4]

It was against this backdrop of monumental errors that
Didi would be embarking upon her career as a wireless
operator.

CHAPTER 10

An Uncomfortable Journey

On 26 March, nearly a month after she had arrived in Paris, Didi took her wireless set to its new home. Although she was concerned about taking the train, she knew that there was danger in whichever way she decided to travel. The wireless was too heavy to carry all the way from Porte Champerret to Bourg-la-Reine and in such cold weather, and there was also a danger that she would attract far more attention to herself if she had to keep stopping to catch her breath along the road. She had already travelled by herself on the train from Orléans to Paris without any problems, although being in the capital was obviously more dangerous.

She bought a ticket and waited for the train to arrive. As it pulled in she spotted a carriage that was almost empty and climbed on board, keeping her case close by. Then just as the train was about to leave, the door was flung open and a small group of German soldiers clambered in. They sank, out of breath, on to the seats opposite Didi. She turned her eyes towards the window and ignored them. She might have to travel on the same train as them but she didn't have to look at them. She was an attractive 23-year-old and she did not want to have to fend off unwanted attention; indeed her lack of experience of situations like this was one of the things that had worried her sister.

Suddenly the young man sitting opposite her began to speak. She heard him greet her in halting French and turned her head to find that he was smiling at her. Not wanting to encourage him, she smiled politely and turned away again. The young German would not be put off. Again he spoke to her, asking, 'What do you have in your case?' She turned back in confusion and he, believing that she had not understood his question, pointed to her case. Trying to appear confident, although feeling very frightened, she glanced at it and replied, 'Oh that? It's just a gramophone!', praying silently that he wouldn't ask to see it. He didn't, and Didi thought that she had diffused the situation.

Her relief lasted for only a moment. As she turned her face towards the window again, the young man tried to strike up a conversation with her once more. Fumbling in his pocket, he produced a packet of cigarettes and held it out towards her, asking in the same hesitant French if she would like one. Didi turned back to him and gave him what she believed was an icy stare and refused his offer, informing him that she didn't smoke. As soon as the words were out of her mouth she regretted having said them. The German's face fell, his smile vanished and he stared at her hands, folded in her lap, the fingers stained by nicotine. She knew at once that she had made a big mistake. In her haste to remain aloof she had told a silly lie. Her heart sank. She felt sick and cursed her stupidity. How could she have been such an idiot? Too late she realized that he had just wanted to chat to her but, by snubbing him in front of his colleagues, all she had done was humiliate him. He was now looking at her with contempt and she was frightened that he would turn on her; her cover would be blown and all the effort she had put into reaching England and joining the SOE would have been for nothing. Her mind raced as she tried to think of a way to recover the situation. Glancing at the other soldiers, she could see that they were making fun of him and the look on his face told her that he wasn't taking their teasing very well. He said something in German that she couldn't understand and they all looked at her. This time none of them was smiling.

Didi knew that she had to keep calm and not let them see that she was becoming nervous. They were now distinctly suspicious of her but if she left the train at the next stop they might realize that she was making her escape, so she decided that she must remain where she was. It was all she could do to stay in her seat as the train came to a stop. She turned her head towards the window and watched the people who were leaving: people who were free to do as they pleased – or as free as anyone could be in an occupied country – while she remained surrounded by enemy soldiers, carrying a piece of equipment that would mean her certain arrest, if not death, if discovered.

The train began to move again and she knew that she couldn't remain on board any longer. As the train pulled into the next station, she stood up, hoping that none of the soldiers would offer to help her with her case, and smiled weakly at the one she had offended. He just glared at her, so she said goodbye, picked up the case, trying hard not to show how heavy it was, and stepped on to the platform. Expecting to feel a hand on her shoulder at any moment and to hear a demand for her to open her case, she walked quickly towards the exit. Her legs felt weak and her heart was beating so fast that she was sure everyone would know she had a guilty secret. But the train began to move off again and although she glimpsed the young men glaring at her through the carriage window, she had not been followed. She almost collapsed with relief. She didn't even know where she was and had to stop for a moment to work out which way she needed to go from there. One thing that she was sure of was that she wouldn't be catching another train that day, however far away she was from Bourg-la-Reine.

Having discovered that she was about four stations short of her destination, she began walking. The incident had shaken her badly. It was yet another reminder of how careful she had to be and she thanked God that she had come through the ordeal unscathed. As she walked she remembered the advice given on her training course that wireless operators should not transport their wireless sets themselves, as operators were more valuable than sets. She thought it was well-meaning nonsense. Why on earth would anyone voluntarily put themselves through what she had just undergone knowing what the consequences might be if they were caught? In any case she had no idea where she would have found someone to carry her wireless set.

When Didi finally reached the Dubois house in Bourg-la-Reine she quickly set up the wireless and the aerial, fervently hoping that she wouldn't have any trouble communicating with London. With relief she found that everything was in good working order and the frequency she had to use for her broadcasts was very clear. She sent the message telling London that she and Savy had arrived safely, that she had met her contact and that everything was in place, ready for her to begin her work. With her first message completed she dismantled the aerial and carefully packed away the wireless set, ready for the next time. Then she returned to the city, this time without the heavy case and with a lighter heart.

Every day since 1940 the BBC had broadcast a programme on its French service that contained many pre-arranged, seemingly nonsensical, messages. The programme always began with the words 'Ici Londres – les messages personnels de la BBC' and continued with messages such as 'It always rains in England', 'Hear my heart crying', 'I like Siamese cats' and so on. Although they sounded like rubbish to any of the general public who listened to them, they represented a lifeline to the Resistance and to agents such as Didi. These messages were used to pass on all sorts of information. They told agents when to begin sabotaging various targets like railway tracks or factories; when to expect a drop of supplies or people; when not to expect them because of unforeseen conditions; and other similar instructions. Sometimes they even gave personal news, such as the birth of a baby.

On the evening after she had made her first transmission to London, Didi hoped to hear a message through the BBC French service that would confirm that her wire had been safely received. Still feeling shaky from the close call she had had with the German soldiers, she was uncharacteristically in need of some company, so she went to spend an hour or so with Louise and her family at their home in the Place Saint-Michel, to listen to the messages. This in itself was dangerous. When the Germans had discovered that the BBC was making these broadcasts and that they had no way of knowing what they meant because they were not in code but were just fixed phrases, they banned the use of personal wirelesses. To ensure that this ban was heeded, they sent direction-finding vans on to the streets to tour the area, listening for any indication that wirelesses were being used. Nevertheless that evening Didi and her friends listened carefully for the words that would confirm that her communication had been received. Eventually with huge relief they heard the message that they had been told to listen out for, which was believed to be 'Happy to know that the duck has had a good trip'.[1]

The day had ended better than Didi could have hoped. She was still safe and had learnt a lot from having made that awful train journey. She felt that she was better prepared for what she might encounter from now on and if she ever needed company she knew that all she had to do was walk past Louise's apartment in the Place Saint-Michel to know that people who cared about her were there, just behind those walls.

From that moment Didi resolved never to be caught out again. When in the street she kept a constant watch on anyone who seemed to be walking behind her for very long. Years later she said: 'I wasn't nervous. In my mind I was never going to be arrested. But of course I was careful. There were Gestapo in plain clothes everywhere. I always looked at my reflection in the shop windows to see if I was being followed.'[2] If it looked as if she was being followed she would quickly turn around and walk the other way, or enter a shop to see if the stalker followed her. Although she was often suspicious, these fears never amounted to anything. When entering a train she was very wary and rather than pick a seat in an empty carriage, as she had done before, she would try to choose a carriage that was nearly full, with few seats free for any German soldiers who came aboard. She also tried to avoid places where she knew there would be Germans, such as the street news-stands, which were full of German newspapers and magazines. Her solitary life was, as she described it, a life in the shadows, and gradually as she became used to it, she also started to enjoy it. The work gave her a sense of purpose and whenever she transmitted a message to England she felt pride in what she was doing.

Jean Savy, meanwhile, had been having a difficult time. As well as often meeting Didi and sending messages that she coded and transmitted, he had been working tirelessly to try to salvage and resurrect some of Major Antelme's contacts, and to establish more of his own. It was not an easy task. He knew that the Allied invasion of Europe could not be very far off and, with his friend having been arrested, much of the responsibility for the financing and provision of food for the troops rested with him. Then one day, while he was out and about trying to recruit new supporters, he stumbled across some information so shocking that he felt it was too sensitive to relay by wireless. He asked Didi to send a message to London as soon as she possibly could to ask for an aircraft to be sent to fetch him and take him back to England. The information he possessed could only be relayed in person.

The Deadly Discovery

Four hundred kilometres to the south and still unaware that her sister was in France, Jacqueline refused to stop working. Her health had not improved; on the contrary it was getting worse, and Southgate was becoming more and more concerned about his courier. He knew that he had to get her back to England as soon as possible but his own workload was increasing daily. He was worn out himself and, following the arrest of Auguste Chantraine and the subsequent loss of his land for aircraft operations, the Stationer circuit still had no dropping or landing zones, which meant more travelling for its leader and for Jacqueline when she was part of a reception committee, or had to escort a new arrival.

Southgate had hoped that the appearance of James Mayer (*Frank*), Georges Audouard (*Martial*) and Pierre Mattei (*Gaetan*), the three agents he had received on 11 February just after his own return from England, would have provided some respite but all it did was cause him more problems.

Mayer had remained in Tarbes, close to where they had landed, and fitted in very well with the local Resistance members, including Charles Rechenmann, who was setting up a new circuit called Rover, which would reduce the enormous size of Stationer. Mayer became Rechenmann's second-in-command. Audouard had been sent to Terrasson and told to join another agent, Jacques Dufour (*Anastasie*),[1] and help him form a group there under the leadership of a Monsieur Delord, who owned a clothing depot. When he visited the group, Southgate was very disappointed with what had been achieved. Delord seemed to have no authority over the agents and Audouard only obeyed orders when he felt like doing so. Despite his poor performance, Southgate had to send him on to Châteauneuf, south-east of Limoges, to instruct the group there in the use of bazookas, booby traps and mortars, for which he had been trained in England. While he was away, trouble started in Terrasson over the killing of two Resistance members by the Milice, the Vichy French volunteer paramilitary organization, and Dufour asked Southgate to send Audouard back to him to help calm the situation. The agent refused to return and missed an appointment in Limoges soon afterwards, so Southgate, by now at his wits' end, asked London to order him back to England. Then he discovered that when Audouard had told him of things he had done, he had been lying – he had been with his mistress all the time; and when Southgate discovered her true identity, he was sick with worry, saying of her, 'This woman frightens me to such an extent that I may find myself obliged to send her to a better world.'[2] He didn't disclose her identity but it is believed that she had Nazi sympathies, which would account for his anxiety.

He told Audouard that he was sending him back to England and that he would be leaving soon. Audouard replied that he wasn't going anywhere. That was the final straw. Southgate sent a report to London, telling HQ:

You remember the operations on grounds Rose and Violette. You sent a plane and that plane returned to base without finding the reception committee. And it had a good reason. After having sent *Martial* [Georges Audouard] with the messages for the reception committee, and after having seen *Martial* again and learnt from him that the messages had been delivered, I heard after enquiry that *Martial* had never even set foot on Rose or Violette ... he told me later that the orders and messages had been given. Instead of which he was with his horrible and dangerous mistress. And that is why a plane and its crew came here for nothing.

... I am rather afraid that your orders to make him return to you arrived a little too late, for *Martial* and his mistress had to be executed Sunday night. I shall give you later the exact details and take all responsibility for this military execution, by military men, of a military man ...[3]

Despite this report, the execution of Georges Audouard and his lover hadn't actually taken place. Southgate had given the wayward agent one last chance to redeem himself, ordering him to leave his mistress and await his own arrival the following Friday, but of course Audouard wasn't going to hang around to see what Southgate would do. He escaped with the woman and was later arrested by the Germans. Luck was with him a second time as, although he was imprisoned, he survived the war.

The situation in the Stationer circuit was becoming untenable and for Southgate there were more problems to come. Agent Mattei had been tasked with finding new grounds that could be used as dropping or landing zones for agents and supplies. Southgate had sent him to Poitiers with an introduction to the bursar of Poitiers boys' school, who would help him, and had also told him to contact another agent, Pierre Hirsch (*Popaul*) in Montluçon, who he hoped might be able to suggest where he could look for landing zones. Mattei went back and forth looking for suitable grounds before contacting Southgate to tell him he couldn't find any. Exasperated, Southgate sent him away and nothing was heard from him for a week or two. Then Hirsch received a letter asking him to get either Pearl or Southgate to meet Mattei at the station in Poitiers. He mentioned a date and time but Southgate was in Montluçon at the time and when he received the cryptic message, it was too late to keep the appointment. Had it not been, it is doubtful whether he would have gone anyway, as he felt that 'the whole letter and story seemed phoney'.[4]

Eventually Pearl was sent to see the bursar at the school to find out if he knew what had happened to Mattei. She returned in an agitated state and told Southgate that when she had arrived the concierge stopped her going into the building and told her to leave as quickly as she could, as the house was full of Gestapo officers, and the bursar and his wife had been arrested. Southgate heard nothing more from Mattei. He too had been arrested and was imprisoned for much of the remainder of the war, but he eventually escaped and managed to get back to England. In 1946, he was awarded a Mention in Dispatches for the work he had done in Corsica, where he had been before being sent to the Stationer circuit, and because 'After his arrest [in Poitiers] he conducted himself with the utmost bravery and in spite of extreme pressure did not give away any of the people or addresses known to him.'[5] In truth he knew very few names and addresses of the agents in the Stationer group, but had the letter received by Hirsch arrived a little earlier and been believed, he might have been responsible for delivering Maurice Southgate, the biggest prize of all, to the Germans. Hirsch certainly believed that he himself was in danger of being betrayed, as he had met Mattei and passed on the message to Southgate. He was so concerned that the circuit might have been blown that he changed his name and obtained new documents in the name of Pierre d'Hamblemont.

Ironically, Mayer, the only one of the three agents to give Southgate no problems at all, was the only one who did not survive. He was arrested in May 1944 and a few days later so too was the Rover chief, Charles Rechenmann, who had given such sterling service to Southgate and Stationer. They were both taken to Fresnes and then on to Buchenwald concentration camp, where they were executed on 14 September 1944.

Because of the number of problems Southgate had had with the circuit and the fact that Mattei had not identified a landing zone before his disappearance, Jacqueline remained in France throughout March, even though back at SOE headquarters Buckmaster was still demanding to know when she was going to return home. She was becoming steadily weaker, although still working and maintaining that she was fine. To add to Southgate's woes, Pearl was also ill, suffering from rheumatism, which kept her immobile for a while.

Then Alexandre Schwatschko (*Olive*), a 24-year-old Romanian-born aircraft expert, arrived. Southgate reported that he was 'a big fellow, risks anything, (a bit too much even) who thank goodness can take care of himself ... very helpful in his work. I gave him carte blanche and a few weeks later his first Lysander operation was a success.'[6] This operation had been to organize a ground where a tiny Westland Lysander aircraft could land and take off, and then get London to send the aircraft to fetch Jacqueline and take her back to England.

For in April, she had received yet another order from Buckmaster to return to England. This time she knew when she was beaten and for the good of her health agreed with a heavy heart to leave. The last thing she wanted to do was to endanger the circuit to which she had devoted the past 15 months but, in a last act of defiance, she confirmed her intention of returning as soon as she felt better. She made one last exhausting journey to Paris, still unaware that her sister was there. They had been apart for nearly a year and a half, and it would have been wonderful for them to have spent even a few hours together, especially as the demands of the task Didi had undertaken there meant that she was living a very isolated, lonely existence. But their reunion was not to be and soon Jacqueline was heading south for Montluçon, where she stayed at the home of the Bidet family, a trusted safe house, while waiting to hear from which field she would be leaving for England.

At last news came through that a Lysander would be fetching her from a landing ground at Villers-les-Orme, a few kilometres to the north-west of Châteauroux. So she said goodbye to the Bidet family and went to stay at another safe house, a farm close to the ground, to await the aircraft's arrival. Here she met one of the two people who would be her travelling companions, a Frenchman known only to Jacqueline by his code name, *Regis*. The name meant nothing to her; she had never met him before and had no idea of his true identity or the work he had been doing for the SOE. She therefore did not know that *Regis* was the Wizard circuit leader, Jean Savy – Didi's boss.

Savy was going back to England because of what he had discovered. This was the trip that he had asked Didi to arrange for him so that he could personally deliver information too sensitive to relay to London by wireless. While travelling in northern France near Creil, approximately 60 kilometres north-east of Paris, he had come upon a quarry at Saint-Leu-d'Esserent, used by the Germans as an ammunitions dump. After talking to his contacts and looking for himself as much as he was able, he had discovered that the quarry actually contained around 2,000 rockets, ready to be fired at southern England.

It had been known for some time that the Germans were developing a rocket capable of carrying a 1.25-ton warhead that could travel long distances and destroy large areas of London and other towns and cities in southern England. In August 1943 the site at Peenemünde on the Baltic coast, which was believed to be at the heart of the experimental development, had been hit by bombs dropped by the RAF, and the feeling was that this had put back the programme for a considerable time. The truth was that while the damage to the site had been great and several hundred workers had been killed, production had been disrupted for only a matter of weeks and the rockets, known as V-1s, remained a serious threat. In the winter of 1943 further launch sites for the V-1s had been discovered in the Pas de Calais area but still no rockets had been launched against England and no one knew when it was planned to launch them. Savy realized that a haul as large as the one he had found had the potential to destroy much of London.

Horrified, he was anxious to get to London as soon as he could to make the authorities aware of this.

Savy and Jacqueline remained at the farm near Villers-les-Orme for three days, waiting for the aircraft to arrive. For some reason – Jacqueline never found out exactly what it was – they could not listen to the messages broadcast by the BBC, which would have told them when to expect their transport. It may have been because the farm owners were nervous about using their wireless set when there were workers around. They certainly didn't want the farm hands to know that Jacqueline and Savy were at the farm, which meant that the pair had to spend the first two days concealed in one of the outbuildings. On their third day it was thought too dangerous for them even to hide in an outbuilding and they were concealed in the hay until nightfall, only being allowed back into the farmhouse for something to eat at around 10 p.m.

Even if security had been less strict, and Jacqueline and Savy had been permitted to speak about their own work and that of their circuit members, it is unlikely that she would have discovered from him that Didi was working with him in France. Perhaps Savy knew that Didi had a sister but would not have been told that Jacqueline also worked for the SOE in France. Even if he had suspected that she did, he would never have realized that Jacqueline and Didi were sisters as they did not resemble each other physically. And so the three days passed slowly and Jacqueline never knew that that her companion could have told her how her young sister was coping in enemy-occupied Paris.

The other passenger who would be travelling to England arrived close to the departure time. She was Josette

Southgate, the wife of Maurice, who was leaving her home-land, having remained in Paris while her husband travelled around the country with his Resistance work. Mrs Southgate had given all the money she had, 200,000 francs (then equivalent to approximately £1,000), to her husband to use for Stationer. It was agreed that this would be regarded as a loan and would be repaid in London so that she would have some money with which to keep herself while in England. She intended to stay with her mother- and father-in-law, who were by then living in Slough at 33 Sussex Place.

When the Lysander finally landed Jacqueline was amused to see a chalked message on the side of the fuselage, which Buckmaster had written himself, hoping that it would ensure her compliance. It said, 'Jacqueline must come. This is an order.'

As the three travellers watched the small aeroplane taxi-ing towards them and saw the inbound passengers scramble to the ground with their baggage as it stopped, Jacqueline was amazed to see that one of them was her best friend from her days in the SOE training school, Lise de Baissac. The two women hardly had time to say a quick hello as they passed each other before Jacqueline, Josette Southgate and Savy climbed on board. The door was quickly closed and they were soon rattling across the field; then the pilot, Robert Taylor of 161 Squadron, lifted the Lysander up into the darkness of the night sky and headed towards England.

The Lysander was due to land at RAF Tangmere on the south coast of England, but when it approached the area the pilot found that the airfield was covered by a blanket of fog, so he continued inland until he reached the airfield at Dunsfold in Surrey where, now low on fuel, he made a good landing. Home at last, Jacqueline returned to Stamford Hill to try to pick up the pieces of the life she had left and regain her previously good health. Josette Southgate went to Slough to her in-laws' house and Jean Savy delivered the news of his deadly discovery.

As a result of Savy's revelation and the first-hand details he provided of the quarry and its contents, the RAF, after more than one bombing raid, completely destroyed the site and the flying bombs. But the quarry at Saint-Leu-d'Esserent was only one of the sites containing the rockets and, in the early hours of 13 June 1944 the first of the V-1 rockets, which came to be known by Londoners as 'doodle-bugs', was launched against London, from another site in northern France. It landed in Grove Road, Bow,[7] and destroyed a railway bridge, which carried the main line from London to the east coast, and several houses, killing six people. The first few raids were undertaken to test the range of the V-1s but soon they were raining down on the south at regular intervals, causing terrible damage. During the first two weeks of the doodlebug raids, 1,600 people were killed and 4,500 seriously injured. Given the panic that was caused by these rockets, and the large number of casualties in London and the south-east of England, Savy's rush to stop at least one of the sites from launching its weapons had been completely justified and he had brought the news not a moment too soon.

Savy's hurried departure had, however, left Didi in limbo. Four days before he left, another wireless operator, Jean Gerard Maury (*Arnaud*), had been sent from England to assist in receiving and sending the numerous messages that were expected in the run-up to D-Day. With Savy gone, the Wizard circuit had two wireless operators but no leader and no one to do the work that had prompted its being set up in the first place. After the flurry of activity during the first few weeks of Didi's time in Paris, she suddenly had nothing to do. While she had become used to her solitary existence, part of what made it bearable was the knowledge that her work was making a difference to the course of the war. Time weighed heavily upon her and she found it difficult to fill the endless empty hours each day. Her only wish was that she would quickly be assigned to another circuit, but she could not be certain that it would happen. When she checked for messages each day she prayed that she would receive news of a new assignment and would not be returned to England.

CHAPTER 12

A Bad Decision

A week after her return to England Jacqueline was called to SOE headquarters for the customary debriefing that all agents had to undergo on coming home. Still extremely tired, she patiently answered questions and gave information about the workings of the Stationer circuit, its agents and the agents of other circuits with whom she had come into contact. The debriefing was a painstaking process; each piece of information that Jacqueline was able to give, however small, painted a vivid picture of life in the field. While operating in France the agents did not have time to cover every angle of their work in their reports. They managed to sort out most of their problems themselves and couldn't waste time reporting back to London with details of every incident that had occurred. But it was vital for London to know all available information about the difficulties their people suffered, if only to ensure that the mistakes of the past didn't happen again.

For hour after hour Jacqueline described the long, exhausting journeys that she made from one town to another across the huge Stationer area. She told the officer conducting her interview, for instance, how she had quickly discovered that season tickets were available on the railway and how it made her life so much easier to have one, as it meant she didn't have to queue for a ticket each time she travelled and didn't draw attention to herself by constantly appearing at the ticket office, where she would soon have been recognized.

Jacqueline also explained that there were always lots of German soldiers around the railway stations and on the train there was the constant risk of being picked out for

Jacqueline's rail card.

questioning by plain-clothes Gestapo officers. She described how during one rail journey a woman sitting next to her had been singled out for a Gestapo grilling, and been obliged to hand over her papers and handbag for scrutiny. She herself had always managed to avoid this, but she said that by the time she left France the controls were becoming much tighter and the searches more frequent. She advised the officer conducting her debriefing to make sure that new agents were told not to keep any incriminating papers on their person when travelling and to ensure that their personal documents would pass muster. She also mentioned that when she had traded in her fake identity card and obtained a genuine one, and had been asked to produce a photo for this, she did so but requested that the picture be returned to her so that she could give it to her fiancé, to ensure that the photo was not kept and that there was less likelihood of her being recognized sometime later. She felt more secure with the genuine identity card. She had been with Maingard on the Boussens–Toulouse–Tarbes train when he had been searched, Jacqueline said, but he didn't have any problems because he had very good papers.

As time passed she had found it more and more risky to take express trains anywhere. When she first arrived she used to travel from Toulouse to Pau on the Toulouse–Tarbes–Pau express, which left Toulouse at 10.20 a.m. and arrived in Pau two hours and ten minutes later. But increasingly the express trains were filled with plain-clothes Gestapo men, often accompanied by uniformed officers, so when in Toulouse she usually got up early and took the slow train, which left at 5.20 a.m. and didn't arrive until 11.00 a.m. It was a boring journey but at least the Gestapo avoided travelling on the slow trains.

When speaking about her colleagues, Jacqueline always called them by their code names. They were the only names she knew them by, and when she gave the officer conducting her debriefing information about people she had come across in the course of her work she didn't really know whom she was talking about; nor did she know their links to other people. She recalled that she had heard about the fate of an agent called *Alice*, who had gone into a shop to speak to one of her contacts and the Gestapo had come in while she was there. Instead of remaining calm and just leaving the shop, she went outside in a hurry and then hid in the house next door. Although the neighbour let her in, she became worried when the Gestapo returned to the shop and told them where *Alice* was hiding. Jacqueline didn't know *Alice* personally but thought that she was known to Southgate.

In fact *Alice* was Cecily Lefort, a 44-year-old British woman who was married to a Frenchman and lived in Brittany. She had volunteered for the SOE and had become the courier for the Jockey circuit, led by Francis Cammaerts. Southgate did indeed know her and had a slightly different story about her arrest, saying that she had been visiting a friend of her circuit leader when the Germans arrived and she was caught. Southgate had not been at all impressed by her: 'She was the wrong type for the work, as she was conspicuously British in appearance and drew attention to herself by her behaviour … her laugh could be heard a mile away …'[1] She survived in this role for only three months and, after her arrest, was taken to Ravensbrück, where she died sometime in early 1945.

Another agent of whom Jacqueline had details had, unbeknown to her, already been discussed by Maurice

Southgate in a report he had sent to London. Jacqueline told how, sometime the previous summer, possibly in June or July, she had received a message from an agent called *Gaby*, asking to meet her. Since the message had come via another agent she knew to be trustworthy, she had agreed to the meeting. *Gaby* told Jacqueline that she had arrived the previous week but had had no reception committee waiting for her. Not knowing what to do, she had gone to the address in Clermont-Ferrand that she had been given, probably 37 rue Blatin, and asked for Jacqueline. When the women met, Jacqueline agreed to take *Gaby* to Maingard in Châteauroux, where *Gaby* left her bag before going on to Marseilles to start her work as a courier for the Monk circuit. She didn't retrieve her baggage for three months and when she returned to Châteauroux, she told Maingard that she wasn't worried about her bag, which contained most of her clothes, as she was the 'queen of the black market' in the southern French port. When she had spoken to Jacqueline she told her that she was a widow but then said that she had not been widowed. She told Maingard that she had been married and divorced three times, which was another lie. Had Southgate taken Jacqueline and Maingard into his confidence, they would have discovered that *Gaby* had given him yet another story. Southgate suspected, but was not able to prove, that she had embezzled the large amount of money given to her by the SOE to take down to the Monk leader, Charles Skepper. She certainly didn't have any of it on her when she was taken to her circuit in Marseilles. She told Southgate that because she hadn't had anyone to meet her she had buried the money, along with her parachute, on a farm near where she landed and took him to the farm to retrieve it. It wasn't found, and the farmer and his family had no idea what she was talking about. Southgate even contrived to search the farm with another member of his circuit, both dressed as German officers, and it was clear to him that the farmer and his family were not lying. So was she an embezzler or had she simply mistaken the place where she had hidden the cash? No one ever discovered what had happened to the missing money.[2] In March 1944, just before Jacqueline was brought home and the day after Charles Skepper was detained by the Germans, *Gaby* was arrested. The 27-year-old agent was executed in Dachau in September 1944. Her real name was Eliane Plewman and she was the sister of Albert Browne-Bartroli, who had arrived in France on the aircraft that had then taken Jacqueline's brother Francis to England the previous autumn.

Jacqueline's debriefing lasted for a long while. As well as talking about her journeys and the people she had met while in France, she described the sabotage raids undertaken by the circuit, and the supply drops that sometimes went wrong and left the agents either missing parcels or looking for those that had never existed. Satisfied that he had received all the information that she could give, the interviewer told Jacqueline that she would be passed on to another section, the training section, and that after she had had a rest, she would be undertaking a refresher course. He completed his report, noting that Jacqueline was 'a very capable, intelligent, highly reliable woman, who has operated in the field for a considerable time with marked success'.[3]

*   *   *

Stuck in Paris with no circuit leader and no real work, Didi went every day to the house in Bourg-la-Reine and, at the times she had been allocated, listened for any incoming transmissions that might give her information about what was going to happen to her and to Maury, the wireless operator who had arrived in Paris just as Savy was leaving.

Then one day, a week or so after Savy's departure, Didi received the message she had been waiting for: news of her next assignment. She and Maury were being transferred to a new circuit called Spiritualist. The best news was that it was in Paris. Didi had worried that she would be sent elsewhere and would have to search for new accommodation for herself and her wireless, but Spiritualist operated in the east of Paris and in the *département* of Seine-et-Marne. It was better news than she could have hoped for and she looked forward to meeting her new circuit chief. Although she had enjoyed working for Savy, it was by no means certain that he would be returning to France and Didi needed to keep busy.

Although both were from well-to-do backgrounds, Didi's new boss, René Dumont-Guillemet (*Armand*), was about as different from Jean Savy as it was possible to be. While Savy had been a hardworking, serious lawyer, Dumont-Guillemet had been a playboy before becoming a Resistance fighter. Born in Lyons on 5 April 1908, he had had a privileged upbringing. Although he attended a good school, he wasn't a diligent student and didn't complete his studies. Instead he left school and concentrated on his sporting interests. He loved skiing, his favourite ski slopes being in the Jura mountains, and when he was a little older took up motor racing. Summer weekends were the times he liked the most, and he spent them all enjoying himself with his friends on the beaches of the Riviera and swimming in the Mediterranean. Eventually he decided the time had come for him to find some sort of work and, being a fan of the movies, he became a set designer, working for several film companies, including Paramount.

When the war began in 1939 he enlisted in the French Army but was demobilized in 1940 after the fall of France. He then started his own truck company, based in Paris, where he and his wife, Raymonde Rougeaux, lived in the rue de Monceau with their son, Michael, who was born in 1941. In the autumn of 1942 a pre-war British friend, Sidney Jones (*Elie*), arrived by felucca to run a Resistance sabotage circuit named Inventor to be based in Marseilles, and Dumont-Guillemet was recruited to help him. The following year Jones suggested that his friend should be taken to London for SOE training. He left on 16 October in a Lysander of 161 Squadron, piloted by Flight Lieutenant McCairns. He had only one travelling companion on the trip, the chief of the Stationer circuit: Jacqueline's boss, Maurice Southgate, known to him only as *Hector*.

While Dumont-Guillemet was in England his friend Sidney Jones was arrested, along with his courier Vera Leigh (*Simone*), both victims of the double agent Roger Bardet (whose presence at the departure of the aircraft in which Francis Nearne had come to England had caused such a heated argument). After his arrest Jones was sent to Mauthausen concentration camp, where he was executed in September 1944. Vera Leigh died in the concentration camp of Natzweiler-Struthof in the Vosges mountains in France sometime in July the same year, along with three other female agents: Andrée Borrel (*Denise*), Diana Rowden (*Paulette*) and Sonia Olschanesky (*Tania*). All four women were given lethal injections and their bodies were cremated immediately. There is strong evidence that they were not all dead when they were taken to the ovens.[4]

After the successful completion of his training, Dumont-Guillemet returned to France to set up the Spiritualist circuit in Paris, accompanied by a wireless operator, Henry Diacono (*Blaise*), an Algerian-born British officer of Maltese descent. Part of Dumont-Guillemet's remit was to unite the small factions that remained of the Prosper and Farmer circuits. Prosper had been based in Paris under the leadership of Francis Suttill, who had been arrested in the middle of 1943 and was to die at the hands of the Nazis in Sachsenhausen concentration camp in 1945. Michael Trotobas, the Anglo-French chief of the Farmer circuit in Lille, had been killed in a gun battle with the Germans in November 1943. In the absence of both leaders, the two circuits had become largely fragmented.

The former playboy Dumont-Guillemet had at last abandoned his hedonistic lifestyle and found an occupation in which he really believed. Perhaps because of his incomplete education and his energetic lifestyle, he was a man of action rather than words. He had returned from England with a few specific projects to attend to: arranging a mass breakout from Fresnes prison, which was his own idea and which he subsequently abandoned as being unworkable; kidnapping a German V-1 rocket engineer; a sabotage attack on the Bosch Lavelette works; and re-establishing contact with the members of the Farmer network in Lille.

The kidnap of the German V-1 rocket engineer was in the final planning stages when the Germans decided that they would move the man to more secure premises, so the kidnap attempt was ditched in favour of things more achievable.

Undoubtedly the most important task given to Dumont-Guillemet was that of re-establishing contact with the Farmer circuit in Lille. This he managed to do, and it had enormous benefits to the Resistance groups in the north and east of France, where supply drops had become extremely difficult. Because Dumont-Guillemet had the means, via his truck company, to transport goods from the drops being made closer to Paris, the agents in the Lille area were able to maintain an efficient, strong Resistance network. This network contributed greatly to the destruction of German communications both up to and after D-Day, provided vital information about the V-1 rocket launch sites in the area and carried out many sabotage raids.

Dumont-Guillemet also had a task of his own. He had a burning desire to find out what had happened to his friend, Sidney Jones. While conducting some careful but extremely dangerous enquiries about the fate of Jones, he managed to uncover several double agents, whom he eliminated.

Because of his enormous energy and the large number of Resistance fighters he led, there was plenty of work for the wireless operators Didi, Maury and Diacono. Didi quickly re-established her routine, sending messages to England from the house in Bourg-la-Reine. Although when she had begun transmitting from the Dubois house everything had been quiet in the area, after a few weeks she noticed that the number of Germans she spotted had increased, as had the direction-finding vans that they used to locate wireless operators. Maury, who had also seen and heard an increase in the number of Germans, agreed with Didi that it was becoming unsafe to continue using their former safe houses for broadcasting, so he began searching for another location. He eventually found a room in the west Paris suburb of Le Vésinet where, 20 years earlier, Didi's elder brother Francis had briefly gone to school.

The new room was about the same distance for Didi to travel as it was to Bourg-la-Reine. Despite this, for a time Didi preferred to make her transmissions from the old, tried and tested location. Maury had already gone to Le Vésinet and had told her that the reception there was not too good. To try to ensure her own safety Didi always made certain that she arrived at the house with plenty of time to spare before her skeds (the planned times for receiving or transmitting messages). With the regular work that she was doing for Dumont-Guillemet she had become much more proficient at Morse code and could send a message very quickly. Whenever she thought about the danger she was in, she always believed that she would survive; she was sure she would never be captured. Her belief in God had helped her adjust to her lonely life and now that her position within the Spiritualist circuit was secure, she relished the life she was leading.

By the latter part of July 1944 she had sent a total of 105 messages and had been working for four months, more than two months longer than what was statistically believed to be the maximum time a wireless operator could operate safely. She had already stayed in Bourg-la-Reine for much longer than was safe; she knew that she couldn't delay her departure for Le Vésinet any longer. Having made the decision to move she was given an urgent message to send for Dumont-Guillemet, and was again torn between her usual location and the new one. She decided to make this transmission the very last one from the Dubois house. She could get a good reception from there, whereas Maury was still having difficulties at Le Vésinet.

She set off, in the rain, for her last trip to Bourg-la-Reine on the afternoon of 21 July. When she reached the house she found that the district was in the middle of a power cut, so she decided to remain there for a while, hoping that the power would soon be back to normal. But it was off for so long that she missed her sked and chose to sleep there so as to be ready for her next one in the morning. When she awoke she found that the power was back to normal, so she retrieved the pieces of her wireless, quickly assembled the set and checked the aerial. Everything was in order and she began tapping out her message.

She had almost finished it when she heard the sound of a car engine nearby but had no premonition of anything untoward. As she completed the transmission, however, she was suddenly aware of shouting in the street and car doors banging. She rubbed clear a patch of condensation on the window – it was still raining – and was appalled to see several cars and men who could only be Germans streaming from them. She knew that the moment she had believed would never come had, in fact, arrived. It suddenly occurred to her that the first noise she had heard might have been a direction-finding vehicle, and she realized that it would only be a matter of minutes before the Germans would be banging on her door.

CHAPTER 13

A Brilliant Actress

As the activity in the street outside the Dubois house became louder and more frenzied, Didi didn't dare waste any more time looking out of the window. She knew that she had a lot to do and very little time in which to do it. The wireless aerial had to be pulled down and hidden, the set itself taken apart and the pieces hidden; her codes had to be destroyed and she had to hide her pistol. Not hesitating for a moment, she rushed to do all these tasks before the dreaded knock on the door. When she had dismantled everything, she took the wireless components into a bedroom and hid them as best she could in a cupboard. She thought that they would be safe if the Germans took only a cursory glance around, but if they conducted a full-scale search she knew that they would be found. Running back into the room where she usually made her transmissions, she snatched up her codes and the paper on which she had coded Dumont-Guillemet's urgent message and took them into the kitchen. The stove was not alight but she stuffed the papers into it, grabbed her matches and struck one, holding it close until they began to burn. It seemed to her to take forever but they were soon blazing away.

She watched the flames devouring the paper until she could see that everything had been completely destroyed and then stirred the ashes with the poker in an attempt to disguise the fact that the stove had been alight that day. At least, if she were arrested, she would have the satisfaction of knowing that the message had been sent, but how she wished she had not used the Dubois house to send it. If only she had just retrieved her wireless equipment and taken it to the new place in Le Vésinet, none of this would have happened.[1] But she knew it was pointless to think of what might have been. She quickly ran through the mental checklist of what she had done and felt that it was just about all she had time to do. Only then did she think of saving herself.

But it was too late. She could hear the sound of heavy boots on the pavement directly outside the house and knew that she had nowhere to go. Suddenly there was loud, insistent banging on the door. Taking a deep breath to calm herself, Didi walked across the room and opened the door. She found a gun pointing directly at her. It was being held by a plain-clothes man, who barked out something in German and then pushed past her into the house.

Didi began to yell at him, asking who he was and what he thought he was doing, barging into the house without having been invited. The German stopped and looked at her as if she were mad. Encouraged that he seemed to be taking notice of what she was saying, she repeated her question, demanding to know what he thought he was doing. The story she had rehearsed so many times since her arrival in France flooded through her mind and she slipped easily into the character of the unintelligent girl her instructor had written about in her finishing report. She knew that her whole future depended on what she did and said in the next few minutes.

As she repeated her question the German turned abruptly and informed her in French that he knew she had been sending messages on an illegal wireless set, and that he was going to find it and prove that she had been working against the Germans. For a second she tried to look amazed; then she forced herself to give a small laugh, telling him to go ahead and see what he could find. She assured him that it wouldn't be an illegal wireless, as she didn't have a wireless set at all, and even if she had had one, weren't wirelesses things people listened to? What did he mean by saying she had been sending messages on one? She was certain she had never seen a wireless that could do things like that – he must be mistaken.

The German hesitated and regarded her with a puzzled expression. Thinking that he was beginning to believe he might have made a mistake about which house contained the unlawful equipment, Didi told him that if he would tell her what this thing looked like she would help him search for it. He walked back towards the front door and for a moment she thought she had fooled him. Then he shouted something, and several more armed men came running into the house and began searching all the rooms. Opening cupboards and drawers, they threw things on to the floor and kicked them aside as they went further into the house, opening doors to the other rooms and ransacking the entire house.

In a very short time they had found the pieces of the wireless set that Didi had hastily put in one of the bedrooms. They brought them back into the room where she was being held and waved them in her face. The first man asked what she thought they were, if they were not pieces of a wireless set. She feigned surprise but could see that the situation had been lost. Even if they had any doubts about her own link to what they had found, she knew that they would interrogate her about anyone else who might use the house and whose equipment it could have been, so she decided not to speak any more.

She had been rather loud up until that point so, taking her unexpected silence as an admission of guilt, one of the men produced a pair of handcuffs and Didi was arrested. She was marched unceremoniously into the street, where she was pushed into one of the seven waiting cars. A total of 17 Gestapo agents had been sent to find the wireless operator they had been monitoring for some days and now their job was done.[2]

The car carrying Didi took off at speed along the road that led back to Paris; the six other vehicles followed behind it. Pedestrians crossing the road jumped on to the pavements in alarm as the motorcade sped past them and screeched around corners. As the cars approached the city the cars began to slow down. They headed towards an address in the 8th *arrondissement*, the name of which put fear into the hearts of all agents in Paris: 11 rue des Saussaies, the building that the Gestapo had commandeered as its headquarters.

When Didi realized where she had been taken, she knew at once that she would be in for a rough ride. She began praying silently that she would be able to withstand whatever she had to endure and that she would not betray any of her colleagues in the Spiritualist circuit. She was terrified but determined that whoever was sent to deal with her would not see her fear. The words that had been drilled into her during her training – never be afraid, never let them intimidate you – went round and round in her head like a mantra.

She was put into a small room and the door was slammed shut. After several minutes two men came in. They were not those who had arrested her and were more polite, greeting her quite courteously. One of the men told her that they needed to ask her a few questions about what had been going on at the house in Bourg-la-Reine and that she must answer their questions truthfully.[3] If she did, she would come to no harm. Keeping up the pretence of being a simple country girl, Didi nodded and gave her name as Jacqueline du Tertre. The Germans wanted to know if she was French and she told them, 'Of course I am. What else would I be?' They asked if she had a job and she began stalling for time while she gathered her thoughts, simply telling them that she worked for a company. When they pushed her for more details she told them that her work involved sending messages to the various sections of the company, for a businessman. They then enquired as to the nature of the company and she replied, 'How should I know? I just send the messages.' Trying again, they asked what the company actually did and what the messages were about, but Didi gave them a disinterested look and told them that she didn't know and the messages were always coded so she didn't understand what they said. She confided that when she had been employed she had been told that she would have to learn how to code but she had made such a mess of it that her boss thought it best if he did it himself and she just transmitted what he had written. Giving them a slight smile, she said that she too thought that was best; the boss was always very secretive and she knew he was worried about competition, so she didn't want to be blamed for anything that went wrong.

Her inquisitors appeared to be thoroughly confused by this seemingly quite stupid young woman. She had been arrested at a house where wireless equipment had been found and had now admitted that she sent wireless messages but insisted that they were for a businessman, and seemed to think that what she had done was quite normal and nothing to be worried about. Didi could see that neither man understood her attitude and she sensed that they might be starting to believe she was telling the truth. Perhaps they really thought her to be completely foolish. She had tried to appear incredibly naive, as she wanted them to think that in an occupied country in wartime, no one would do what she claimed to have done unless he or she was really dim-witted and telling the truth.

After pausing for a few moments, they began to use another approach. Playing what has come to be known as the good cop/bad cop routine, one of the men spoke kindly to Didi, telling her that her boss must have tricked her into working for him; he was clearly a spy and she shouldn't allow him to get away with it. He also suggested that if she had been lying about him it must be because she herself was the spy and she would be well advised to admit to it now, before it was too late for him to do anything to help her. Before she had the chance to reply the other man rushed at her, yelling, 'You are a spy, you lying, dirty bitch,' and smacked her hard around her face, knocking her sideways on her chair.

If she had been lying, this was the moment when she would have been likely to break down and confess to her treachery, so, instead of being cowed, she made a huge effort to show that she was outraged at their behaviour towards her. Refusing to be intimidated, she shouted that she was not a liar and she was definitely not a spy.[4] The look on her face must have displayed so much contempt for them that they seemed to Didi to be considering the possibility that she really had been telling the truth; and, as she watched their confusion, a feeling of satisfaction came over her. She was almost enjoying the deception and she also felt that by keeping the questioning going without admitting to anything, she would give those in the Spiritualist circuit time to find out about her arrest and take any measures they felt were needed to ensure the safety of the group. Each time she was asked the same questions, she just gave the same answers.

The Germans tried many interrogation techniques over the next few hours but her story never wavered. The only changes were in the way she replied: the tone she adopted was sometimes conciliatory, sometimes exasperated, sometimes even rude. Each time they accused her of being a spy she strenuously denied it, but still they kept questioning her, trying to break her, until eventually she shouted at them, asking, 'What do you want me to say? I keep telling you the answers and you keep asking me the same questions. I don't know why you bother if you are not interested in what I am saying.'

Eventually Didi was hauled to her feet and marched out of the room and down a corridor to another room. It was small and had no furniture; instead there was a bath filled with water. She knew that she was about to suffer what she called 'the treatment of the baignoire': she was going to be pushed under the water and held there in a final attempt to get her to talk.[5]

CHAPTER 14

Torture

Maurice Buckmaster could, perhaps, be forgiven for being a little smug about his decision to override the opinions of Lieutenant Colonel Woolrych who, two years earlier, had said of Jacqueline: 'Mentally slow and not very intelligent ... Little depth of character – in fact, she is a very simple person.'[1] Buckmaster had been proved right in his belief that as an SOE agent Jacqueline was 'one of the best we have had'. Her tireless work during the 15 months she had been in France had been invaluable. Having returned to England for a much-needed rest, she had successfully completed a revision course at Roughwood Park, earning further praise. Her instructor said:

> Her experience in the field had taught her a great deal about personal security. She appreciated the value of the revisionary lectures and exercises. She appears to be a most competent and level headed person.
>
> ... Her orders as leader are always clear and sound and she has a great deal of self confidence and personality that makes people obey her orders. Always worked hard at schemes and obeyed her orders conscientiously.[2]

Now she was about to embark upon yet another course, which would give her the ability to organize reception committees herself, receiving agents and supplies, when she returned to the field.

It was now the middle of July 1944 and things were looking up for Jacqueline. Although she was still painfully thin, she was beginning to regain her health and she no longer felt the overwhelming exhaustion that she had been experiencing when she arrived in England in April.

She had been glad to see Francis once more. She knew that he had had problems in coming to terms with how close he had been to being caught by the Gestapo prior to his departure for England. Even though he was relatively safe in England, he still had nagging worries about what would have happened to his wife and little boy if he had been arrested; and now, after being away from them for nine months, all he wanted to do was to get back to France to look after them both. When Jacqueline had asked him to undertake ad hoc courier missions for the Stationer circuit he had readily agreed and had performed them well but it was only now, and with great guilt, that she realized what a strain it had put upon him. Alarmed about his physical and mental state, she also knew that she would never have been able to forgive herself if anything had happened to him.

Then there was the concern she felt about Didi. She was upset when she discovered that her wishes had been ignored and that Didi had gone to France as an agent. She knew that the task of a wireless operator was much more hazardous than that of a courier. Knowing that it was said that the average time a wireless operator could work before being arrested was about six weeks, she was uneasy about

Didi having been put in so much danger when she had tried hard to prevent it and she worried about how she was getting on.

But there was little time to dwell on these anxieties and Jacqueline knew that she must put them to the back of her mind so that she could concentrate on her next course, which was being held at Howbury Hall in Bedfordshire. The hall was in the hamlet of Water End, which formed part of the village and parish of Renhold on the river Ouse. Situated in attractive, peaceful countryside, it was the perfect place for Jacqueline, a place where she could relax as well as learn.

Jacqueline threw herself into the course wholeheartedly. Now that she was feeling better, she was anxious to get back to France as soon as possible and she knew that with the course under her belt she would be of even more use to her circuit than she had been thus far. The technology that had been developed, about which she was now going to learn, would make it much safer and easier to receive new agents and supplies.

In the past when an aircraft approached a dropping zone, the only method of letting the pilot know where the drop should take place was by the use of three lights held by agents on the ground in a straight line, indicating the direction of the wind. The reception committee leader held a fourth light, with which he flashed an agreed letter in Morse code. If the letter was that which the pilot expected to see, he knew that he had arrived at the correct dropping zone and that it was safe for the agents, or supplies, to drop. The problem with this system was that there was always a danger that the Germans might manage to infiltrate a circuit, or capture a member and obtain the code letter. If this happened the drop would be made into the arms of the enemy, and several agents had been lost this way. Even if there was no breach of security, there was the risk of the lights being spotted by the Germans or the Milice, with the same devastating results.

In order to reduce this threat, SOE scientists from the organization's Signals Directorate had developed a two-way wireless system that they called an S-Phone. This allowed the pilot of an aircraft and an agent on the ground to talk to each other, as Southgate had when receiving three agents arriving from England. The device itself was heavy and cumbersome, and had a short range, but it was better than the light system and, should there be a suspicion of German infiltration of a circuit, it allowed a UK-based agent who knew the person on the ground to travel in the aircraft and monitor the agent's voice to check whether or not it was who it was purported to be.

Another device, even heavier, was a radar system that was developed to give the air crew greater accuracy in finding the dropping zone. This consisted of two parts: a beacon transmitter called Eureka for use on the ground, and a receiver called Rebecca that was fitted inside the aircraft, allowing the navigator to find the destination without needing flashing lights or maps.

The students learnt how to use and maintain both devices on the course, which was quite short but intensive. When Jacqueline had completed her training, her report, dated 19 July 1944, gave the following details:

S-Phone: Has worked well and has a fair theoretical and good practical knowledge. Qualified to operate. Should give a little further practice to maintenance.

Eureka: Good pass. Qualified to operate and maintain a Eureka in the field.

R.C. work: Has worked well. Has a good all round knowledge and should be useful in the field.

General: A pleasant, hardworking student who showed keenness and acquired a satisfactory knowledge of all branches of R.C. work. Recommended as an s-phone operator and Eureka operator on a R.C. operation. Do not recommend her as a leader but, with her knowledge she would be an asset to any Reception in which she took part.

She finished her advanced course on 19 July, four days before Didi was arrested.

Despite their suspicions that Didi was, after all, a very stupid girl who had had no idea of what she was actually doing, her captors refused to take any chances. By observing her reaction to the sight of the water-filled bath they were certain that, if she had been lying, she would now try to save herself by telling the truth. With a man on either side of her, holding her arms tightly, they asked her one more time about her wireless broadcasts. She refused to answer. So, giving her no chance to take a breath, they suddenly lifted her and plunged her into the bath, holding her head under the icy water. She began to choke and struggle for breath but succeeded only in filling her mouth and nose with water. Trying hard not to panic, she was again remembering what she had been taught – never be afraid, never let them dominate you – when suddenly she was pulled up, coughing and spluttering.

The questioning began again. Who was she working for? Where was she sending her messages? Didi just gave them a defiant look and again refused to answer. Once more she was thrust into the water and a heavy hand ensured that her head was completely submerged. Unable to move, she began to fear that she would not be pulled out in time but, at the point when her lungs felt as if they would burst, she was again dragged out of the water and asked about her spying activities. She remained silent, determined not to let them win even if it cost her her life. Back she went underwater.

By now she was sure that she was going to die. A calmness came over her and she felt as if she were beginning to lose consciousness. As her body started to become limp, her torturers knew that they would get no information from her in that state and pulled her out abruptly, thumping her on her back. Fighting for breath, she coughed, spewing water over herself and her persecutors, and then began taking painful, rasping gulps of air until finally she was able to breathe again. Slumped on a chair, bent forward and dripping water on the floor, she could hear the Germans talking. She didn't understand what they were saying but she thought that they sounded angry and frustrated, and she knew that she had beaten them, if only for a short time. Her spirits soared. She had remembered what she had been taught and although she had been very afraid, she had not let them dominate her. Despite feeling very unsteady and weak, she was triumphant.

Seeing that she had revived, one of the men asked, 'Have you had a nice bath'? Looking him directly in the eye, Didi replied angrily, 'Excellent. I will be complaining at the Town Hall about what you have done to me!' This defiant remark seemed to convince the men that she was telling the truth. Their questioning began again but this time concentrated on the businessman for whom Didi had said she worked.

When one of the interrogators asked her to tell him how she had met her boss, she quickly took up the story of Jacqueline du Tertre, repeating much of what she had told him before:

I was bored at home and wanted to come to Paris to look for work but when I got here I couldn't find anything at all to do. Every day I went to a café and bought a drink to have while I looked at the vacant jobs in the newspaper. I was desperate. Then one day – I had almost run out of money and was thinking I must go back home – there was a man in the café who kept staring at me. I didn't know what he wanted so I didn't look at him but he came to the table and said, 'You are worried? Are you all right?' I told him I was looking for a job and said I couldn't find one and I had no more money so he said he might be able to help. He bought me a drink and sat down with me and we spoke. He said, 'I am a businessman and I need help with my business. I won't tell you what it is now but I will later – I don't like people to talk about my business, it's not good, but I think I can help you.' Then he gave me some money to be able to get by and said he would see me in a few days in the café.

The German interrupted Didi's account to ask her if she didn't think it odd that a stranger would offer her a job and then give her money before she had done anything for him. She pretended to consider what he had asked and replied: 'No, he said he would be back and I said I would be there – I was desperate, with no money until he gave me some so I went back and wanted to work for him. There was nothing else I could do. And he was nice to me – he was very polite, you see.'[3]

The German abruptly changed the subject and asked how Didi had learnt to use a wireless set. Her preparation and mental rehearsals for this entire situation, although she had thought it would never arise, had been thorough, and she immediately replied that she had worked for the post office at home and they had trained her to transmit messages using the wireless and Morse code.[4] The man was sceptical, but she told him that it was a normal procedure in a French post office and he seemed satisfied.

Then the other man asked her if she knew about the British spies in the country. She adopted a puzzled look and said that she didn't know what he meant. Shouting at her now, he told her that she was a very stupid girl and that the man for whom she had been sending messages was a British spy. He had been using her, to save himself being caught. Feigning disbelief, she replied, 'No, you are mistaken. He is a businessman ...' but then she stopped. Her expression changed and the look of understanding on her face told the German that she had at last realized that what he was saying was true. It was a masterly performance. Colonel Buckmaster had told her that she was a good liar and she had proved that he had been right. She found, as she was telling the German this fiction, that she almost believed it herself and that despite the horrors they had put her through that morning, she was now actually enjoying herself.[5] Although her torturers did not know it, she felt that she was in control of the situation. Nothing she was telling them was true, yet she had succeeded in fooling them. When they asked her for her boss's address she gave them one but insisted that she had not been there herself. They then wanted to know about her next meeting with him and she said that it was at 7 p.m. that evening in a café opposite the Gare Saint-Lazare.[6]

There was no time to lose. Although her clothes were still damp from the bath, Didi was bundled into a car and driven to the Gare Saint-Lazare. She was told to wait for her boss in the café and warned not to tell him that they were also waiting for him at another table. Now expressing her anger at being duped by this man, she agreed readily, but said that she would at least have to buy a drink if she were to wait there and asked for some money. She then sat down to await the arrival of a man who existed only in her imagination.

Although she was delighted to be the cause of the Germans running around Paris after an imaginary man, she didn't want to be anywhere near them when they realized that she had been making fools of them. As she sipped her drink she could almost feel their eyes boring into her back but had no idea how she would be able to get out of the situation she had made for herself. The minutes passed and no one arrived. Suddenly Didi stood up. One of the Germans also jumped to his feet and came towards her. She told him she needed to go to the lavatory. He nodded but told her that he would go with her. While in the lavatory she looked around for a way to escape but there was none except a window that was too small and too high for her to reach, so she unlocked the door. As she was doing so, an air-raid siren sounded. Although it offered no chance of escape, it at least gave her a reason for the non-appearance of her boss. Pretending to be annoyed with him once more, she told her captors, 'Well, it is too late for him now. He won't come if there is an air raid, you know.'

Back they went to the rue des Saussaies. Didi was left in an office with an armed guard, an arrogant young Frenchman whom she believed to be a member of the Milice, while her captors went to see if her boss had been found at his address. When they returned, she was informed that the address she had given them didn't exist. She expressed no surprise, telling them that it must prove that he was an agent. Why else would he have given her a false address?

Shaking his head in exasperation, one of the men told her: 'We are going to give you the benefit of the doubt.' Then, seeing the beginnings of a smile appear on Didi's face, he added: 'We are sending you to a concentration camp. You'll have a good laugh there. Yes, it won't be like here; it'll be your punishment for having worked against us.'[7]

The euphoria that Didi had felt vanished. She might have been able to fool the two bullies, who were grinning broadly at her reaction to the news they had just given her, but what good had it done her? She was still going to be imprisoned and her work as a wireless operator was over. Worse still, she began to wonder if she would ever see her sister again. It was unbearable to think of the distress that Jacqueline would suffer when she discovered what had happened to her. If only she hadn't sent the message from

Bourg-la-Reine and had gone to the new house in Le Vésinet. Her only consolation was that she hadn't betrayed any of her colleagues. She hadn't said a word about Dumont-Guillemet, Maury and Diacono or any of the others, so she knew that at least she had saved the Spiritualist circuit. But it had been at a high price to herself.

Annoyed that they had wasted so much time on this stupid French girl, her interrogators called for a car to take her to Fresnes, to the infamous prison south of the city, to await deportation. As they drove through the streets of Paris, the city that had been her first home when, 21 years before, she had come to France as a small child, Didi looked at the sights that had become so familiar to her and she felt like crying, wondering if this might be last time she would ever see them. The car sped along the rue du Faubourg Saint-Honoré and, as it turned right into the rue Royale, she twisted around in her seat, looking in the opposite direction and hoping to catch a glimpse of the magnificent neoclassical Roman Catholic church of the Madeleine, before the car turned on to the Place de la Concorde, across the bridge over the Seine and along the boulevard Saint-Germain. Didi knew that they were now very close to Louise's apartment and tried not to think of how she used to walk past the building knowing that the people inside cared about her, as she didn't want to give a hint that she knew anyone there. Then the car took a right fork, away from where Louise and her family lived, and headed south along the boulevard Raspail towards Fresnes and the prison. From there she would be sent to a concentration camp, where she knew the chances of survival were, at best, slight.

A wave of misery swept over her as she finally understood the depth of her predicament. There was simply nothing left for her. In despair, she began to pray silently, asking God for the strength to withstand whatever she now had to suffer. The prayers helped and as she arrived at Fresnes she began to have a small glimmer of hope that she would survive and realized that if she were to do so she must remain optimistic. So, turning her attention to what she knew must be her next task, she began to plan her escape.

CHAPTER 15

Didi Vanishes

The day after Jacqueline had returned to England the Stationer circuit was sent a new wireless operator. René Mathieu (*Aimé*) arrived to take over from Maingard so that the latter could become Southgate's aide-de-camp (ADC). Mathieu, who had his base in Montluçon, assumed all responsibility for the circuit's wireless transmissions, thereby freeing Maingard to take up the position of ADC immediately.

At the end of April Southgate had been due to meet Capitaine René Antoine, the military representative of the Armée Secrète (AS) in Châteauroux, and narrowly escaped being apprehended by the Germans, as Maingard, who had heard about the arrest of Antoine, cycled at breakneck speed to tell him not to go anywhere near the AS man's headquarters. Several arrests had been made in Châteauroux and, since the town seemed to be becoming more dangerous, Southgate and Maingard decided to move to Montluçon themselves, if only until the furore had died down. They took a train and arrived in the town at 11.15 p.m. on 30 April.

The following morning the pair set out for Mathieu's house on the rue de Rimard. Southgate left Maingard there to look at the two dozen messages that had arrived from London during the previous week and to take them back to their lodgings so that he could read them later. Several newly arrived agents had also recently come to Montluçon, and before meeting Mathieu himself Southgate had lunch with them. When he eventually got to the rue de Rimard he was very tired and quite preoccupied. He therefore failed to notice several men walking up and down the street, endeavouring to look inconspicuous. Had it been at any other time he would have immediately recognized them for what they were – Gestapo agents – but he had so much to think about that he didn't notice them or the obvious members of the Milice who were also hovering around the area. Southgate, one of the best of all SOE circuit leaders, who had always been so security minded, went to the house where Mathieu was staying and, for the first time in his SOE career, knocked on the door before making even the most cursory of security checks. It was what he had feared Jacqueline might do in her exhausted condition and, in a similar state himself, he made what was to be both his first and his last major mistake. The door flew open and he was dragged inside by armed men, who proceeded to search him.

When nothing incriminating was found on him, he was taken to Gestapo headquarters in the town. Here he was placed in a small room with several other people who were being guarded by young Frenchmen, members of the Milice. Southgate described how he was treated by these young hoodlums:

I was robbed of everything I had, watch, wallet and all personal belongings. After being handcuffed I was told to face a wall in a small room with about a dozen other people who had been arrested in the town. We were heavily guarded by young Frenchmen from 18–20 years of age. These Frenchmen took great pleasure in annoying us by getting hold of our hair, pulling it and bashing our faces against the wall, just for the fun of it. I received a severe knock on my forehead and passed out. I came to a moment later, stood up again, and much to my horror I was called a 'Zazou'. The ordinary police methods were used. They would ask your name and, if you gave it, hit you on the head and tell you to shut up; and if you did not speak, you were still hit and asked why you did not speak.[1]

To be called a zazou, one of a group of young people prevalent in Paris at that time who wore baggy, knee-length jackets, tight trousers and thick-soled suede shoes, was a huge insult to Southgate. He complained as much about being classed as a zazou as he did about the physical violence to which he was subjected. The treatment that he received, although it irritated him intensely, was not as bad as that which his companion had to suffer. While Southgate was merely insulted, Mathieu was beaten up by the young thugs.

Although the Germans had previously put a price on Southgate's head, they did not realize that it was he whom they were holding. Nor did they know the identity of Mathieu. The pair spent the next few weeks being interrogated and physically abused in a number of different locations until finally they found themselves at 84 avenue Foch in Paris, the home of the counter-intelligence section of the Gestapo, known as the Sicherheitsdienst.

Having been taken to the sixth floor of the building, they were given chairs to sit on in a corridor, whereupon Southgate caught sight of someone he knew well in one of the small rooms off the corridor: his school friend John Starr, who appeared to be very much at home in the place. Southgate was disturbed by the sight but, although his friend was obviously receiving special treatment from the Germans, he couldn't believe that there was anything sinister in Starr being there and felt that there must be a logical reason for him to be cooperating with the enemy.[2]

Mathieu and Southgate were transferred to the prison at Fresnes, but Mathieu never really recovered from the injuries he had suffered at the hands of the Milice and died sometime later that year, never having regained his freedom. Southgate had just started to get to know his two cellmates at Fresnes when he was abruptly returned to avenue Foch. The Germans had discovered his true identity.

Arriving once more at the offices of the Sicherheitsdienst, Southgate was met by three Germans: Dr Josef Goetz, the language expert who was in charge of wireless broadcasts, a colonel whose name he didn't know, and another man known as Ernest, who spoke fluent French and was the first to greet him, saying, 'Well, Mr Southgate, the game is up.' Southgate was amazed that they had discovered who he was so quickly and wondered what had happened:

Believe me, you could have knocked me down with a feather. Once more I could not help thinking of Capt. Starr. Later on I was told by Ernest himself that one of our own agents recognised my photograph on my identity card under the name of Maurice Leblanc, and he quite openly said: 'Oh, but this is Southgate, alias Hector.'

... One thing that made Ernest furious was that London on the 2nd or 3rd May broadcast to all concerned: 'Beware of Hector's whereabouts. At Montluçon a big police operation has taken place.'[3]

Southgate was pleased that all the circuit members would have known of his arrest so soon after it happened. He didn't want to believe that it was his old friend who had denounced him at the avenue Foch, but he couldn't think of anyone else it could have been. There was more bad news. When the German colonel began to interrogate him with the help of an interpreter he asked many questions about the organization of the SOE, and it was clear to Southgate from the documents he showed him that the Germans already had a lot of details. Southgate told him that it seemed to him that they knew more about it than he did. The Colonel's reply shocked him: 'We know much more; documents that are sent to your country are read by our people before yours.' Southgate listened in horror as the Colonel continued by asking him if he knew *Claude* (Henri Déricourt). He admitted that he did, having met him in London, and the Colonel told him, 'Claude is a very good man of ours. From him we get reports, documents and names of people.'

With his true identity now known Southgate could no longer pretend to the Germans that he had nothing to tell them. He knew that because it was a significant time since his arrest and news of it had undoubtedly reached the Stationer circuit, anything that he now disclosed would have little bearing on what happened to it. As a safeguard he confused his story by making up false details and describing them as having happened to actual people but in locations where they had never been. The Germans soon tired of listening to him and realized that what he told them was no longer of any use to them, but still he was kept at the Sicherheitsdienst headquarters.

While in avenue Foch, Southgate saw a lot of John Starr and had many opportunities to speak to him. Certain things about his friend confused him and led him to think things he would rather not have considered:

> Capt. Starr was engaged in making out charts from documents handed to him by the Germans, and I asked him why he was doing that, and his answer was the following: 'If I don't do it somebody else will, and in doing it I am gathering very valuable information which may come in useful sometime.' I must say I was a little disturbed by his attitude, although I refuse to think there is anything wrong with the man, as on the day of his arrest he tried to escape, and received two shots in the thigh. He also tried to escape with a girl [Noor Inayat Khan] ...[4]

Eventually on 20 June Southgate left the avenue Foch and was taken back to Fresnes prison, where he remained until August. Then, just before the liberation of Paris, he was sent to Buchenwald concentration camp. In Southgate's mind the one good thing to arise from the trip to Germany was that he was part of a group of 36 men, one of his travelling companions being Lieutenant Arthur Steele (*Laurent*), the wireless operator of the Monk circuit, to which courier Eliane Plewman (*Gaby*) had belonged. During the journey Steele told him that 'he had recognised my photograph and identity card at H.Q., Paris, and by that I know that Capt. Starr had nothing to do with my denunciation'.[5] While Southgate was relieved to receive what he thought of as proof of his friend's innocence, there were many who disagreed with him, although there was no absolute proof of any treachery. Nor was it proved that Steele was the real culprit. All he had told Southgate was that he had recognized his photo; he never said that he had told anyone. Southgate seemed to feel no animosity towards Steele for his perceived betrayal – or none that he admitted to – and it begs the question of whether by naming Steele he was simply trying to save the reputation of his old school friend, John Starr. By the time he made the report in which he named Steele as the one who had recognized his photo, Steele was dead, having been executed in Buchenwald concentration camp in September 1944. John Starr survived the war and the accusations of those who believed he may have been a traitor. He died, an old man, in 1996.[6]

When Jacqueline heard the news about Southgate she was very sad. The role of a courier was generally regarded as being at best boring, and at worst dangerous and exhausting. Jacqueline had had 15 months of this existence and only two things had made it bearable for her. One was, of course, that she knew she was doing something useful for the war effort. The other was the companionship she had shared with the people with whom she worked in the Stationer circuit, especially Maurice Southgate. She knew that his loss was a tragedy for those who remained in France. He was a well-respected man who also commanded the loyalty and affection of the people with whom he worked, and she wondered how they would manage without him. She was also apprehensive about what her role in the circuit would be when she went back to Stationer after finishing her courses.

But within a few weeks of learning of his arrest, all thoughts of Southgate and Stationer were wiped from Jacqueline's mind as the terrible news about Didi's arrest reached her. It was what she had feared from the moment she had discovered that Buckmaster had reneged on his promise to keep her sister away from the action. Although she had been distressed by the situation that Francis had found himself in and believed that she was to blame for it, her distress was nothing compared with the anguish she felt when she heard about Didi. She was appalled by the thought of her naive young sister having been taken away by the enemy and terrified by what she knew might happen to her. Jacqueline, who had always displayed such dignity and self-control, who could always be relied upon to remain calm in the face of any difficulty, fell apart at the news of Didi's arrest. It had arrived at SOE headquarters in a message, sent on 26 July, by one of the two remaining Spiritualist wireless operators, Jean Gerard Maury. In it he simply said, 'Rose arrested 22nd about 11 o'clock at her work.' With no other news it seemed that Didi had just vanished.

Francis was not faring too well either and the news of his sister's disappearance only added to his misery. He had received the news about Didi at the Barkston Gardens Hotel in London, where he had been staying, courtesy of the SOE. After all this time, the organization was still trying to think what could be done about him and he was miserable, knew no one and had nothing to do.

When Buckmaster had sent a note about Francis to the Director of Finance back in March, he received a reply that told him that something had to be settled soon, because there was nothing further that the SOE could do for the young man and that it would not even, therefore, be able to continue paying for his board and lodging. It was not what Buckmaster had wanted to hear. He decided that he had a job for Francis after all and wanted him to be enrolled again in the organization, as he planned to use him in an unspecified role after D-Day.

Although the Director of Finance was happy with this arrangement, those in the training section were not. In reply to Buckmaster's claim to have a job in mind for Francis, the section sent a terse note, which rather annoyed him, as it informed him that:

> I understand that it is suggested that this man should again be put into training. I personally feel very strongly that he is totally unsuitable from the point of view of intelligence and emotional instability, and I cannot feel that we are justified in training a man of this type, who would be useless to us and a danger to others, to oblige his sisters.
>
> I had a long talk with Major Jacobs after he saw Nearne some weeks ago, and he was most definite and convincing.[7]

To prove his point, a copy of Major Jacobs's report was forwarded to Buckmaster. The doctor had said:

> This man's condition remains much the same. There is still evidence of marked nervous instability.

Opinion: The long period of waiting with nothing defi-
nite to do had certainly not improved his nervous state.
I agree that he would be better employed in some job
which does not involve severe strain. I do not think he is
fit to undergo strenuous paramilitary training. Once
again I suggest that he should be interviewed by the
Psychiatrist.[8]

Several further memos were sent back and forth concerning poor Francis, with Buckmaster involving more people
from the organization at ever higher levels. Less than a
month after learning that Francis was judged to be unsuitable for either training or a job, Buckmaster fired off a note
to the Director of Operations for North-West Europe,
Brigadier Eric Mockler-Ferryman, copying in all positions
below, up to and including Brigadier R. E. Brook, who
directed western European operations. The note concluded
with his opinion: 'I regard as a matter of principle, the right
of the Country Section to take responsibility for choosing
the agents which it sends to the field, subject, of course, to
advice and guidance from the Administrative Sections
interested.'[9]

The F Section head was clearly infuriated by the replies
he had received to what he regarded as being his business
alone, and only wanted to accept the advice and guidance
from the Administrative Sections if that advice coincided
with his own wishes. The whole situation was becoming a
battle of wills and it was a battle that Buckmaster was
determined to win at Francis's expense, although, as time
went by, his enthusiasm for the fight began to fade. He
admitted that the details of the job he had had in mind for
Francis earlier in the year had not, at that time, been clear

in his mind but was at pains to point out that, contrary to what many in the SOE thought, 'It is not at all the family consideration that induces me to recommend him again.'

Vera Atkins also became involved in the impasse in the summer of 1944, when she told Buckmaster, 'This unhappy man is still at a loose end. He registered for military service and underwent his medical over a month ago. He has heard nothing since.' Buckmaster, by now having grown completely uninterested in Francis and his problems, merely replied, 'Sorry, I can't help it. He is a British subject.'

Atkins then suggested that perhaps they could simply put Francis on to a plane back to France, as they had done with two other unsuitable agents in the past. Buckmaster's reply, written in the margin of the note, was three lines high, in capital letters, and had been underlined four times. It said simply: 'NO'.[10] He was clearly annoyed with the suggestion, possibly because he had realized, too late, that he could easily have done what she suggested had he thought about it a few months earlier. In February 1944, anxious to rid himself of Francis, he had pushed the problem of what to do with him on to Selwyn Jepson who, it will be remembered, had arranged for him to be officially 'landed' in the UK on 14 March. Having done that, it was too late to remove him covertly because he was now known to be in the country and was therefore, under the terms of the National Service (Armed Forces) Act of 1939, liable to be called up for military service.

In August Didi was still languishing in a damp, dark prison cell in Fresnes. She kept herself busy by thinking of the many different ways she could attempt to escape if only the right opportunity presented itself. But the prison, built in the latter part of the nineteenth century, was believed to be impregnable. It was an immensely solid structure from which it was unlikely that anyone would be able to escape unless the building were bombed. Even the audacious Dumont-Guillemet had deemed arranging the breakout of prisoners from Fresnes to be an impossible undertaking and had refused to try it, despite it having been his initial idea and having had orders from London to do so.

In the days before the liberation of Paris, it had become clear to the Germans that they would soon be leaving the capital. Following the failed plot to assassinate Hitler on 20 July, the Wehrmacht's senior officer in Paris, General Karl Stülpnagel, who had been implicated in the plot, was replaced by General Dietrich von Choltitz, whom Hitler ordered to defend the French capital whatever the cost. The General, until that point a loyal supporter of Hitler, could see no sense in this instruction and could not decide what his next course of action should be. He knew that if an Allied attack were to be made on the city he would not have enough troops to counter it but he thought that he might be able to defeat the Resistance. He was wrong.

On 10 August, the day he took office, the French rail workers, many of whom supported the Resistance, went on strike. They were followed by the Paris police, who began their first ever strike and then refused to obey von Choltitz's order to lay down their arms. Although the police had mainly supported the Nazis, there were among their number approximately 3,000 officers who supported the Resistance. They were buoyed by the action of the rail workers, which gave them the opportunity they needed to show that they were no longer going to pay lip service to the occupiers of their city. Von Choltitz's orders were further disregarded when the prefect of the police ordered the gates of three prisons, the Roquette, the Santé and the Tourelles, to be opened to allow political prisoners to leave. The following day the city's civil servants also decided to strike. By this time the Germans knew that all was lost and they began to withdraw. In the rue des Saussaies, where Didi had been held, the Gestapo agents were hurriedly dumping their records in the street. When the pile was big enough they set fire to it and the citizens of Paris, who had, when possible, avoided the street for the four years of the German occupation, came out in droves to see the Nazis on the run.

The French Army's Second Armoured Division, commanded by General Philippe Leclerc, had been given the honour of liberating the French capital and had been told to take the most direct route into Paris, through the forest of Rambouillet to Versailles. Leclerc had a better idea. He sent a small group this way, entering the city through the Porte de Sèvres as a diversion; but his second force entered through the Porte de Vanves and the final, main thrust came from the south through Longjumeau and Fresnes to the Porte d'Orléans.

By the time the Second Armoured Division passed by the prison at Fresnes on its way into the city, many of the prisoners from the various Resistance circuits around France had been brutally executed there. Others had been moved out by their German guards once it had become obvious to them that their occupation of Paris was coming to an end.

Didi was one of them. In the early morning of 15 August, just ten days before the French capital was liberated, she and hundreds of other prisoners, male and female, left the prison at Fresnes on board buses that took them through the still-sleeping streets of Paris to the railway station at Pantin on the north-east edge of the city.[11] Freedom had been so close. Now a whole new set of horrors awaited her.

CHAPTER 16

The End of the Line

The Stationer circuit had always been too big for the number of people who undertook its work. Had it been smaller, Jacqueline would not have worn herself out both mentally and physically by the amount of travelling she had had to do in order to accomplish all her given tasks. She was also convinced that Southgate would not have been arrested had some of the burden of Stationer been taken off his shoulders earlier. He had borne his responsibility bravely but he was only human, and humans are fallible.

Plans had been prepared,[1] detailing what should be done if the worst happened and Southgate, Jacqueline and wireless operator, Amédée Maingard, were captured. These plans included roles for Auguste Chantraine and Charles Rechenmann, but by the time of Southgate's arrest, both Chantraine and Rechenmann had been captured themselves and Jacqueline had gone back to England. This left just Pearl Witherington and Maingard to cover the whole area, and look after the hundreds of Resistance members in the circuit by themselves.

Those in charge in London finally came to their senses and accepted that Stationer could no longer function as a single entity. It was decided to split the circuit into two, with two new leaders: Shipwright, run by Amédée Maingard, and Wrestler, which was put in the hands of Pearl Witherington, a surprising but good choice for an organization that rarely appointed women to senior positions. Her appointment as a circuit leader would have been approved by her training instructor, who had commented in her finishing report: 'This student, though a woman, has definitely got leaders' qualities. Cool and resourceful and extremely determined. Particularly interested and suited for active work. She has had a good influence on the course and has been a pleasure to instruct.'[2] Although it is doubtful that the feisty Pearl would have appreciated the words 'though a woman', the instructor's opinion clearly alerted F Section to her suitability and helped to ensure her appointment as leader of Wrestler.

When Jacqueline heard what had been decided, she was left to wonder where she would fit in to this new set-up upon her return to France. The news that her rightful role, the one she had worked so hard to fulfil, was being taken by Pearl, who had been in France for a much shorter time and, at that point, had done far less work than her, must have been a bitter pill for her to swallow.[3] When she managed to speak to Maurice Buckmaster about Stationer and asked which new circuit she would be assigned to, he told her that it was unlikely that she would be going back to France at all, despite her excellent training results.

Her reaction to the arrest of Didi may have been instrumental in the decision not to send her back to France. She had been so distressed by the news that it was obvious to all with whom she came into contact that she was not ready to resume her heavy workload. Buckmaster advised her not to worry about the work but to concentrate on regaining her health and strength, as he had another task for her in mind. Like the task he had had in mind for Francis, the one that he wanted Jacqueline to do was still being formed in his head. He couldn't give her any hint of what it would entail until much later, he said, so Jacqueline remained at a loose end in London with nothing to do except worry about her siblings and blame herself for the situations in which they both now found themselves.

She could see the torment that poor Francis was going through, and had no idea where Didi had been taken or what she was going through. No one seemed to know; nor had they managed to find out any details of how she had been apprehended. Although she tried to ignore it, the lack of information about Didi preyed upon her mind. Would she ever see her sister again? With so many empty hours to fill, Jacqueline sometimes thought back to the days of her childhood, remembering the little girl who had hero worshipped her and tried to tag along with her wherever she and her friends went. Although Didi was now a grown woman, Jacqueline still regarded her as her little sister, spirited, brave but rather unworldly. She knew that without her influence Didi would not have thought of coming to England in the first place. She would still be in the family home in Grenoble with her parents, waiting for the war to end so that she could train as a beautician and begin her adult life; perhaps she might even have got married and had children. Jacqueline hated the war that had caused so much heartache for her and her family. Although she would never confront him with the question, she couldn't understand why Buckmaster had taken no notice of her views before sending Didi to Paris, of all places, one of the most dangerous cities in the country, but she knew there was nothing she could do about it except wait and pray fervently for Didi's safe return.

At the end of September 1944 Vera Atkins bumped into Francis, who told her that he had just been called up into the British Army. She in turn reported this to the F Section finance officer, Mr I. D. Lloyd, telling him, 'This man ... is, therefore, really not any longer employed by us.' But the problem of Francis Nearne would not go away. He soon turned up again at SOE headquarters with a request for help in transferring to the Intelligence Corps. He explained that unless he could obtain this transfer he would soon be posted, and said that he had spoken to his company commander who, in view of his work in France, had suggested that he ask the SOE for help. Francis also requested help in obtaining permission for Thérèse and Jack to be brought to England, as he was still worried sick about how they were managing without him and had not heard from his wife for some time. Brigadier Mockler-Ferryman, Director of Operations for North-West Europe, acted promptly and helped secure the position with the Intelligence Corps that Francis had requested. He was posted to Rotherham in Yorkshire and ended the war there as a lance corporal. At last the SOE had done something good for Francis, even though Thérèse and Jack had had to remain in France.

But by October 1945 Francis had another problem. Although the war was over by then, in both Europe and the Far East – VJ day was 15 August 1945 – Francis was not eligible for demobilization. His military service had been too short for him to be immediately considered and his time at the SOE and the many months afterwards that he had spent in limbo, begging to be sent home but having to wait to be called up, were not counted as service. He had been told that he was to be posted overseas and the most likely place that he would go to would be India, where there was still fighting going on between the different religious factions, prior to the country's independence.

Francis had just about managed to cope with service in Rotherham, although he found the north of England very different from what he was used to in France. But the thought of being sent halfway round the world, away from everyone and everything he knew, to a land he couldn't even imagine, when he had not seen his wife or son for two years, filled him with horror. He had spoken to his commanding officer about the position he now found himself in and although the CO sympathized, the best he could do was to give Francis compassionate leave so that he could return to France briefly to make sure that all was well with Thérèse and Jack.

On his arrival in England after his brief trip home, Francis was told that he had approximately two weeks before he would be departing for India by boat. In a panic he telephoned the SOE office and spoke to Vera Atkins, telling her what was now happening to him and asking for her help. Vera was of the opinion that there was little that could be done, but then Francis mentioned that while he had been in France he had visited a former employer, who had offered to give him his old job back. Suddenly Vera saw what she thought might be a way out of all his difficulties. She told him to make an application to his CO for his release from the Army and to leave the rest with her. She promised him that she would see what she could do. In view of the previous attitude of the SOE, although admittedly not of Vera herself, Francis had very little confidence that this particular problem would be solved, but what more could he do except put his trust in Vera to try to sort something out for him?

Vera went straight to Buckmaster's office to tell him what needed to be done for Francis. He agreed with her and sent a note to the officer in charge at the Directorate of Finance and Administration. He told him of the difficulty that Francis was having and reminded him that

> he was finally out-posted to the I. Corps on the understanding that we would try to obtain his release at the end of hostilities ...
>
> ... he thinks he is going to be shipped to India. He is very upset at this and wishes to apply for release on compassionate grounds and asks us now to help him in this. His wife and child in France cannot live on his Army allowance of 470 francs per week. When he was there a few days ago his old firm, Marassi, rue Condorcet of Grenoble, offered him his job back provided he could return to them shortly but they were unable to hold it open for him indefinitely ...
>
> I asked him to make application for release to his CO at Rotherham and I should be glad if you would take whatever steps you think best in order to help him in this matter. He is definitely an SOE responsibility since we brought him to this country.[4]

Two days later Vera, now Flight Officer Atkins, having eventually been given the commission in the WAAF that she had long sought, wrote to Francis: 'Following our

THE END OF THE LINE

telephone conversation, I have taken up in the proper quarters the question of helping you to obtain your release on compassionate grounds and I understand that a memorandum has been sent to the War Office branch concerned ... Please keep me informed of how things are going.'[5]

The memo about the sad case of Francis Nearne eventually reached the right person at the War Office. In accordance with Buckmaster's request, Francis was demobbed and was able to return to his wife and son in the tiny corner of France that would remain his home and his safe haven for the rest of his life. Had the SOE not brought him to England, he could have remained with his family throughout the war. But the moment Francis set foot on British soil all that changed and he began what was undoubtedly the most unhappy time of his life. Had he known what would happen to him, he would never have consented to make the trip to London; after all, he had only made it to get some training. It was unfortunate that he was not considered suitable for the course. The right thing to have done would have been to return him to his home with all haste, not leave him alone in a strange country with little money and no real purpose, and then conscript him into the Army. Had Buckmaster not asked Selwyn Jepson to deal with Francis, and had he not been in the temper that he obviously was in when he dismissed Vera Atkins's suggestion that they should simply fly Francis home, perhaps the poor young man would have had a more settled life.[6] All he had wanted to do was to help the Allies fight the Germans the way his brother and two sisters had done; in return for this patriotic gesture he had been ridiculed, belittled, humiliated and made to feel that he was a complete failure. The

SOE's handling of Francis Nearne was not one of the organization's finer achievements.

Jacqueline had also received news. The task that Buckmaster had had in mind for her had come to fruition and she had been told that she was to become a film star.

It had been decided that after the war had been won, the British public should be told about the secret work that had been done in France. Since nearly every document relating to the SOE was classified, and would remain so for many years to come, the only thing to do was to make a film about the organization – a sort of drama/documentary that would give a flavour of what had happened across the Channel during the war, without disclosing anything top secret. The filming, undertaken by the RAF Film Production Unit, began in 1944 and was paid for by the Central Office of Information. Jacqueline was cast as the female lead, playing an SOE wireless operator called Miss Williams (*Cat*). The male lead was taken by Harry Rée who, as Captain Brown (*Felix*), was an agent and the boss of the circuit.

Rée (*César*) was well suited for the role, having joined the Acrobat circuit in eastern France near the Swiss border before becoming the head of the Stockbroker circuit, based near Belfort. Other SOE agents were used in supporting roles, one of whom was Brian Stonehouse who, like Jacqueline, had been born in England but had spent part of his childhood in Boulogne-sur-Mer. The two became life-long friends.

The film, initially called *School for Danger* but later renamed *Now It Can Be Told*, was released in 1946, and showed some aspects of SOE selection, training and life in occupied France. Jacqueline was filmed doing much of the physical exercise that, in reality, she had missed by not being sent on the paramilitary course. She also acted out the part of a wireless operator – her sister's role, and not part of her remit at all. Heavily dumbed down, in order to spare its eventual audience the more gruesome details of what might have happened had the agents been caught, the film was nonetheless an interesting interpretation of contemporary history. It was also all that the general public would be told until the SOE personal files, with the true facts, began to be released in March 2003.

Didi was now on the next stage of her journey to the camps. At Pantin station the prisoners stepped off the buses and were directed by numerous guards on to a platform, where a huge goods train was waiting. Watching the proceedings, to ensure that they were conducted in a proper manner, were the Swedish consul and the president of the French Red Cross. Their presence gave the prisoners confidence that nothing bad would happen to them and they resigned themselves to an uncomfortable journey with an as yet unknown destination.

They were put into wagons that were normally used to transport cattle. Despite the hour, the sun was already shining and it promised to be a beautiful, hot day. There were no seats and most of them had brought some items of luggage, so each wagon was crammed with people and bags. Some tried to find a small space on the floor on which to sit, while others stood so that they could see through the small, barred openings at the top of each wagon, hoping to be able to identify stations along the way and perhaps work out where they were being taken. Some believed they were heading to Germany; others pointed out that since there were no toilet facilities in the wagons, they were obviously only going to make a short journey.

By mid-morning the train still hadn't left and with the sun blazing down on them the prisoners, locked in the wagons, were becoming extremely hot and irritable. Because of the circumstances of her arrest, Didi had no baggage and was able, when the opportunity arose, to shuffle around in the wagon unhindered, sometimes managing to get a breath of fresh air from the opening at the top of the wagon. Those who had elected to stand were thankful that they had done so, as they too managed to catch a little cooling breeze, but it was exhausting being packed into such a small space with so many other people. The German guards ignored their pleas for drinking water.

At last, just before midnight on 15 August, the train began to pull out of Pantin station. By now many of the prisoners had been locked in the wagons, in the fierce heat of a summer day, without food or drink, or any toilet facilities, for over 18 hours. Some of the older prisoners were in a very bad way, but the young ones like Didi fared a little better and, although they suffered, were able to recover more quickly. Didi certainly felt that, should an opportunity present itself, she would still be able to try to escape. It was only the thought of escaping that kept her going throughout the nightmare journey that was to follow.

Slowly, very slowly, the train started to move. It took most of the night to reach its first stop. During the hours of darkness the temperature inside the wagons was almost bearable; but when the sun started to rise the next morning those inside the wagons began to fear for their lives. Then, amidst much clanking of wheels and hissing of steam, the train suddenly stopped. After a journey lasting the entire night they had reached the station at Lagny, a distance of approximately 40 kilometres. The guards got out of the train and unlocked the wagon doors, telling everyone inside to get out quickly. Many of them were dazed and dehydrated but they all tumbled out, to discover that the reason for disembarking was that the Resistance had blown up part of the rail lines and the train could go no further. It was lucky that this had happened, for many of the prisoners would have died of the intense heat had they not been able to walk in the open air for a short while.

Beyond the platform at Lagny was a field, bordered on one side by trees. Although her legs felt stiff from having been crammed into the train, Didi thought that she might be able to reach the trees if she ran fast enough. It wasn't the best plan she had ever made but it was all she could think of at short notice. She set off as fast as she could, leaving a small group of women staring after her, obviously horrified by what they could see was about to happen. One of the guards had seen her break out of the group and began running towards her, brandishing a rifle and shouting at her to stop or else he would shoot. For a split second Didi was tempted to carry on and take her chance, but knowing that she and her legs were no match for a bullet she stopped. The guard rushed up to her and, grabbing her by her arm, dragged her back to the group of frightened women. He shouted at them all, telling them that if any of them did that again they would be shot with no warning.

The march continued towards a part of track that was still intact and to which another train had been sent. While the prisoners walked they were seen by farm workers in the fields, who noticed how much they were suffering. Many of them produced bottles of water, which, ignoring the guards, they gave to the grateful prisoners.

Soon they were being crammed into the wagons of the other train. With the Red Cross official and the Swedish consul no longer observing what was happening to the prisoners, their tormentors felt able to bully them and managed to get everyone back on board much more quickly than the previous day. When they were all locked in, the guards walked along the platform shouting at the tops of their voices to let the captives know that anyone who tried to escape again would be shot and that everyone in the same wagon as that person would also lose their lives. Didi could feel the eyes of all those around her, looking at her and forbidding her to try another escape. She knew then that she would not be able to get away just yet: she knew she couldn't live with the deaths of the others on her conscience. The thought of escape had been the one thing that had sustained Didi during her imprisonment, so it was with a heavy heart that she abandoned her plan.

Having been given water the prisoners now all needed lavatories but there were none in the cattle trucks. The only facilities that had been provided were some old tins, placed in the corners of the wagon so that the contents could be tipped through the barred openings in the top of the wagon. In theory it was a reasonable idea; in practice it didn't work, especially as when the train rounded a bend or hit a rough piece of track, the tins fell over, depositing their contents all over the floor. It was only when the guards needed a lavatory themselves that the train stopped and the prisoners were also allowed to squat on the track, flanked by two guards who ensured that there were no more escape attempts.

The afternoon light eventually faded and still the train made its way across France, through the pitch black of the night and into the next morning when, as the first rays of the sun began to brighten the sky, it crossed the border into Germany. If the sight of so many Germans in France had horrified her, Didi was now terrified by being in their homeland. Everywhere she looked there were Germans. They seemed like ordinary men, women and children but they were her enemies. She knew that if it had been difficult to escape in France, it would be almost impossible in Germany, where there would be no one she could trust. She couldn't even speak the language.

The journey lasted for another few days and when they next stopped they discovered that they were in Weimar. Large groups of men were removed from the train and formed into lines for the march to the concentration camp at Buchenwald, a few kilometres away. For some of the female prisoners this was the first sight that they had had of their husbands, fathers, brothers or sons, and although it was heartbreaking to feel as if they had been lost again as soon as they had been found, it comforted many of the women to know that their men folk were still safe and well.

On the last day of the journey, as the sun began to set, the train pulled into the station that was their final destination. The women were now only a short walk from the camp where they might be spending the rest of the war. Some would, in the course of the next few months, be moved on to other places and other camps, where life would be dangerous, the work hard and the conditions unbearable. But for some of these unlucky women, this camp would be where they would remain for the rest of their short lives. For them there would be no more freedom, only backbreaking work, disease, starvation and death at the hands of some of the most brutal people known to man. This was Ravensbrück concentration camp.

CHAPTER 17

Lost Opportunity

When Didi saw the setting in which the camp had been built, she was heartened. It was not what she had imagined a prison camp would be like at all. Despite the women being tired and hungry after the ordeal of the train journey, the march from the railway station, a distance of about 3 kilometres, had not taken long, and they had skirted around the edge of the pretty village of Fürstenberg, with its elegant villas and gardens stretching down to the lake – the Schwedtsee. Of course, it would have been much more enjoyable had they been free women and not prisoners. Before the concentration camp had opened its gates to women prisoners in 1939, the area had been a place where people came for holidays or days of relaxation, messing about in boats or having picnics on the banks of the Schwedtsee, which was surrounded by pine forests. For Didi the trees and the woodland represented the place in which she planned to hide when she managed to get out of the camp, for she was still determined to escape.

As the column of women reached the outer gates of the camp, though, it became depressingly clear, even to Didi, that escape was probably never going to be a realistic option. For Ravensbrück concentration camp stood behind a vast wall, at least 5 metres high, which was topped by electrified barbed wire. As the women poured through the gates they found themselves in an open area that they later discovered to be the *Appelplatz*, the place where, several times each day, they would be made to stand in all weathers to be counted. To the left was a long, wooden building surrounded by barbed wire. This was the canteen where all the SS guards and the female overseers (*Aufseherinnen*) gathered in their spare time and were served food by prisoners, who were not allowed to eat even a tiny fraction of what they consumed. On the right, opposite the canteen, was another long, wooden barrack, which housed the showers and the kitchen; behind it was a narrow passageway, bordered on the other side by a bunker used to house prisoners in solitary confinement, in the dark and without even the most basic facilities. The passageway would soon become one of the most feared places in the camp for the new arrivals, as this was where prisoners were executed by a shot in the back of the neck. With typical German efficiency, at the other end of the passage was a crematorium, which enabled the guards to kill a woman and then dispose of her body in record time.

On the other side of the *Appelplatz* was a wide path, the *Lagerstrasse* or Camp Street, on either side of which were more wooden barracks. Two of those on the left were used as a hospital, the *Revier*, another feared place, where patients were just as likely to be killed as they were to be made well again. The other huts, known as the *Strafblock*, a prison within the prison, were where those who committed a misdemeanour, or what was regarded as one by the guards, were punished. Behind these buildings was the morgue, while the huts on the right of *Lagerstrasse* housed the prisoners.

Although the camp was primarily for women, there were a small number of huts, a kitchen and a hospital set aside for male prisoners. Ravensbrück had been built by men from the nearby camp of Sachsenhausen, and when repairs or more buildings were required, the men had to be brought from there to do the work; and in 1941, it had been decided to have a small number of men living permanently at Ravensbrück. This small camp-within-a-camp was initially planned to house only the 350 men necessary for the work, but by the end of 1943 there were between 8,000 and 10,000 men living there.

To complete the camp set-up and make the transportation of inmates and supplies efficient, two railway tracks bordered the camp: one to the north, the other on the south side running straight past the Siemens factory, where many of the prisoners were forced to work. To the east, after the railway lines had passed the camp, the lines gradually merged.[1]

There was another smaller facility built to the south-east of the main site. It was officially called Uckermarck but was known as the *Jugendlager* – youth camp – as its original purpose had been to house German juvenile delinquents. At the time of Didi's arrival at Ravensbrück, Uckermarck was being evacuated in readiness for conversion into an extermination camp that would allow the Germans, in what was left of the war, to obliterate all evidence of what had gone on in Ravensbrück by murdering as many of the women prisoners as they could. It was to be an impossible task for them. Even with the two ovens in the crematorium burning night and day, they were losing their battle to clean up the camp. Geneviève de Gaulle Anthonioz, who had belonged to the Resistance and was a niece of Charles de Gaulle, was a prisoner at Ravensbrück around the same time as Didi. She recalled how the smoke from the crematorium was 'becoming worse. Acrid smoke fills my cell … one of the furnaces had been overloaded with dead bodies and has caught fire.'[2]

In this hellhole Didi spent the first few weeks of the autumn of 1944. She was put into a hut with Frenchwomen, as she was still claiming to be French. She had told no one of her real identity and the women with whom she became friendly only ever knew her as Jacqueline du Tertre. She quickly learnt to trust no one. Even the most loyal person could be persuaded to betray a friend when confronted by starvation or the wrath of the guards and overseers.

The guards were mainly men from the Waffen SS who lived in houses outside the camp wall. They escorted prisoners when they were being moved to and from sub-camps and other work facilities, and also provided security for the camp perimeter, ensuring that escapes could never happen. They would sometimes aid the overseers, who were all women, recruited from the general public with the promise of high wages and light work.

From its beginning, Ravensbrück was the place where overseers for all the concentration camps were trained. New recruits were taught how to prevent prisoners escaping, how to make them work efficiently and how to punish them for any infringements of camp regulations. The women selected as overseers were a diverse group. Many were poorly educated and quickly became used to the idea of being able to bully women whose education had been far better than their own. Others applied to be overseers out of political conviction and in order to do their best for the Fatherland, while yet more applied for these positions for financial reasons: an overseer was paid very much more than an office worker.[3]

While many of these women were little better than criminal types, they were not all cast in the mould of the ugly harridans that people have come to believe them to be. Even the infamous Irma Grese, possibly the most sadistic, psychopathic overseer of all time, who began her career at Ravensbrück, was, in her earlier days, a physically attractive young woman, although by the time she was executed for war crimes in December 1946 her dissolute lifestyle had left its mark: photos of her at the time of her trial show a haggard, hard-looking woman who appears to be much older than her 22 years. Happily for Didi, although not for others elsewhere, by the time she arrived at the camp Grese had gone on to pastures new at Auschwitz and Bergen-Belsen.[4]

There is no record of Didi receiving any particular ill treatment while in Ravensbrück although she, along with all those in the camp, certainly suffered from the appalling general conditions, the lack of food and medical treatment, and the ever-present threat of specifically targeted cruelty for no apparent reason other than the whims of the overseers and guards.

One of the senior overseers working at the camp during Didi's incarceration was Dorothea Binz. Known to the French prisoners as La Binz, she had come to the camp in 1939 and remained there for the rest of the war, dispensing her violent form of discipline to anyone who happened to get in her way. Whenever La Binz appeared, accompanied by a large dog, the prisoners were on their guard. Binz was a small, blonde woman with a vicious temper who regularly beat prisoners or whipped them simply because she enjoyed it. She often used to deliver her beatings in multiples of 25. Twenty-five lashes from a whip or a strong stick were just about survivable; 50 could sometimes be survived by the most robust of prisoners; but no one survived 75. On one occasion, having beaten a prisoner to death, La Binz was observed standing on the woman's legs, gently rocking back and forth. When she eventually went on her way, her boots were covered with her victim's blood.[5]

La Binz was not the only sadistic overseer at the camp. The 36-year-old Greta Boesel was another. Although a trained nurse, she was in charge of work details. Her favourite saying, when referring to the unfortunate souls in her charge, was: 'If they cannot work, let them rot.' As part of her remit she sent prisoners to be murdered at Uckermarck, and when the gas chamber was opened at Ravensbrück in December 1944 delighted in selecting those who were to be gassed. The head nurse at Ravensbrück was 58-year-old Elisabeth Marschall. Despite her original choice of occupation, Marschall was not interested in attending to the health of the prisoners. Instead she too helped select those who were to be murdered and also attended the doctors who conducted medical experiments in the camp, causing untold suffering to the women, which resulted in painful, lingering deaths. Marschall was assisted by Vera Salvequart, a 25-year-old Czech-born nurse who had spent much of the war as a concentration camp prisoner herself and, as a prisoner, had been sent to work in the *Revier*, where she dispensed poison to the patients.

In the Ravensbrück trials conducted after the war, Binz, Boesel, Marschall and Salvequart were among 11 criminals from the camp who were sentenced to death for the atrocities they had committed. Several others, including women, were given long prison sentences. Salvequart petitioned George VI, asking him to grant her a reprieve and stating that she had been a prisoner and had, earlier in the war, passed secrets to the British. Her reprieve was not granted and she, along with the others, was hanged by Britain's chief executioner, Albert Pierrepoint.

The commandant of Ravensbrück was a 36-year-old married man with children, SS Obersturmführer Fritz Suhren. He arrived at the camp in October 1942, taking over from Commandant Max Koegel, and remained in charge until the end of the war. Suhren was responsible for the deaths of thousands of women. He adopted the policy of *Vernichtung durch Arbeit* (extermination through work) and was also responsible for the building of the gas chamber.

Life in Ravensbrück was a nightmare. The women were in constant fear for their lives and had no control over their own futures. If they rebelled they were punished; even if they behaved as they were instructed to and did nothing to antagonize the guards and overseers, they were also punished. Some of the women simply lost the will to do anything. In the camps there was a term for people like this: they were called *Muselmänner*. They spent their days shuffling around, not speaking or even seeming to see their fellow prisoners or the guards, totally indifferent to anything and everything that happened to them. By the time they had reached this state most were on the brink of death, too far away from the reality of their situation to be able to recover. Didi could not imagine ever being reduced to this pitiful state herself but, in the world she now inhabited, nothing was certain and her instinct told her that despite the odds against it happening, she had to keep believing she would survive. Unlike some who felt that they had been abandoned by the Almighty, Didi had a faith in God that remained strong and it was this that allowed her to keep going through the dark days she spent in Ravensbrück.

She was put to work in the camp garden for a short time, growing vegetables for the staff and inmates, although the former received most of what was produced. She was made to work hard but it was nothing compared with what she would ultimately have to do.

Soon after her arrival she bumped into Yvonne Baseden, a young Women's Auxiliary Air Force officer (WAAF). Yvonne had also trained as a wireless operator and had been arrested in the summer of 1944 in a safe house set up in a cheese factory in southern France, having attended a daylight drop of arms from the United States Army Air Force (USAAF). She had a French mother and an English father but, like Didi, had decided not to admit to having anything to do with Britain, believing her chances of survival would be greater if she was believed to be French.

Ravensbrück was fast becoming a place for reunions, as three more SOE agents, known to the other inmates as the 'little paratroopers', suddenly turned up. They were wireless operators Lilian Rolfe (*Nadine*) and Denise Bloch (*Ambroise*), and courier Violette Szabo (*Louise*). Didi knew Violette slightly and she had left England for France on the same day as Denise, who was returning for her second mission, having first been recruited in France. While on the first mission Denise had been tasked with escorting a British wireless operator, Brian Stonehouse (*Celestin*), to help him with his French. He could speak it perfectly well but with an English accent. Stonehouse was the same person who had been the childhood friend of Jacqueline Nearne while they all lived in Boulogne-sur-Mer. Denise was actually French but was believed to be British because her two companions were British. She didn't correct the error, perhaps thinking that she would be treated better if the Germans didn't know her true nationality. Violette certainly wanted to stress that she was British despite having a French mother; it would have been easier for her to be believed anyway as she also spoke French with a marked English accent.

The sight of the three other agents made Didi really nervous and she tried to keep out of their way as much as possible, as she didn't want to let anyone know that they were already acquainted. For some reason many of the prisoners were interested in the 'little paratroopers' and Didi was aware that if she were not careful one of the guards or overseers would realize that she was avoiding contact with them and want to know why. If that happened she would not be able to keep up the pretence of being Jacqueline du Tertre and her entire cover would be blown. So Didi contrived to meet Violette and told her that she was posing as a French girl. While it was sad to meet under such difficult circumstances, the two girls caught up with each other's news and Violette was horrified to hear about the torture Didi had suffered in the rue des Saussaies. She urged Didi to admit that she was British, telling her that when she herself had admitted to the Germans she was English, she hadn't been mistreated at all;[6] she was sure that it was because they were frightened of doing anything bad to British nationals in case of reprisals once the war was over. Didi, however, refused to change her mind but did agree on one thing: that should one of them formulate a plan to escape, she would share it with the other and they would abscond together, along with Lilian and Denise.

Before long all four women were moved to a work camp at Torgau, where they were employed in a munitions factory. It was delicate, dangerous work but they hoped they would not have to do it for long, as Violette had met someone there who helped her get a key for one of the gates in the camp wall. When Violette told Didi the good news, Didi was ready to drop everything and leave immediately, but Violette was more wary and thought it best to plan the escape properly before rushing into anything. It would be the one decision she would forever regret. While the four girls were planning their breakout, another prisoner overheard what they were discussing. Hoping to earn some privileges for herself, she immediately went to one of the overseers and told her what she had heard. Luckily another girl realized what was going on and found Violette to warn her of the other prisoner's treachery. Violette knew that she would have to throw the key away and did so quickly before she could change her mind or the overseer could come and search her. It was a bitter blow to them all, as it had been the best chance they would ever get of escaping.

Soon afterwards Didi went on to another camp in Abteroda while Violette, Denise and Lilian were sent to a work camp at Königsberg in eastern Prussia, 700 kilometres away, to help build an airfield.[7] The four never saw each other again. It was a bitter blow for Didi, for she was fond of Violette, saying: 'She was a very solid person, a tomboy, but very kind. She would have done anything to help anyone else. I would have liked to have gone with her.'[8]

Separated from her friends – people whom she knew she could trust – Didi was alone once more. But unbeknown to her, a worse fate was in store for the 'little paratroopers' when suddenly, early in 1945, they were taken back to Ravensbrück.

They might have avoided the torture that Didi had suffered, but Didi had been right to keep up the pretence of being French. With the end of the war in sight, the Germans wanted all trace of the English girls ever having been there to be removed. One evening, at the end of January or beginning of February 1945, they were sent for by Fritz Suhren, who read out a statement ordering their execution. They were taken to the passageway behind the camp kitchen and, one by one, forced to kneel and shot in the back of the neck by SS Sturmmann Schult. Their bodies were taken to the crematorium, but not before their ragged clothes had been removed and put into the camp store to be recycled for some other poor women.

In Abteroda Didi knew nothing of what had happened to her SOE friends and she had no time to think of what their fate might have been, as she had been taken there to work in the BMW aircraft-engine works, making parts for Messerschmitt aircraft. The Germans particularly liked having girls working for them in the factory, as their smaller fingers were more suited than men's to putting together the tiny parts of the complicated aero engines. Every day she became more and more exhausted. The work was backbreaking, the hours long – 12-hour shifts – and the concentration required to complete the task properly gave her a headache and made her eyes hurt. While she worked, she considered ways to escape but try as she might, she could find none.

Day after day she laboured, hunched over a bench, until one day it occurred to her that if she couldn't escape, she could at least refuse to work. That day she told the guards that she couldn't work. She said that she was too tired and in any case didn't see why she should help them when they were fighting against her own country, France. They shrugged their shoulders and told her that if she refused to work they would shave her head – a common punishment for disobedience – and she would not be given any food. Since the food was nothing more than a bowl of watery soup, she didn't hesitate. She told them they could do what they liked, so they dragged her away from her work bench and shaved off her brown hair. Minutes later, and now completely bald, she was taken back to the bench and told to get on with her work. She again refused. This time one of the guards, armed with a rifle which he pointed menacingly at her, told her that she had 20 minutes to decide whether she would like to work or whether she would prefer to be shot. Didi finally relented. It would have been a futile gesture to lose her life in such a pointless way, so she began to work again; but in a show of resistance she did so at a very slow pace. Her industrial action was soon noticed and she was threatened with punishment once more, so she started working at a normal pace but broke parts as often as she dared. She was reprimanded again and again, but excused herself by saying she wasn't used to doing that sort of work and obviously had no talent for it.

The thought that she could still do something to hamper the German war effort gave her a certain satisfaction, as did her blatant show of contempt for the guards. Even if they didn't understand exactly what she was doing, she knew, and it boosted her morale to know that she was still able to thwart their attempts to break her spirit.

Then she was told that she was going to be moved again. The news was unexpected and it suddenly occurred to her that perhaps the guards had understood more than she realized and she was being sent to somewhere even worse than Abteroda as a punishment. Had she gone too far this time? Perhaps this was the end of the line. She knew that sometimes she was reckless in the way she dealt with the Germans; it was the only thing she could do to make herself feel a little bit better about her desperate situation, but was it worth risking her life? She had developed friendships with one or two of the French girls and didn't want to be parted from them, but on the other hand a move to a different camp might possibly provide her with an opportunity to escape. She didn't know what to think and, with a heavy heart, waited to hear what her fate would be.

CHAPTER 18

The Getaway

In February 1945 Didi left Abteroda and was transported for the final time, in one of two groups, to a labour camp in Markkleeberg, 10 kilometres south of the city of Leipzig. Each of the women in these two groups was classed as a political prisoner which, according to the German authorities, was someone who had actively worked against the Third Reich; and the women, 249 in total, were all French, many of them having been arrested for Resistance activities. The camp was one of many sub-camps, several of which were located in the Leipzig area. This one was a sub-camp of Buchenwald concentration camp. Whether the women were moved because of a need for labour or simply to get them further away from the advancing Allies is debatable; it may even have been a combination of both, but whatever the reason, Didi knew that being classed as a prisoner accused of working against Germany meant the camp was not going to be an easy place to survive. Unlike at Ravensbrück, where uniforms had stopped being issued by 1944, on arrival at this camp the women were given dark-grey overalls to wear. Long-sleeved and baggy, they had buttons down the front to the waist and a belt. On the sleeve of the left arm was a red triangle, which identified them as political prisoners.

Markkleeberg was unlike any of the other camps to which Didi had been sent before. The prisoners worked at a variety of jobs. Aircraft manufacturer Junkers had chosen Markkleeberg as the site for a factory, Junkers Flugzeug und Motorenwerke AG (Aircraft and Engine Works), and had taken over a weaving plant from Stoehr & Company in October 1943, in order to build aircraft engines there. Its first employees were the redundant workers from the weaving plant. The town's population, estimated to have been 18,000 at that stage of the war, had not been in favour of playing host to a large aircraft factory, fearing that their homes would be in danger of aerial attack if the Allies became aware of its existence. Their concerns, although well founded, were ignored, as Markkleeberg had good railway links with the surrounding area, which made it ideal for many forms of industry.

After the factory became operational, more labour was needed. At first forced labour was brought in from occupied countries and the workers were billeted in hostelries in the surrounding area. Then the sub-camp was built to house both forced labourers and the slave labourers who were brought from concentration camps. In addition to supplying workers for Junkers, the camp provided workers for at least two other companies: chemical giant I. G. Farben, which held the patent for the Zyklon B crystals that made the lethal gas used in the gas chambers of the extermination camps, and Julius Pintsch, which manufactured lighting for railway carriages, lighthouses and other marine facilities. For the use of each labourer the companies paid a small sum to the SS Economic Administration

Main Office (WVHA). The workers themselves were, of course, given nothing. The SS also operated the policy of *Vernichtung durch Arbeit* (extermination through work), so the conditions in the camp were particularly harsh in order to fulfil this aim.

The only similarity that Didi could see with any of her previous camps was that, like Ravensbrück, it was located in a very pretty area. The town of Markkleeberg itself, on the river Pleisse in the state of Saxony, was small and attractive with flowerbeds and parks, and the townspeople took pride in their surroundings. The scars left by the open-cast mining that had taken place in the area in earlier days had been disguised by careful landscaping, and some of the disused pits were eventually filled with water to form lakes where, in the heat of summer, townsfolk could swim, and picnic at the water's edge. Around the outskirts of the town were dense woodlands.

Built in a residential area on a former athletics ground at the junction of two streets, Am Wolfswinkel and Equipagenweg, and opposite a neat row of houses, the Markkleeberg camp buildings and the electrified barbed-wire fence were mostly hidden by trees.[1] But despite the attempts to camouflage the labour camp, the abundance of trees could not completely hide the town's dark secret. There were watchtowers in three corners of the fence and the foliage did not disguise the large searchlights.

By the time she left Abteroda for Markkleeberg Didi was exhausted. She had been made to tackle all types of hard physical work which, combined with the lack of any decent food, had made her weak and susceptible to the illnesses that were rife in all the camps. The only spark of hope left to her was her never-ending thought of escape.

She had become obsessed with it. Throughout the journey between the two camps, a distance of approximately 230 kilometres to the east of the country, she looked for any opportunity, however slight, to make her getaway, but none presented itself, and the party of prisoners was large and armed guards were everywhere. Even if she had found a chance to slip away unnoticed, she had not really thought what she would do next. She had only a vague idea of where she was in Germany and she couldn't speak more than a few words of the language. These she had mostly learnt in the camps so they were unlikely to have been of much use to her, and had she escaped it was likely that she would have been discovered and recaptured. Had that happened she might have found herself in much worse conditions than she had suffered thus far, or perhaps even been shot.

Given her weak physical condition, it is understandable that Didi's recollections of arriving at Markkleeberg camp and of the time she spent there were sketchy and muddled. She thought she left Abteroda on 1 December 1944, but records of movements to and from Markkleeberg between August 1944 and March 1945 show that no one came from either Ravensbrück or Torgau, and that the only arrivals from Abteroda were of 125 Frenchwomen on 12 February and another 124, also French, on the 26th.[2] The rotten food, the back-breaking work and the treatment meted out by the sadistic guards had clearly begun to affect her mentally as well as physically. She described herself as 'wandering around as if drugged',[3] and in her mind the wretchedness of one camp became confused with the hardships of the others until she was uncertain what had happened at any of them.

She couldn't remember if she had helped to build roads or if she had worked on aviation components in Abteroda. Was it here in Markkleeberg that she had tried to sabotage her work by drilling the wrong-sized holes in aircraft parts or had that been in Abteroda as well? Her hair was now very short, but where had she had her head shaved? The first group of French political prisoners to be sent to Markkleeberg on 12 February had had their heads shaved on arrival. The second group who arrived on 26 February were not shaved,[4] so if Didi's memory of having short hair in Markkleeberg is correct, she must have arrived in the second group.

The work at Markkleeberg was extremely hard. The ground Didi was told to dig had been frozen throughout the winter and it was almost impossible to make a dent in it, much less prepare it for the building of roads. Even the guards could see that malnourished, exhausted women were unlikely to be able to do very much building. But it made no difference to them and the prisoners were still forced to work much harder than they were capable of doing. Many died trying. Others who survived were beaten when they did not reach the levels of achievement that the camp authorities expected.

If the backbreaking work wasn't bad enough, through-out the winter months Didi, like many of the other women, suffered from dysentery – the debilitating illness was rife in the insanitary conditions of the camp – and she also had a chest infection and a hacking cough that she could not shake off. Naturally in a camp that worked to the principle of *Vernichtung durch Arbeit* there was very little medical attention. The diet – the standard fare at Markkleeberg was a thin, watery soup and dry crust of bread – and the long hours of hard labour took their toll on her 5-foot 6-inch frame and she became severely emaciated.

Didi was beginning to think that she would never escape from Germany or see her family again. She became so weak that she could hardly move, but she had to try to carry on because those who did not work did not live for very long. She existed through those final few months of captivity in a daze. With her strength failing, she knew that she had to save as much of her energy as possible if she were to have any chance of survival. The days ran into each other as she battled to hold on to her sanity and her life and avoid the anger of the brutal female SS overseers, who took particular pleasure in using their rubber whips on those women who tried to resist.

The only light in this sea of darkness was the bonds she formed with the French political prisoners who had arrived with her in February. To the other prisoners in the camp they seemed different. They had stuck together and still kept their sense of humour, while some of the other nationalities had not. The group of girls who had had their heads shaved on arrival refused to be upset by it; some even made jokes about the way they looked. This was a completely different attitude to that of the other nationalities, some of whom had been so upset by it that they'd committed suicide rather than have to suffer the embarrassment of having no hair.[5] For Didi, being surrounded by women who had retained their sense of humour and love of life despite their appalling treatment was the best medicine; these women helped her to get through each day and gave her some hope for the future. They were certain that France would survive as a sovereign nation, and that they would eventually return to their homes and take up the lives they had left behind when they had been arrested. Every evening before collapsing into what passed for beds, they affirmed their belief in France by standing and singing the Marseillaise.[6] For other prisoners – Jews, Eastern Europeans, some both Jewish and from Eastern Europe – the future wasn't so certain; even if they survived the camp and the war, they couldn't be sure that their homelands would still exist come peacetime.[7]

Apart from her friends, it was still Didi's belief in God and her iron will that kept her alive. Describing her final days at Markkleeberg, she recollected: 'The most important thing was the will to carry on. You could never let them see that they were winning. You just had to cling on to the will to live, however long it took. I always had hope that it would soon be over.'[8]

Winter slowly turned into spring and with the warmer weather came renewed hope of escape. Although very weak, Didi had survived and she knew that the war must be coming to an end. She had heard the rumours that abounded in the camp about the Allied troops advancing towards Leipzig – the Americans from the west and the Russians from the east. The guards were aware of this too but, unlike the prisoners, knew that they were more than mere rumours.

In April 1945 the women were told by one of the guards that the American president, Franklin D. Roosevelt, had died and that the war would soon be over. He went on to say that he and the other guards would soon be leaving the camp and the prisoners would all be free. The French girls were delighted and spent the next few minutes hugging each other and singing the Marseillaise. The Hungarian prisoners, of whom there were many, were more practical. They hurried off to the huts where the food was kept, broke in and took everything they could find that was edible. The French girls suddenly came to their senses and managed to get the Hungarians to part with some of the food they had stolen. Then, before any of them had a chance to do anything else, the camp siren sounded and the commandant's voice boomed over the loudspeaker: 'I have received an order from Berlin. We are leaving on foot in 20 minutes. Those who are sick will be taken by cart and you will all follow. No one can remain in the camp.'[9]

The prisoners' euphoria was instantly shattered. The guard, in what one must assume was a final taunt, had lied. They were not free; nor were they ever likely to be free. The Germans were moving out of the camp to avoid being captured by the Americans or the Russians, and they were taking the women with them to hide the evidence of their abhorrent behaviour. It was unlikely that they would let any of them survive to be able to tell what had happened to them in Markkleeberg.

There were less than 20 minutes left to grab what possessions they had, and for Didi and her friends to try to regroup and decide what to do. They managed a hurried conversation, in which they all agreed that if they were to have any chance of survival they must try to escape on the way to the next camp. The guards then pushed and shoved those who were thought well enough to walk into a long column, while other guards rushed back and forth, dumping the sick prisoners in carts. There was an underlying air of panic amongst them as they hurriedly counted the prisoners and then began to move them out of the camp for the last time, under cover of darkness.

The prisoners were told that they would be taken to another camp 80 kilometres to the south – although Didi couldn't recall its name, this might have been Chemnitz, approximately 80 kilometres to the south-east of Markkleeberg – and from there they would be sent to yet another camp. Many of the women who survived the march went on to the concentration camp of Mauthausen in the Austrian state of Oberösterreich (Upper Austria), 20 kilometres from Linz.

Turning towards the south, the women were led through the residential area of Markkleeberg and out on to a road, bordered on one side by thick woodlands. Although weak and emaciated, and barely able to move themselves, the women were told to push the carts containing those prisoners too ill to walk. Had any of the residents of Markkleeberg looked out of their windows on that moonlit night, the column of women would have made a sorry sight indeed.

Didi's hopes soared when she saw the woods, thinking they would make a wonderful hiding place. The guards marched backwards and forwards along the lines of exhausted women, prodding their backs, urging them to move faster and pointing their rifles at them to show what would happen to them if they didn't obey orders. Didi watched their movements and judged that she might be able to leave the column if she moved directly after a guard had passed her and before the one behind reached her. She knew that she would have to be very quiet and move quickly. Trembling in anticipation she waited until a guard marched past, and then grasped the opportunity and headed towards the woods. Finding a reserve of strength she didn't know she possessed, she started to run and on reaching the nearest tree, hid behind it.

She half expected to hear the roar of a guard's voice or the sound of shots being fired in her direction, but she knew that this might be her last chance of survival and it was a chance she had to take. She rested for a moment, hardly daring to move and terrified that her rasping breath would be heard. All the while she remained there she could hear German jackboots stamping up and down, and the softer shuffling feet of the women, on the surface of the road. The sounds went on and on; the shambling convoy seemed endless. But there were no loud voices, no shots, and no one seemed to have missed her. Eventually there were no more footsteps. All was quiet and she knew that, for the first time since that terrible day in Paris the previous summer, she was no longer a prisoner.

A few moments later she realized that she was not alone. Two pairs of eyes were peering at her through the darkness. They belonged to two girls she knew from the camp. One of them was her friend Yvette, who had been at the camp at Torgau with her and with whom she had stayed ever since, moving from there to Abteroda and then to Markkleeberg. In later life, Didi was unable to be sure of the name of the other girl, although she knew that she had also met her in Torgau and thought her name was Suzanne.[10] Yvette and Suzanne had also managed to drop out of the marching column and had slipped into the woods.[11] Didi and Yvette hugged each other in excitement, wondering what had happened to another of their friends, a girl named Monique who had been on the same transport from Fresnes to Ravensbrück as Didi in August 1944, and had then followed the same path as they all had to Torgau, Abteroda and Markkleeberg.

For the first time in many months they had a chance, however slight, of reclaiming their lives. Standing in the quiet, peaceful woodland, still hugging each other – this time to keep warm – they could hardly believe what had just happened to them. Despite the dangers that they knew they would still have to face, they had escaped; they were free at last.

CHAPTER 19

A Narrow Escape

Knowing that they were still close to the town of Markkleeberg, Didi and her two friends retraced their steps. They had to find somewhere to rest and make plans for what they should do next. They didn't want to go anywhere near the marching column in case the guards found them, and the most logical place to head towards was the camp, which they knew would be empty.

The people of Markkleeberg had been right to think that the presence of the Junkers factory in their town would attract Allied bombing raids. The Markkleeberg area had been bombed several times, and while heading back towards the town the girls came across a deserted house that had been damaged during a raid. It had a hole in one of the side walls that they managed to climb through, and they collapsed, exhausted, on the floor. They rested for a while and then explored the house, finding that although it was damaged, it was still relatively secure. It was the perfect place to spend the night. Although it was April, it was still bitterly cold and there had been sporadic snow showers. The girls were still wearing their thin, grey overalls but they had brought their ragged camp blankets with them, so managed to cover themselves, and they slept fitfully through the intensely cold night, huddled together on the bare floor.

The next morning they awoke hungry and thirsty, and knew that they would have to find some food if they were to be able to continue their journey. Clambering through the hole in the wall into daylight they were able to see exactly where they were, and discovered that there was what appeared to be a smallholding along the road. Setting off towards it in the hope of finding something to eat, they hadn't gone very far when a dog started barking. It had obviously heard them approach and, terrified that they would be discovered, they turned and fled back to the bombed house, still hungry. It was too risky to try to find real food, so they had to make do with some dandelion leaves that they found along the road, quenching their thirst with the sprinkling of snow that covered them. Although not the feast that they had long dreamed of in the camp, it was better than nothing and would do until they managed to get some real provisions.

Frightened by the encounter with the dog, the girls decided to remain in the house for another day while trying to decide what their best course of action would be. They were still worn out and bitterly cold, but at least they could rest and stay sheltered from the wind and the snow flurries. They knew that it was vital to remain alert and they listened for any sounds that might suggest that their hiding place was in danger of being discovered. By now it was likely that they had been missed by other prisoners, and perhaps by the guards if they were still doing a roll call each day. Although it seemed improbable, they couldn't dismiss the possibility of there being a search party out looking for them. At intervals throughout the day they could hear the sounds of vehicles and people, but none came close enough to cause them any real concern, so they decided that the bombed house was as safe a refuge as they could expect to find and that they could remain there for another night.

They spent their time that day talking to each other about their lives and the hopes they had had, before the war had robbed them of their dreams for the future. It was a luxury they had not had in the camp, where they had been hard at work during the day and too tired in the evenings to do anything but collapse into their beds before the whole exhausting process began again the following day.

Didi still did not want to admit to anyone that she was not French and had actually been working for the British. It was not that she distrusted her companions; she simply felt that she must keep up the pretence until she knew for certain that her disclosure would not create problems for any of them. She had no difficulties in passing herself off as French, and Yvette and Suzanne had no suspicions that she was anyone except who she said she was. Her French was faultless, and all her memories of her childhood and of growing up in France were real, so there was plenty to talk about without telling the girls her real identity. The only thing that she had to remember was that she was Jacqueline du Tertre, but that story was so imprinted upon her mind that it required almost no thought at all.

Yvette came from Caen and had been a prisoner of the Germans for longer than either Monique or Didi. She had been a sub-lieutenant in the Air Force (l'Armée de l'Air) but, after the fall of France and the splitting of the l'Armée de l'Air into two sections – those who had escaped from France and joined the Free French Forces (Forces Françaises

Libres) and other military units, and those flying for the French Armistice Air Force on behalf of the Vichy government – she was without a position. She decided to join the Resistance and, in July 1943, became a member of a group called the Velite-Thermopylae, a Gaullist intelligence network that was part of the RF, the Free French Section of the SOE, where she served as an intelligence agent and a dispatch rider. Her important but dangerous role had lasted for only four months before she was betrayed, by whom she never discovered. She was arrested by the Gestapo and kept for 48 hours in the prison in Caen before being sent to Paris on 8 November 1943, where she spent another few days at the prison in Fresnes.¹ After she left Fresnes she was taken to Ravensbrück, where she remained for almost a year before going on to the camp at Torgau with Monique, Didi and Suzanne, and others such as the 'little paratroopers' – Violette Szabo, Lilian Rolfe and Denise Bloch. When the latter group was returned to Ravensbrück, Yvette, Monique and Suzanne were all sent to Abteroda, along with Didi, and there, like Didi, Yvette worked in the aircraft engine factory, before all four girls were transferred to Markkleeberg in February 1945.²

Yvette knew more than Didi about Monique, as she lived a mere 20 kilometres from Monique's family home at the Château d'Audrieu in Normandy, between Caen and Bayeux. Monique's father was the French pilot Philippe Livry-Level, who flew a Mosquito with the Royal Air Force in England and had taken part in the famous raid on the prison at Amiens in February 1944. He had been furious when he discovered that his daughter had been recruited by a British Army officer, Captain Attlee, for a secret mission, despite him refusing to give his permission.

He had been so angry that he had written a letter of complaint to Air Vice-Marshal Broadhurst, the Air Officer Commanding No. 83 Group, which was one of the main parts of the 2nd Tactical Air Force, providing support to Allied forces during the invasion of Europe.[3] The letter had been passed to the senior intelligence officer at the headquarters of 21 Army Group, who stated in a letter that 'they have had full knowledge of the case and have had all their intelligence officers and agents looking for your daughter but that they have not yet made contact with her but that they will not cease to try and do so'.[4] The letter was dated 3 September 1944, which was nearly three weeks after Monique had been transported to Ravensbrück concentration camp. It was small wonder that the 21 Army Group men had had no luck in trying to trace her.

It was thought that the reason Monique had agreed to work for the British, without her father's permission, was that on 8 June, two days after D-Day, a ghastly event had taken place, which she knew she would never forget. Twenty-six Canadian soldiers had been executed at her family home after being taken prisoner by a reconnaissance battalion of the 12th SS Panzer Division Hitlerjugend. Monique had been in the grounds of the château and had seen some SS officers take three of the captured Canadians at gunpoint towards a wooded area. When one of the Canadians hesitated at the edge of the woods, she witnessed him being hit with the butt of an NCO's rifle. The young man staggered after his comrades into the trees, and a few moments later Monique heard three shots and then saw the SS men return without their prisoners, the NCO loudly boasting that it was he who had killed them. A similar scene was going on no more than 100 metres away and, not wanting to see any more, Monique rushed back into the château, where she tried to calm herself by reciting the words of the funeral service in Latin. After that, she could do nothing except join the British when asked and try to avenge the young Canadians' deaths.[5]

If Didi learnt anything about Suzanne that day in the bombed-out house, she did not recall what it was. The lack of food and her poor state of health had weakened Didi considerably more than her companions, and although she was now free and should have been uplifted by that, her mental state was still so fragile that she found it hard to retain much of what she was told. She still had the cough she had suffered from for several weeks, and Yvette and Suzanne were concerned about how they would cope if she collapsed and was unable to continue walking with them. They urged her to rest as much as possible and were pleased when the next morning all three felt sufficiently rested to be able to continue their journey.

Crawling once more through the hole in the wall, they found a road and began to walk along it, judging the direction from the rising sun. They had made up their minds to go to Leipzig and, if the advancing Americans had not yet reached the city, find somewhere to hide until they did arrive. Soon Didi's energy began to fade and she was desperate to rest. Her legs ached and she wheezed with every breath. She knew that she was in a much worse condition than her friends, but didn't want to let them down and refused to stop. The will power that had sustained her throughout her captivity came to her aid once more and, although she walked very much more slowly than she would have liked, with the help of the two French girls she managed to keep moving.

For some hours they made very slow progress along the road that they hoped would take them to Leipzig, telling themselves that each step brought them closer to the advancing Americans and freedom. Then, rounding a bend, they saw with sheer dread a road junction ahead with a small group of German soldiers standing on one corner. They couldn't turn back without arousing suspicion and were sure that whatever they did, their escape attempt was now drawing to a close. The Germans would surely recognize their camp overalls, despite the thin blankets they had draped over their shoulders in an attempt to keep warm and disguise their appearance. At least the red triangles on their left sleeves were covered. After a few hurried words, and with heavy hearts, they decided to go on. There was nowhere else to go.

As they reached the junction, one of the soldiers stepped forward and barred their way. He demanded to see their identity papers. Trying not to appear nervous, they explained that they were French workers who had volunteered to come to Germany to help with the war effort; they hadn't yet been given any papers, as they were on their way to join their first work party and had been told they would receive everything they needed once they arrived. The story sounded weak even to them, but they could think of nothing else to say that might convince the Germans to let them go. They stood for several minutes while the men talked amongst themselves, obviously trying to decide what to do with them. Didi knew that they only had to look at her and her companions to see that they were not what they claimed to be. All three girls were extremely thin; their overalls, unsuitable for the time of year anyway, were stained and threadbare; and she knew that if they came a little closer, the guards would undoubtedly spot the lice that had made their home in the matted hair of all three. It had to be obvious to the soldiers that they were escaped prisoners and they waited for the handcuffs to be snapped on to their thin wrists.

Unbelievably that didn't happen. After another quick conversation with his colleagues, the soldier told the girls that they were free to go. Incredulous, they smiled, thanked him and went on their way as quickly as they could, fearful that he might change his mind.

The girls never really understood how they had managed to avoid arrest. Their best guess was that the soldier had known that they were escapees but that, in view of the imminent arrival of the Allied forces, neither he nor his colleagues had the time or inclination to do anything with them. There was also another possibility: the men may not actually have been soldiers. At this stage of the war the troops in the area consisted of Wehrmacht, SS and a group called the Volkssturm, a shambolic collection of boys as young as 16 and older men who had not been called up elsewhere. The Volkssturm could loosely be described as the German version of the British Home Guard but were not as well trained; nor did they have proper uniforms, as they had only been formed the previous autumn, but, sporting armbands, some of this ragtag bunch wore uniforms from their civilian occupations and could be mistaken for regular troops. If these 'soldiers' were in fact from the Volkssturm, it might explain why they let the girls go: they would not have wanted to have three starving prisoners to feed and may not have had anywhere to take them, even if they had been able to arrest them.

Whatever the reason, Didi and her two companions were amazed at their good fortune but, knowing that they could not rely on it lasting, resolved to travel through woods where possible rather than use the roads. For the rest of the day they hid themselves as much as they could, and at the faintest sound they ducked behind bushes or fell into ditches to avoid having to speak to anyone again.

They had no further contact with the enemy, but by the time they reached a village on the outskirts of Leipzig the light was fading and, with it, the hope of finding food. Their stomachs were aching with a hunger that was even worse than it had been in the camp, where they had at least had the thin soup and dried bread to sustain them. They were all exhausted, mentally and physically, and by now barely able to support each other. It was imperative that they find somewhere to stay for a few days to rest and regain their strength. They came across a church and hid in the grounds, huddling together against the cold so that they could sleep for a few hours during the night.

The next day they knew they would have to look for another shelter. It was obvious that the Germans were still in control of the area but they were hopeful that the Americans would soon reach Leipzig. When they found it was a Catholic church in whose grounds they had sheltered, Didi persuaded her two companions to trust the priest not to betray them. They went looking for him and found him praying inside the church. The good Father regarded the three frail figures in horror and, with the help of hand signals, as he did not seem to speak French, shepherded them into the rectory. His face showed the shock he felt at the sight of their emaciated bodies and their ragged clothes; and when the blanket slipped from the shoulders of one of the girls and he saw the red triangle on her arm, he knew for sure that they were what he had suspected, escaped prisoners, and he could see that they had been treated very badly. With a lot more hand signals and a few odd words of French, the priest let them know that they could remain in the rectory until the arrival of the advancing Allied troops. Then he called his housekeeper and said something to her that the girls did not understand. She looked at the dishevelled, filthy creatures, nodded, and then quickly went out of the room, returning several minutes later with a large tray. On it were bowls of thick, steaming hot soup and some pieces of bread – not the hard, stale bread that they had become used to but fresh, soft bread that tasted wonderful.[6] Didi's instinct to trust the priest had been right. Still, they had been extremely fortunate, as there were many clergy who, whatever their true beliefs were, had taken the easy option and sided with the government.

When the girls had eaten and drunk some water, the housekeeper led them to a room in the rectory, where she made up beds for them, and then showed them into the bathroom, where they found soap and clean towels. It was the first time in many months that they had been shown any kindness at all – for Yvette it was the first time in well over a year – and they couldn't quite believe what was happening to them. The housekeeper didn't seem to understand why they stood looking at her in bewilderment, and began miming and pointing to the towels to show them that they could have a wash. Then she left them and, amidst tears of relief and joy, for the first time since they had been captured they were able to get themselves clean and begin to clear the lice from their hair.

For the next few days they remained at the rectory, where the priest and his housekeeper treated them with great kindness. They slept a lot and in a very short time, Suzanne's and Yvette's health began to improve. But Didi's chest infection did not clear; indeed she seemed to be getting very much worse. She was finding it hard to breathe, still had the painful cough and slipped in and out of consciousness until the priest, who was obviously worried, went off to find a doctor he could trust to treat her. With the medication the doctor prescribed she began to improve.

By the time they heard the approach of soldiers and tanks, Didi felt well enough to go out and greet their liberators. The priest urged caution, as there had been Red Army soldiers in the area and he didn't want the girls to fall into their hands. But soon it was obvious that the Americans had arrived. The city of Leipzig and the surrounding area were captured by the 2nd and 69th Infantry Divisions of the United States First Army on 19 April 1945.

Didi and her friends tearfully thanked the priest for all his help. He was a true Christian who, with his housekeeper, had done everything he could for them. They would never forget his kindness. But now it was time for them to start the long journey home. Didi recalled that she told the Americans 'I was English and asked them if they would show us where the Red Cross was. However, they would not do this but put us in a house for one night.'[7] No longer frightened, the three girls slept really soundly for the first time in many months, secure in the knowledge that their ordeal was finally over and they were safe at last.

The following day they were taken to a building that the United States Army had commandeered to use as a temporary prison camp and were invited to tell their stories. The two French girls explained that they had been members of the French Resistance and had been captured and transported to Germany. Didi told them that she was a British agent, and that she had been held at the labour camp of Markkleeberg until she and her companions had escaped while being evacuated. Didi recalled: 'The captain of the camp interrogated us with a lot of SS in the room. When he had heard our story he presented us to the SS and told them that as they had treated us so badly they would have to pay for it but the SS said they knew nothing about us.'[8]

The day after their interview Suzanne and Yvette were sent to join other French nationals in a Red Cross transit camp, where they would stay until they could be sent back to France. The three girls were sad to part but vowed to keep in touch when they were all back in their own homes. Yvette made Didi repeat the address she had given her until she could do it with no mistakes, and then they hugged each other and said goodbye.

Didi was taken to another camp to be questioned further about her role as a British agent.

I was interrogated by someone in the American Intelligence Service. They asked me my number and I told them I had no number; they asked for my papers and I told them my story how I was arrested and that naturally the Gestapo had taken my papers away. I told them I was a wireless operator and that I knew Colonel Max Baxter [Maurice Buckmaster]. They were not convinced and told me I would have to go through many more camps before I was passed by the British authorities.

At the last camp I was again interrogated and told them exactly the same, how I was landed in France and arrested by the Gestapo. They expressed great surprise at a plane being able to get there in the night. They were very curious and asked me a lot about the organization, schools etc. and I did not want to give too much away so they said I was a German agent. They told me they would send a message for confirmation and for the time being I would have to stay in the camp with the Nazi girls.[9]

It is inconceivable that even though Didi's account of what had happened to her was muddled, the Americans couldn't see beyond her fragile mental and physical state, and recognize that she was a victim of the Nazis, not one of them. Because the work, and especially the organization of the SOE, had been secret it was unknown to the American occupying troops, it is perhaps understandable that they assumed it didn't exist and that the details Didi had given them were lies. But it is incredible that they believed that a woman who was seriously malnourished, painfully thin, visibly ill and wearing filthy, ragged clothes could be a Nazi when all the Nazi women in their custody were well fed and clothed, and seemingly in good health.

Didi herself wondered how they could possibly think that, when it should have been obvious to them that she had been a victim of Nazi brutality. Even if they were suspicious, was it really too much to ask that she be given the benefit of the doubt while her story was checked? 'They said they were sorry but there were so many German agents they had to be careful. They said even if they did have a message saying I was English it would not prove anything as I might still be a German agent.'[10] It was not fair, either, that they should disbelieve her because of their ignorance about what had happened to Allied prisoners in concentration camps. Unlike many of her fellow prisoners, who had not been able to withstand the deprivation of life in the camps and had yielded, not living to see the end of the war, Didi had survived; her belief in God, her iron will and her fierce need to survive had kept her from giving up during the long months she had been imprisoned. But now she was so distressed by the reactions of the Americans that she was perilously close to giving up. At the very point when she had finally believed that her ordeal had come to an end, the freedom that she longed for seemed to be slipping away from her once more.

CHAPTER 20

Allies or Enemies?

By the time the US First Army captured Leipzig on 19 April 1945, the Americans had liberated at least three Nazi camps. Two of the sub-camps of Buchenwald – Ohrdruf and Dora-Mittelbau – were freed on 4 April and 10 April respectively. The US forces had then gone on to liberate Buchenwald itself on the 11th. A news report about the visit to the camp at Ohrdruf, by American generals Eisenhower, Bradley and Patton, on 12 April, said:

> As they toured the Ohrdruf concentration [*sic*] camp today, Eisenhower and Bradley burst into tears. General Patton, the most battle-scarred of them all, was overcome by the sight and smell of the piled-up corpses; gagging at each fresh horror, in the end he simply bent down and vomited.
>
> ... The GIs cannot believe their eyes. There are piles of unburied corpses, stacked higher than a man, at every turn ...[1]

General Dwight D. Eisenhower added to the description of the horrors they had witnessed:

I have never felt able to describe my emotional reactions when I first came face to face with indisputable evidence of Nazi brutality and ruthless disregard of every shred of decency. Up to that time I had known about it only generally or through secondary sources. I am certain, however, that I have never at any other time experienced an equal sense of shock.

I visited every nook and cranny of the camp because I felt it my duty to be in a position from then on to testify at first hand about these things in case there ever grew up at home the belief, or assumption that 'the stories of Nazi brutality were just propaganda'.[2]

Despite Generals Eisenhower, Bradley and Patton having discovered what the guards had done in these camps, the news doesn't appear to have reached the American troops who captured and occupied Leipzig until much later. The German prisoners were treated well by their American captors and this encouraged them to expect favours. Unconcerned about the frail men and women they had mistreated only a few weeks before, the camp guards and overseers behaved as if it would soon be recognized that their actions had been justified. They were relaxed, the female overseers especially friendly with the American soldiers, flirting and begging cigarettes from them, and inviting them into their rooms.

Didi remained in American custody, sharing her accommodation for most of that time with the female Nazi inmates. As if it were not bad enough to be regarded as one of them, she also found their behaviour intolerable. She was furious that these brutal, sadistic women were now receiving better treatment than she, who had spent nearly five months in

Jacqueline (*top*) and Eileen (*bottom left and right*) – or Didi as she was known to her friends and family – as young women living in Nice, France, before the Second World War set their lives on such dangerous paths.

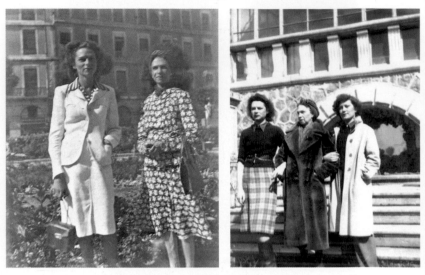

Jacqueline with her mother, Mariquita (*above left*),
and joined by Eileen (*above right*).

John 'Jack' Nearne, the girls' father.

The girls' brothers: Francis, the eldest of the Nearne children, in his Army uniform (*top*), and Frederick (*bottom*).

Preparing for war: Jacqueline (*top left and bottom left*) and
Eileen (*top right and bottom right*) in the uniform of the FANY
in 1942. Only two years later, both girls were working
undercover in France.

(courtesy of Mrs Murray Anderson)

(© Ian Ottaway)

Flight Lieutenant Murray 'Andy' Anderson, the pilot who flew
Eileen to France from England in 1944. The plane he flew was
a Westland Lysander, similar to the one above. Note the fixed
ladder, which enabled agents to disembark and board the
aircraft in the quickest possible time.

Eileen's friend Yvette Landais, with whom she escaped from the labour camp at Markkleeberg.

Yvette Landais just after VE Day, wearing her Markkleeberg camp overalls. Note the triangle on the left sleeve that identified her as a political prisoner.

A rather thin and fragile-looking
Eileen in London after the war.

Jacqueline at a UN function in
New York with her boss Captain
Johan de Noue, Chief of Protocol
and Liaison (*right*).

Jacqueline and Eileen, with one of Eileen's paintings.

Eileen (*left*) with fellow SOE agent Odette Hallowes at a ceremony in Ravensbrück in 1993 to unveil a plaque commemorating all those who lost their lives in the camp.

Eileen with her niece Odile in Teignmouth. Eileen passed away the following year.

(© Nick Randall)

The blue plaque in honour of Eileen outside her home in Lisburne Crescent, Torquay. A fitting tribute to an extraordinary woman.

great danger working in occupied France for the Allied cause, and another eight months as a concentration camp inmate. But she would not behave as the German women did, making advances to gullible young soldiers in return for better conditions, and she refused to have anything to do with them. They must have known that she wasn't one of them, but didn't bother to tell anyone and in turn simply ignored her. Didi demanded to see a senior American officer and reported to him everything that was going on. She was pleased to see the following day that one of the German women had had her head shaved by her comrades. No one admitted to knowing why this girl had been singled out but they must have suspected that it was she, not Didi, who had told the officer in charge what had been happening.

Didi was again interviewed by an American intelligence officer. She was asked the same questions as she had been before, and again told her interrogator how she had flown into France one night in a small aircraft that landed in a field and remained there only long enough for her and her companion to disembark and for two other agents to board the plane to be taken back to England. To all his questions, Didi repeated the answers she had already given, but once again the officer made it clear that he didn't believe a word, especially about the aircraft landing.

It is odd that the Americans, especially those in the Intelligence service, professed to have no knowledge of how the British had landed their people, as well as parachuting them, in enemy territory. The Americans themselves had participated in flying agents to occupied countries, including France, and must have known that in order to repatriate agents to the UK by air, they had to have been able to land the aircraft in France in the first place.

Nevertheless, a report about Didi made by the intelligence officer on 2 May 1945 and sent to the commanding officer of the American Intelligence Centre four days later shows a complete ignorance about the life lived by captured agents. Having heard that she had been tortured and suffered in a concentration camp, the officer should not have been surprised that Didi's account was confused, incomplete and contained some errors. He wrote:

SECRET
HEADQUARTERS
FIRST UNITED STATES ARMY
OFFICE OF AC OF S, G-2
INTERROGATION CENTER

MEMORANDUM:
TO: Officer in Charge, Master Interrogation Center.
SUBJECT: NEARNE, Eileen, alias DUTERTE,
   Jacqueline, alias WOOD, Alice, alias ROSE.

1. Subject claims to be a British subject by birth and to have worked in France for the British Intelligence Service until she was arrested by the Gestapo on 25 July 1944.

2. Subject stated that she has lived in France with her family since the age of two; that in March 1942 she was issued a passport by the British Consul in GRENOBLE, France, to return to England; that she went to LONDON via BARCELONA, MADRID, LISBON, GIBRALTAR, and GLASGOW, in company of her sister Jacqueline NEARNE; that almost immediately after her arrival in LONDON she and her sister joined the Information Service FANY where she was trained as a W/T operator; that she subsequently

entered another Intelligence organization, run by a Col. Max BAXTER (British Army); and that she received training as a W/T operator and cryptographer in a school near OXFORD.

3. In the end of February 1944, Subject stated she was flown to a field near ORLEANS, France, from where she made her way to PARIS. She was in company of another agent, whose name she does not know, and whom she met twice daily in PARIS in order to obtain from him the reports she had to transmit to England. Those reports were written in clear and Subject encoded them. Subject signed her messages 'ROSE', but claims she has forgotten her agent's number.

4. In July 1944 Subject's transmitter was detected and Subject was arrested by the Gestapo on 25 July. Subject claims she was not asked to continue her transmission. She claims, moreover, *that despite being tortured* she did not reveal any information detrimental to the British Intelligence Service or its agents.

5. On 15 August 1944 Subject was sent to the extermination camp of RAVENSBRUCK (970 Km N of BERLIN) where she stayed for two weeks, from there to TORGAU, then to ABTERODA, and finally to MARKELBERG near Leipzig. From that last camp, Subject claims, she managed to escape on 13 April 1945.

6. Subject creates a very unbalanced impression. She often is unable to answer the simplest questions, as though she were impersonating someone else. Her account of what happened to her after her landing near ORLEANS is held to be invented. It is recommended that Subject be put at the disposal of the British Authorities for further investigation and disposition.[3]

SECRET

One positive result of her meeting with the senior American officer was that Didi was moved away from the Nazi women and spent the final part of her imprisonment in a cell with a French girl called Paulette, whose account of her life with the Resistance and in the concentration camps the Americans had also disbelieved. Like Didi, Paulette was furious with her treatment by the people she had believed were the allies, not the enemies, of France.

Happily for Yvette and Suzanne, after they separated from Didi they did not have the same problems with the Americans, being repatriated soon after they were placed in the hands of the Red Cross.

Monique, Didi's other friend from the camp, also managed to escape from the forced march out of Markkleeberg as Didi, Yvette and Suzanne had, but she did so further away from the camp. Three days into the march, a group of Belgian workers passed close by the emaciated prisoners and two of them helped Monique to get away. She was taken to a farm where a group of French prisoners of war was working, and given food and a dress by the woman who owned the land. Now dressed as a German peasant, she discarded her camp overalls but cut off the red triangle and her camp number and kept them safe.

Nearly three weeks after leaving Markkleeberg, during which time she had sometimes had to hide in fields to avoid being seen by German troops, she stumbled across Red Army troops, who treated her well. One was obviously attracted to her but she knew that she could not trust him to help her get back to France, so, hearing that the Americans were also close by, she stole a bicycle and made her way to American-held territory, where she too had some difficulties making the Americans understand her position. A few days later she came across a Frenchman with a list of missing persons and found that her name was on the list. She also learnt that her father, RAF pilot Philippe Livry-Level, was in Leipzig, staying with the American officer commanding the area while trying to find her; he had been driving around the area looking for her in a car belonging to the French army. When they finally met up with each other they had a very emotional reunion. Leaving almost immediately, they set off for Paris, where the rest of the family were waiting for news of Monique, and arrived on the evening of 8 May – VE Day – in time for a celebratory family dinner.[4] A week later Philippe received a cable from one of his old American friends (who would five years later become the father-in-law of Robert F. Kennedy). The cable said: 'CONQUERING THE BARBARIANS AND YOUR DAUGHTERS SAFETY AS WELL AS YOUR OWN IS SUFFICIENT GOOD NEWS FOR A SINGLE LIFETIME VIVE LA FRANCE – GEORGE SKAKEL.'[5]

Yvette returned to her home in Caen to recover from her ordeal. Just after VE Day she put on her camp overalls for the last time so that she could have a photograph taken as a lasting memory of what she had lived through, and she then got on with the rest of her life. In November 1947 she was demobilized from the Air Force after having been awarded the Médaille Militaire, the Croix de Guerre with palm, and the Légion d'Honneur by a grateful France. She later married and had two children, Danielle and Yvan, but if she and Didi kept in touch after the nightmares they had endured together, no record of their friendship remains. Didi remembered both the name and the address of her friend, but there were no letters from Yvette amongst the papers found in Didi's flat in 2010.

On 6 May, the American authorities in Leipzig forwarded the damning report about Didi to the British for their comments. By the time it was received on 12 May the war was over, and Vera Atkins was making lists of those agents who had been accounted for and those who were still missing, including Didi. Buckmaster already knew that Didi had escaped from Markkleeberg; the news had reached him in an unattributed note, which he signed and placed on her file. It said: 'Known to have escaped into woods Markleberg near Leipzig April 12/13th. Probably using name Jacqueline Dutertre. 5th Corps First US Army asked to trace her.'[6]

As Didi's claim to be an SOE agent had been given a low priority by the Americans, their report hadn't been compiled until she had already been in their custody for three weeks. Happily for her, the SOE acted much more rapidly. On reading what the American officer had said about her, it was immediately evident that it described one of their missing agents. Despite having asked the 5th Corps, First US Army, to trace Didi, it was not the Americans but Vera Atkins in London who recognized the veracity of her story. Didi had been found at last.

On hearing the news, Buckmaster added another note to Didi's file: 'Not the same stamp as her sister, but a conscientious worker. Rather apt to frivol and difficult to keep on a serious plane, but she did all that was asked of her and we are truly thankful to hear of her reported safety.'[7] Why Buckmaster formed such an opinion of Didi, before she had returned from Germany and been through the debriefing process and given a full account of what she had been through, is difficult to fathom. To say that she was 'not the same stamp as her sister' seems to disclose more about

Buckmaster's opinion of Jacqueline than it does about Didi.

Once the war was over the task of locating and repatriating missing agents had begun. The SOE sent two two-man teams to Germany, each team carrying a long list of the people they were hoping to find. One of the men in each team was tasked with keeping the list chained to his wrist at all times and each list contained approximately 600 names. When it was discovered that Didi was in Leipzig, being held by the Americans on suspicion of being a German spy, one of the teams was contacted and went immediately to rescue her. The two Army officers, Major Denis Newman and Captain Rollo Young, had already reached Weimar in their search for agents, and, according to Captain Young, it was his colleague who found Didi. They had

spent some time at nearby Buchenwald concentration camp and were now touring smaller camps individually.

We had accreditation to the American forces and he [Major Newman] had no difficulty extracting her and bringing her to the Christliche Hospice where we were billeted. We got her some informal American WAAC [Women's Army Auxiliary Corps] uniform and she stayed with us I think for two nights. We then got her on a plane to England but I don't know where.

There was a poignant moment on the first evening. We depended on American rations but had got some small addition locally, eggs I think. As we set out to cook supper, she said in a tiny voice 'Could I do that, it will be heaven to be in a real kitchen'.

She spoke of her sister Jacqueline but did not know much about what had happened to her.[8]

The officers listened to everything that Didi was able, or wanted, to tell them about what she had been through and she recalled that they were 'extremely nice and very sympathetic'.[9] They took her to the aircraft that would bring her back to England, telling her that another Army officer would meet her at the transit stop in Brussels and he would ensure she got to England as soon as possible. Captain Young gave her a note to carry, to safeguard her from further difficulties:

> The bearer Cadet Ensign Eileen Nearne is a British Officer employed by MOI (SP) war office. She has been given instructions by me to report back to London and in view of the treatment she had received while a prisoner in German hands may she be given every help please.
>
> Her credentials may be verified by telephoning Major Sherren at Welbeck 7744 London.
>
> R.S. Young CAPT. (BR) 'T' Force. Att. 12 Army.

When she arrived in Brussels the officer was there to greet her and listened to her story. Then he waved her off on the final part of her flight to England, where she arrived on 23 May 1945. The document given to her by Captain Young also had a small pencilled note that said '15.45 Croydon'. Whether it was written by him or by the officer in Brussels, it is likely to be the time that Didi's flight was due to arrive at Croydon airport, which was still the main airport for London in 1945. Didi recalled how, after the aircraft landed and the doors opened, she 'had the joy and emotion of seeing my colonel [Buckmaster], who came to greet me'.[10]

The bearer Cadet Ensign Eileen Nearne is a British Officer employed by MOI(SP) war office. She has been given instructions by me to report back to London and in view of the treatment she has received while a prisoner in German hands may she be given every help please. Her credentials may be verified by telephoning Major Sherren at Welbeck 7744 London.

R. V. Young.
Capt. (BR)

'T' Force. Att. 12 Army.

Left 25. 2. 44

Didi's war was now officially over. She had only been away for 15 months but the horrific experiences she had endured during that time would haunt her for many more years to come – perhaps for the rest of her life.

CHAPTER 21

Thoughtless Demands

When Maurice Buckmaster arrived at the airport to greet Didi, he had not long returned from the Continent himself. After the liberation of Paris in August 1944 he had planned a trip which, on 25 September, took him back to France, where he had remained for the next seven months, travelling around the country, making contact with Resistance members and those who had helped the SOE agents with their work. He gave his project the lofty title of the Judex Mission, after the process used in early Roman law of selecting a citizen to act as a judge, hear disputes and make decisions. Buckmaster may have planned his Judex Mission with such work in mind, and he did receive several complaints from disgruntled members of the Resistance that he quickly passed to other members of his team for investigation, but in reality it was not a fact-finding trip to right wrongs or to arbitrate in disputes. It was a lengthy public relations exercise, in which Buckmaster was received by officials, attended dinners – formal and informal, received praise for the work that had been done by his agents and dispensed gifts to those who had helped them. He was accompanied by several senior staff from London and a record of the visits he made was kept by Captain

R.A. Bourne-Paterson, F Section's planning officer and a former accountant.

While visiting Rennes in Brittany during the first few days of the mission, the party came across eight men working on repairs to the railway line, which had been damaged by RAF bombing raids. They were anxious to clear up something that had been both puzzling and frustrating them, and they hoped that Colonel Buckmaster would be able to provide the answers they sought. Bourne-Paterson's report explained the problem:

> Their first question was to ask us if we could explain why the Germans, who had tortured and maltreated members of the French Resistance, were now being given, as prisoners, a packet of cigarettes a day by the Americans, and rations far in excess of those available to the civilian population. The reply was not, and is not, easy, and the Americans have done themselves a great deal of harm by the lenient way in which they have treated their prisoners. In the eyes of the French, the British and the French are now very close together, as they have both suffered directly at the hand of the Germans, whereas the Americans, who have suffered neither occupation nor bombardment, still do not know what they are dealing with.[1]

The visit to Rennes also highlighted another problem in the way the Americans worked. It became clear that their policy when dealing with anyone whose first language was not (or did not appear to be) English was to arrest and imprison them before asking questions. The party heard how two girls, both very active Resistance members, had crossed the railway line, and been arrested and imprisoned by the Americans for doing so, one of the girls being locked up on her 20th birthday. It seemed a very harsh punishment for such innocuous behaviour. Such an American reaction was found not to be unusual. Their heavy-handedness towards the Allies but liberal behaviour towards the Germans did nothing for relations between the French people and the US troops.

After leaving Rennes the mission entourage went to Paris, where Buckmaster and Vera Atkins set up a 'drop-in' centre for SOE agents who had not yet been brought back to London. They rented two rooms at the Hotel Cecil in the rue Saint-Didier and, for a short while, their makeshift offices were busy. When the agents arrived they were usually seen by Vera, but she was later replaced by Nancy Fraser-Campbell, a member of the FANY and an F Section staff member from London, who had travelled as part of the mission. Vera didn't stay long in the capital. She was concerned that, despite the facilities for receiving agents, very few had actually emerged and so decided to return to England, where she began her self-appointed task of tracing all the agents who hadn't turned up at the Hotel Cecil, including Didi, and who were still missing.

In October the mission visited Lille and met the people who had resurrected the Farmer network when its leader, Michael Trotobas, had been murdered by the Germans. The head of the Spiritualist circuit, René Dumont-Guillemet (Didi's second boss while in France), had been largely responsible for reactivating Farmer and he was there to meet the members of the mission when they arrived on 3 October. The report of the visit to the Farmer circuit recorded:

Outstanding in all our contacts with the various groups was the evidence of a fervent admiration, amounting almost to worship, of Captain Michel [Trotobas] ... of a burning desire to continue to rank as part of a British War Office organisation, and of the development of an esprit de corps which was remarkable. It was in its way a tragedy that part of our mission is to declare the British connection officially ended, although there is no doubt whatever that unofficially it will continue to exist for a very long time to come.[2]

The report also confirmed that not only was Trotobas a legendary figure in the Resistance; so too, to a lesser degree, was Dumont-Guillemet, without whose input, ideas, financial assistance and leadership the circuit that Trotobas had founded would have disappeared, its members scattered and its great work at an end. It was officially recorded that 'Tangible results of this contact were represented by a mass of well-directed sabotage against German communications and a mass of information particularly of rocket emplacements which came flowing in from Lille.'[3] Didi's role in helping Dumont-Guillemet in this task cannot be dismissed, for it was she, along with Spiritualist's other wireless operators Maury and Diacono, who sent the vital information on to London.

The Judex Mission was joined for short visits by agents who had worked in France, and by November 1944 Buckmaster had asked Jacqueline Nearne to join him and take the members of the mission to meet the people with whom she had worked. She left England for Paris on 2 December, not knowing her sister's whereabouts and uncertain if she was still alive. Two days later, having taken a boat across the Channel and then a train, she joined the group, who were producing an itinerary for the next part of the trip, when they would visit south-west France, one of the large areas in which the Stationer circuit had operated. With them went Pearl Witherington, who had married her fiancé, Henri Cornioley, the previous month, and George Jones, the wireless operator of the Headmaster circuit, who had sent messages for Stationer before the arrival of Amédée Maingard.

At Châteauroux they were able to catch up with many of the people Jacqueline and Pearl knew, and Buckmaster handed out cigarettes and made a speech before heading off to La Châtre and then Montluçon, where Maurice Southgate had been arrested. Because of an administrative error there was no accommodation for any of the party there and they had to sleep on the floor of a café. It gave those mission members, such as Bourne-Paterson and Buckmaster, who had remained in England for most of the war a small taste of the difficulties the agents had endured on a daily basis, albeit without the added danger of a Gestapo raid suddenly taking place.

When they reached Clermont-Ferrand, Colonel Buckmaster, George Jones and Jacqueline went to 37 rue Blatin, home of the Nerault family, who had given so much help to the Resistance. They found that the concierge of the building, Maria, was still there. She had bravely stayed at her post after the family had been caught by the Gestapo during the raid that Francis Nearne had narrowly escaped. Sadly Maria had no more news of M. and Mme Nerault, or their daughter Colette,[4] but she gave them good tidings of their son, Jean, who was alive and well and had not been captured. During the visit to rue Blatin, Jean Nerault suddenly appeared and 'scenes of wild rejoicing took place'. The group retired for drinks to the Brasserie de Strasbourg, a favourite haunt of the Stationer circuit. 'The patron was still there and great was his astonishment at seeing Designer [Jacqueline] in FANY uniform. Although he pretended to have known all the time, it was quite obvious that this was not true and all the garçons were brought in to shake hands with us.'[5]

Next, battling through heavy snowfalls, Jacqueline went with Buckmaster and two other officers to La Souterraine, where she introduced the Colonel to an elderly lady, Mme Marie Gillet, who had been a great help to Stationer, providing a safe house for agents, including Jacqueline, until she was arrested just before D-Day and imprisoned for three months. As a result of her incarceration Mme Gillet had lost most of her belongings and was extremely poor, so Buckmaster was pleased to be able to give her gifts to help her get her life back together, 'for which she most pathetically offered to pay'.[6] The offer was, of course, refused.

Lunch at a restaurant called the Lion d'Or followed, and here Jacqueline was able to thank the proprietor, who had also assisted her in her work during her long stay in France. Jacqueline then left the rest of the group, who headed further south while she caught a train to Paris. She was anxious to get to the capital as soon as possible as, although it was unlikely that she would discover anything new, she wanted to see what she could find out about Didi's whereabouts and hoped that there might be someone who had heard something that would give her hope that Didi was still alive. But, as she had feared, no one could tell her anything at all about her sister and it was with a heavy heart that she began her journey back to England.

Buckmaster, who still had a soft spot for Jacqueline, was delighted to have had her with him on the Judex Mission, commenting:

> It was always a matter of great regret to me that Hector [Maurice Southgate] could not be with Jacqueline and other members of his group who, in December 1944, toured with me the area in which they had been working during the war.
>
> ... I shall never forget the warmth of the family embraces which were showered on Jacqueline, and in which I was often included myself. They bore testimony to her popularity and to her unselfishness. Pent up emotion was released in an overwhelming flood of international rejoicing.[7]

When Jacqueline returned to England she made her way back to the home in Darenth Road, Stamford Hill, where she had lived for such a short time with Didi. When the news finally came through in May 1945 that Didi had been reported as escaping from a camp in Markkleeberg she was delighted; but her elation quickly faded when no other news was forthcoming and no one could tell her anything more about her sister's whereabouts. Then came the American report that Vera Atkins had recognized, and Jacqueline knew, with an overwhelming sense of relief, that Didi would be coming back to her after all.

*   *   *

After having been met at the aircraft side by Colonel Buckmaster, Didi was taken by a driver from the FANYs to Stamford Hill, where Jacqueline was waiting. An almost unrecognizable figure staggered through the front door and Jacqueline was appalled by the change that had taken place in her lively young sister. Didi was obviously very ill, and would need a lot of physical and emotional help in order to return to the vivacious girl she had once been.

Gradually Didi was able to tell Jacqueline a little of what had happened to her, but some things were obviously too painful for her to recount so she just told her sister that she had never lost hope of surviving, and that her will power and faith had saved her. Jacqueline could clearly see that her sister's faith remained unshaken but that, despite her effort to try to be cheerful, her spirit had been badly damaged and she was suffering more from psychological problems than physical – something that Jacqueline was powerless to treat.

A week after her return to London Didi was called in to the office of the SOE to be debriefed. Afterwards, a reporter from the *News Chronicle* contacted her for an interview, which was conducted in a coffee shop. In the subsequent article in the paper she was named as 24-year-old Miss Monique V., who had joined the 'French underground' in Paris; the unnamed reporter noted, 'I cannot tell you her name. It is still on the security list.' Although this was undoubtedly true, it was a rather pointless security measure, as the article had a photo of Didi above the headline 'English girl survived SS torture'.[8]

Thankful to have the ordeal of the debriefing and the newspaper interview behind her, Didi was then left alone to adjust to her freedom. As was customary in those days, she was not offered any help in recovering from the trauma she had suffered. Eventually that help would come, and Didi would be referred to various doctors and clinics, but for the first few months after her return from the camps she was left to her own devices to muddle through as best she could.

One day soon after her return she received a letter from Paulette, who had been with her in American custody after VE Day. In the short time they had been together they had formed a friendship and Paulette had won Didi's trust; Didi had even disclosed that she was British and that her name was Eileen, although Paulette had no idea how to spell the name. Her letter, dated 15 June 1945, came from Metz in north-east France.

My dear little Eiline,

I don't know if the letter I sent from Paris reached you but it was sent with an American officer. Dear little Eiline, I'm finally what one could call almost free, I'm back in France, I'm going to be returned to my département, at least I hope so. And you dear, how has your business been arranged, have they finally decided to return you to the English authorities, that was not very nice, after you left I was seriously angry, and told them that I belong to the French and not to the American authorities. My departure followed yours by 8 days, from the camp for Wiesbaden where I was treated better than previously.

Little Eiline I won't forget you and want with all my heart to see you soon, I'd have so much to tell you. For now little Eiline, I don't see much and I'll leave you, awaiting to hear from you and above all to write more to you.

A friend who remembers you in days of misery as
in days of joy and is always with you, your very
devoted,
  Paulette
Best wishes to you and see you soon.[9]

Although Didi kept the letter from Paulette and it was
found amongst her belongings after her death, it doesn't
seem as if they ever met again.

With rest and the help of her sister, Didi's physical
strength gradually began to improve, although Jacqueline
knew that she was still far from having made a complete
recovery. To others, especially those in the SOE, she seemed
fine, but she was again employing her acting skills,
convincing everyone there that she was well and looking
for work. Vera Atkins was fooled by her performance and
tried to help her by writing letters to prospective employers,
one of which was to a Mrs Cooper at the cosmetics
company Helena Rubinstein, asking if there was a position
for her there:

> Miss Eileen Nearne has worked in this Department since
> she fled to this country from France in April 1942. She
> volunteered for special work in France and was captured
> by the Germans.
>
> In view of her extremely valuable war service and the
> hardship which she has suffered at the hands of the
> Germans we are anxious to see her re-established in a
> suitable peace-time occupation. She is extremely keen to
> train in beauty culture and I have no doubt will work
> very hard on making a success of it if she is given an
> opening.

In the circumstances I am taking the liberty of writing you this personal note in order that you may give her application most sympathetic consideration.[10]

But Didi simply wasn't ready for work. When she and Jacqueline had been asked to give accounts of their work in France for a BBC World Service programme to be broadcast in France, and had done so, Didi had been exhausted by the effort it required. Given her condition when she returned to England, she should never have been asked and before long she decided that she wanted nothing more to do with publicizing the work of the SOE.

Yvonne Baseden, the wireless operator who had been at Ravensbrück at the same time as Didi and had been rescued by Swedish officials in April 1945 and returned to England, also tried to avoid having to speak about what she had suffered. She refused interview requests, speaking to very few people about her war experience. Although it was understandable that she wanted to put the horrors of her incarceration in a concentration camp out of her mind, the SOE had other ideas and Vera Atkins persuaded her to agree to appear on the television programme *This Is Your Life* in the 1950s.[11]

Of the three SOE female agents who were incarcerated in Ravensbrück and survived – Yvonne Baseden, Didi Nearne and Odette Sansom – only Odette spoke at length about her experiences. Jerrard Tickell wrote a book about her, which was later made into a film starring Anna Neagle, thus ensuring that her name would be one of the most well known of all the SOE agents.

*   *   *

With the war and the Judex Mission well and truly over, Maurice Buckmaster's thoughts turned to the awards he would recommend for his agents. It was easy to do this for the male agents. Most of them had been members of one or other of the military forces and, as such, were eligible for military awards. The case of the women was, however, different. Most of the women volunteers had been enrolled in the FANY which, although it provided a uniform and worked alongside the military, was actually a civilian organization. There were also approximately 14 other women who had been in the WAAF (Women's Auxiliary Air Force), which was a military service, but since women were not allowed to bear arms, they were regarded in the same way as those in the civilian services. This meant that when it came to medals, the women were ineligible for many that their male counterparts received, even if the circumstances of their actions were similar and, in some cases, virtually identical.

Both Jacqueline and Didi were awarded the MBE (civil) by the British authorities. The citation for Jacqueline's MBE – signed as early as April 1945 by Major-General Colin Gubbins, the head of the SOE – described how Jacqueline had worked tirelessly from January 1943 to April 1944 and had only returned to the UK because of ill health:

> … During her time in the field she helped to build one of the largest and most successful circuits in France. Her work involved train journeys all over Southern France and to Paris; on nearly every occasion she had to pass through German controls and was subject to lightning Gestapo checks on the trains.

Her organiser was later arrested, but it is known that she carried out her highly important work with great coolness and courage over a long and difficult period and in the face of extremely active Gestapo operations at a time when the enemy was particularly anxious to locate and destroy this circuit.

It is strongly recommended that she be appointed a Member of the Order of the British Empire (civil division).[12]

Didi's citation was less detailed but certainly more appropriate than the remarks made by Colonel Buckmaster in her file just before her return from Germany:

This agent was landed in France by Lysander in early February 1944 as W/T operator to a circuit in the Paris region. For five and a half months she maintained constant communication with London from this most dangerous area, and by her cool efficiency, perseverance and willingness to undergo any risk in order to carry out her work, made possible the successful organisation of her group and the delivery of large quantities of arms and equipment.

She was arrested by the Gestapo towards the end of July 1944 while transmitting, and was subsequently deported to Germany.

For her steady courage and unfailing devotion to duty it is recommended that Miss Nearne be appointed a Member of the Order of the British Empire.[13]

RÉPUBLIQUE FRANÇAISE

Guerre 1939-1945

CITATION

EXTRAIT DE LA DECISION N° 12

Sur proposition du Ministre des Armées,
Le Président du Gouvernement Provisoire de la République,
Chef des Armées, Ministre de la Défense Nationale, cite :

A L'ORDRE DE L'ARMEE

- Lieutenant NEARNE Jacqueline - F.A.N.Y. 18268

"Jeune fille britannique volontaire pour des missions spéciales en territoire occupé, parachutée en France le 25 janvier 1943 dans la région de Limoges. A aidé à la création d'un puissant réseau d'action. En qualité de courrier, a rempli de nombreuses missions et participé à des opérations de parachutage et de transports de matériel. Au cours d'une de ces missions, le 23 mars 1943, elle fut arrêtée par une patrouille de Feld Gendarmerie mais parvint à s'évader quelques heures plus tard. Malgré des difficultés de toutes sortes, a toujours fait preuve de courage et a été au milieu du danger, un des meilleurs artisans de l'entraide Franco-Britannique".

CES CITATIONS COMPORTENT L'ATTRIBUTION DE LA CROIX DE GUERRE AVEC PALME.

PARIS, le 16 janvier 1946
Signé : de GAULLE.

EXTRAIT CERTIFIE CONFORME
PARIS, le 19 novembre 1990
Pour le Ministre et par autorisation
Le Chef du Bureau des Décorations

D. CADILHAC

Both girls were also awarded the Croix de Guerre with Bronze Palm by the French, who were less biased about the work done by the women and more generous with their decorations. The sisters were happy to have had their work acknowledged but Pearl Cornioley was not at all pleased when she was also offered the MBE (civil); she refused to accept it and told those who had offered it that she could assure them that she had done nothing civil at all during the war. The powers that be duly reconsidered and Pearl's MBE became a military award, but – rather unfairly, one must argue – Jacqueline's and Didi's MBEs remained civilian awards.

Three female agents were awarded the George Cross, the highest British award that can be given to a civilian. They were Noor Inayat Khan and Violette Szabo, who were given the award posthumously, and Odette Sansom, who survived Ravensbrück by taking the surname of her circuit leader and lover, Peter Churchill, and letting it be known that she was related by marriage to Winston Churchill, which was, of course, a lie. When it was obvious to all, including the Germans, that the war was lost to them, Ravensbrück's commandant Fritz Suhren drove Odette in a fancy sports car to the American lines and gave himself up with Churchill's 'niece', in the hope of gaining leniency for himself. Odette told the Americans that he was not the Good Samaritan he purported to be and, unlike those of other agents, her story was not questioned. Suhren managed to escape and remained free for over three years, but was recaptured in Germany and tried by the French in 1949. He was found guilty and executed by firing squad in 1950.

After a time, there were suggestions that Odette had not deserved the George Cross.[14] As well as being given the MBE she had also been given the Légion d'Honneur of France, so her contribution to the Resistance had been valued above those of other women such as Didi and

Jacqueline. The women who received the George Cross certainly did not have an easy time at the hands of the Germans and had shown great courage, but so too had the Nearne sisters. Jacqueline, having been in France for 15 months, had served for slightly more than twice as long as Odette, who was arrested seven months after her arrival, and both sisters operated in the field for much longer than Violette, who spent three weeks in France on her first mission and just three days on her second before her arrest. Although both Didi and Odette had both been ill treated by the enemy, and Odette had spent much of her time at Ravensbrück in solitary confinement, she had not had to do the backbreaking work in the camps that had been Didi's lot. So why were Didi and Jacqueline, and others like them, not given more prestigious awards?

It has been suggested that Odette and Violette were given the highest awards because they were mothers who left their children behind to work for the SOE, but there were other women with children in the organization. Yvonne Cormeau of the Wheelwright circuit had a young child and Madeleine Lavigne of the Silversmith network had two children, while Yvonne Rudellat was both a mother and a grandmother. Perhaps there is a much simpler explanation for how the awards were allocated. Aonghais Fyffe, the Security Liaison Officer, Special Training Schools Scotland, believed that two of the three girls who received the George Cross were favourites of Vera Atkins[15] and Francis Cammaerts, head of the Jockey circuit of the SOE, also claimed that Vera Atkins only helped her favourites.[16] Since Atkins had an influence on Buckmaster, it is likely that it was she who put forward the names of Violette Szabo and Odette Sansom.

Whatever the reason, neither Jacqueline nor Didi seemed to care very much that they had not been given more prestigious awards. They were both far more concerned with getting their lives back on track, making up for lost time together and looking to the future.

CHAPTER 22

Adventures, Problems and Losses

Didi's delight in being reunited with Jacqueline in England, together with her relief that they had both survived the war, seemed to mask the state of her health, which was in fact precarious. In May, just after she had returned, she had been examined by an Army doctor, who listed a string of complaints from which she was suffering and gave the opinion that 'she showed marked evidence of nervous instability probably due to psychological trauma sustained while on active service. It is probable that this patient will be permanently disabled as a result of her war service which involved in her case very severe mental strain.'[1]

As the months went by Jacqueline worried that her sister was still not well but, as she felt so much better than she had when she arrived from Germany, it did not occur to Didi that there was anything wrong. She tried to reassure her sister, but Jacqueline was still concerned, remembering only too well how she herself had felt on her return to England. Her condition – she weighed less than 48 kilos[2] – had been caused by work alone, whereas Didi had been captured and abused by the Germans. Jacqueline could not therefore believe that Didi was as well as she claimed. But Didi was adamant, so they put their wartime experiences to the backs of their minds and tried to return to some semblance of normality.

Although their parents had remained in France, both girls decided not to go back to the family home to live. They didn't want to return to Grenoble and the house they had never really regarded as a home; after everything they had both been through during the war, they did not relish the idea of returning to the kind of sheltered existence they had had before coming to England. Both felt that they had earned the right to their own independent way of living, but not having seen their mother and father for three years, of course they intended to visit their parents and brother when an opportunity arose.

Jacqueline had been looking for work in England since the end of the war, and in the autumn of 1945 she was offered a position as a secretary at the newly formed United Nations Organisation, which had come into being on 24 October that year. She accepted the position and began work in London in November. The following month it was decided that the UN should be based in New York City, and work began on a headquarters building on the banks of the East River, between East 42nd Street and East 48th Street. Until the building was completed in 1952[3] the temporary headquarters was situated at the Sperry Gyroscope Corporation's offices in Lake Success on Long Island.

In April 1946 Jacqueline boarded the Cunard liner *Aquitania*[4] at Southampton docks and set sail for Halifax, Nova Scotia, on her way to New York to begin what would be a very successful career with the United Nations Organisation, having been reassured yet again by Didi that she was doing fine.

For Didi, who had been reunited with her sister for less than a year, it was heartbreaking to lose her again, but she didn't want to stand in the way of Jacqueline's chance of a good career and a new life in America. She knew, of course, that Jacqueline would visit her in England. One of her conditions of employment was that she could take extended home leave every two years and Didi hoped, too, to visit her sister in New York when she finally regained her health.

A month after Jacqueline started her job in New York, Didi attended a medical board arranged by the Ministry of Pensions. The members of the board had been told not to ask her any questions about what she had suffered in the camps; their sole purpose was to see if she was well enough to work or if a disability pension should be awarded. Their conclusion was that Didi's working capacity was 'virtually nil at present. They have recommended, therefore, 100% for twelve months. This is a case which should materially improve at the end of that time, but ... in view of all the circumstances the initial assessment should be a high one.'⁵ The Ministry of Pensions accepted the board's recommendation and awarded Didi the full disability pension of £175 per year for at least twelve months because of her 'exhaustion neurosis', for which she had been receiving treatment from a Dr Pennington Jepson in Harley Street.

Throughout the spring of 1946 Didi went from one doctor to another. Staff Commander Mason of the FANY then sent her to have another medical examination. This revealed several troubling complaints that showed no immediate signs of subsiding, including palpitations, breathlessness, sharp chest pains, sleeplessness, loss of appetite, burning sensations in the stomach, night sweats and hot flushes during the day. She was also thought to have become very absent-minded, forgetful, restless and unsettled. She disclosed to the consultant, Mr J. J. M. Jacobs, that while she was in one of the camps she had developed a sore throat, which she thought had been diagnosed as diphtheria, and she had been given injections by the camp doctor. This revelation was particularly worrying, given the nature of the treatment dispensed in the so-called camp 'hospitals', but there was no way of knowing what she had been injected with. Jacobs gave her a thorough examination and reported:

> She is tense, anxious and apprehensive. She displays some difficulty in remembering dates and is inclined to lose the thread of the conversation. Physically she displays tremors of extended fingers, tongue and eyelids. She swayed on testing for static balance; her palms were very moist; pupils were slightly unequal, the left being larger than the right; her pulse rate was variable 90–100. Though I did not examine her heart at all carefully, the sounds were suggestive of a mild toxic myocardial condition. There was no swelling of the ankles.
>
> This girl is, in my opinion, suffering from an anxiety state following her war service and should be admitted to a Psychiatric Clinic for treatment.[6]

On 22 July 1946 Didi was admitted to the York Clinic for Psychological Medicine at Guy's Hospital in London.[7] When Jacqueline found out, she wished that she had not listened to Didi's reassurances about her health, and regretted that now that she was in the US she was unable to return to help her sister. Odile, the family friend with whom she and Didi had lived in Stamford Hill, took over as Didi's surrogate sister and visited Didi as often as she could, giving her all the support she needed. She was happy to do so, despite having two small children to look after alone, her husband being away in America, and even brought Didi home for a weekend towards the end of her time in the hospital to see how she would cope.[8]

During her time as an in-patient at the York Clinic, Didi had individual psychotherapy and participated in group therapy as well. She was also given electroconvulsive therapy. By the beginning of October her doctors felt that her condition had improved greatly and believed she was well enough to leave, discharging her on 5 October after a stay of two months and 11 days. Their subsequent report said that she was 'No longer depressed. No complaints – eating and sleeping well – mixing with the group and taking part in occupational therapy. This patient still reports weekly to the clinic – she is at present unemployed but she has the promise of a job as Ground Air Hostess at Croydon Airport.'[9]

Jacqueline was anxious to hear how Didi was getting on and to her relief Odile wrote to her the day after Didi's release:

> She looks very well indeed and is so glad to leave the clinic, she was beginning to find it very depressing indeed. You can imagine how glad and happy we all are to have her back again … The doctor spoke to me yesterday before allowing me to go up to fetch her. He said that she was well but *must* be kept busy. He said that if I had any affection at all for her I would make her work all day, *anything* but she must not just sit and think. 'Treat her as your child.'

It would appear that she was very good at modelling clay, and she would do well if she went to an art school for it. Also she seems to be interested in being an air hostess ...

I heard Didi singing in the bath a few hours ago and my heart sang with joy. Just now she has gone with Ricky [Odile's three-year-old son] to play in the park. They are the greatest of friends. He loves Didi very much.

Every night when he says his prayers he thinks of you. I have never had to remind him. He always asks God to bless you.

Jacqueline, meanwhile, was doing very well in New York. She had quickly settled down to her work at the United Nations and was enjoying it immensely; and in her letters she told Odile that she also liked America.

Initially there were only 51 member countries of the United Nations, each one being allocated a liaison officer from the Protocol section. These 51 countries were divided between three women and one man, who became the liaison officers to the countries' delegates. After a short time the man, Mr Podsianko, and one of the women, Sylvia Grove-Palmer, went on to other positions within the organization and the countries were divided between four women. Jacqueline was responsible for the representatives of Belgium, the Dominican Republic, Egypt, France, Greece, Haiti, India, Lebanon, Luxembourg, the Netherlands, Poland, Saudi Arabia and Syria. Her colleagues – Mrs C. K. Young of China, Rosita Escala of Ecuador and Janine Blickenstaff of France – each had a fairly even number of representatives to look after from the other 38 countries.

A letter written by Odile Nearne to her aunt Jacqueline,
discussing Didi's health.

The liaison officers were there to handle any problems
the delegates had, as well as arrange accommodation,
transport and secretarial assistance. They also helped to
organize parties and receptions on behalf of their own
delegates. In this they were helped by Sylvia Grove-Palmer,
whose new title was Special Assistant on Social Functions.
Jacqueline proved to be good at this particular task and
was soon working alongside Miss Grove-Palmer in
organizing other social functions in addition to her other

duties. In order to help the representatives of her designated countries, each liaison officer had to have a thorough knowledge of the workings of the UN so that she could give proper advice to those in her care, and she was also responsible for making introductions that would help her representatives with their work within the United Nations.

At the beginning there were many unanticipated problems that had to be quickly resolved. Captain Johan de Noue, Chief of Protocol and Liaison, was particularly annoyed about the ceremony for the signing of the World Health Organisation Constitution in July 1946, and wrote to Andrew Cordier, the executive assistant to the UN Secretary General, Trygve Lie, complaining:

> To use the words of the Acting Secretary General, the signing of the World Health Organisation Constitution, was an example of how not to carry out an official function. Of course, it must be recalled that the choice of the Henry Hudson Hotel Ballroom for such a meeting could not be worse. The acoustics, the size, the air-cooling system, all helped to create disorder, confusion and lack of dignity ... It might also be considered advisable to notify the different officials concerned, for example, the Security Officer, Officer of the Day, Officer in Charge of Room Arrangements, etc. of the part played by the Chief of Protocol, since nobody yesterday seemed to realize that I had been made responsible at the last minute for the ceremony.[10]

It seems that the delegates were not always aware of what facilities were available to them, and Jacqueline and her three liaison colleagues often had to sort out difficulties created by delegates who, not having thought to contact their own particular officers for help, had instead fired off letters of complaint to those higher in the chain of command.

Gradually everything quietened down and the Protocol section began to function very efficiently.[11] It must have been a strange situation for Jacqueline. Since she had spent the war in such a dangerous and important role the sometimes very petty concerns of the UN members must have seemed trivial in comparison. But she tackled her various UN tasks wholeheartedly, with efficiency, tact and diplomacy. She not only enjoyed her work, but also thought it important and one of the best ways to unite countries to ensure that wars like the one she had just lived through would not be allowed to happen in the future:

> I know of nothing more desirable than peace and I wholeheartedly believe in the United Nations as a means of preventing wars. I decided when I left the service that I wanted to be definitely connected with, and work actively for, the organisation's future. Of course I am only a small cog in a big wheel but I feel the same about this work as I did about my underground work in France. I believe people like myself are just as necessary to a successful United Nations as the top delegates. We keep the wheels in motion.[12]

While the position of liaison officer was primarily a job, it also became a lifestyle. There were often occasions when Jacqueline was required to work at weekends, and Captain de Noue had decided from the start that liaison officers should always be on the guest lists for all social functions and should attend as much as possible, as it was hoped 'that not only can they enjoy themselves at such parties, but that they can take those opportunities to become better acquainted with the Delegation members and their families, as well as being introduced to the members they have not already met'.[13]

On many of the social occasions the liaison officers were allowed to invite guests themselves. They were charged $1 a head for their guests and Jacqueline used this privilege, inviting people from her ever-growing circle of friends. Over the many years that Jacqueline worked at the United Nations, her name could often be found on the guest lists for luncheon and dinner parties held in honour of important and well-known people; she was also invited to private parties held by some of those people. She attended functions for such luminaries as HM King Hassan II of Morocco, HM King Constantine II of Greece and his wife Queen Anne-Marie, HRH Princess Irene of Greece, and philanthropist John D. Rockefeller III and his brother Nelson who, under President Gerald Ford between 1974 and 1977, became the 41st US vice president.

Every two years Jacqueline took her home leave and returned to England to visit Didi and her brother Frederick, who had also settled in England after being demobbed from the Royal Air Force in October 1946. The first few times she came back to the United Kingdom she did so by ship, sometimes getting permission to add her annual leave to the home leave so that she could also spend time visiting her family, and friends such as Lise de Baissac, at their homes in France.

When she made her first trip home in the autumn of 1948 she went to France, having been invited to a ceremony at the town hall in Boulogne-sur-Mer on 27 November by the Mayor, Jean Febvay. During the ceremony she was made an honorary citizen of Boulogne in recognition of her wartime service, the city's population regarding her as one of their own because she had lived there for six years as a child. When her leave was over she returned to the United States on the SS *America* and, as the ship approached New York harbour, received a shore-to-ship telegram which welcomed her, as an honorary citizen of Boulogne-sur-Mer, to New York.

During her other visits home, she, Didi and Fred also took holidays together in places that brought back memories of their childhood. Later Jacqueline abandoned the cruise across the Atlantic and travelled by air, which gave her more time with family and friends. In the years between

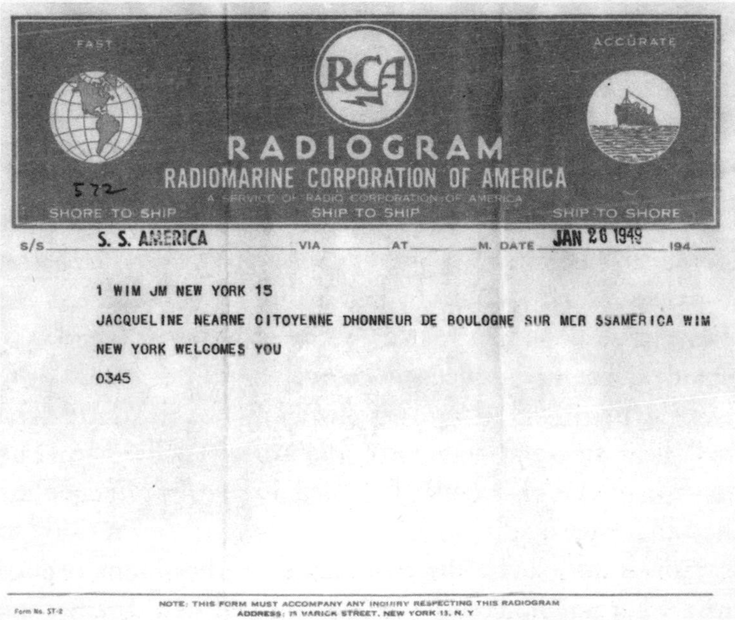
FAST ACCURATE
RCA
RADIOGRAM
RADIOMARINE CORPORATION OF AMERICA
A SERVICE OF RADIO CORPORATION OF AMERICA
572
SHORE TO SHIP SHIP TO SHIP SHIP TO SHORE
S/S S. S. AMERICA VIA ___ AT ___ M. DATE JAN 26 1949 194__

1 WIM JM NEW YORK 15
JACQUELINE NEARNE CITOYENNE DHONNEUR DE BOULOGNE SUR MER SSAMERICA WIM
NEW YORK WELCOMES YOU
0345

Form No. ST-2
NOTE: THIS FORM MUST ACCOMPANY ANY INQUIRY RESPECTING THIS RADIOGRAM
ADDRESS: 75 VARICK STREET, NEW YORK 13, N. Y

her biennial home leave she liked to spend her holidays in Barbados.

Jacqueline had many friends in New York, including artists and playwrights. One of her oldest friends, whom she had known since her childhood in Boulogne, was the former SOE agent Brian Stonehouse, who had also left England in 1946 for America, where he lived in Washington and New York, working as an illustrator for *Vogue*, *Harper's Bazaar* and cosmetic company Elizabeth Arden until 1979, when he returned to England.[14]

Jacqueline liked to spend her spare time with her friends, having dinner, going to the theatre or playing cards, particularly canasta. She attended exhibitions, concerts, plays – sometimes Broadway first nights, at other times plays or musicals written by one of her friends – and she led a very full, happy life in America until her retirement. One of her New York friends, a man named Freddy, recalled attending the opening night of a play written by a mutual friend. It was not a good play and the newspaper reviews the next day were scathing. At 9 a.m. Freddy received a telephone call from Jacqueline in which she said, 'Poor X. All alone in his apartment with these ghastly notices. Someone really ought to telephone him.' Freddy thought it would be better to leave the playwright to digest the bad notices first but Jacqueline believed that all his friends would think the same and, as a consequence, no one would call him and the poor man would be left completely alone. She decided to call him straightaway and, according to Freddy, 'The author of the play never forgot that she did.' Jacqueline had that rare quality of always knowing the right thing to say or do at exactly the right time, and her many friends loved her for it. Freddy himself said of her, 'Every time

I saw her, Jacqueline always made me feel that life was a bit better and brighter, more hopeful and more fun.'[15]

Sadly nothing ever came of Didi's hopes to become either a beautician or an air or ground hostess at an airport but, because of her doctor's encouragement and his comments about her clay modelling, she was able to enrol at the Hornsey School of Art in 1947.

One of the effects of electroconvulsive therapy can be that the patient's symptoms gradually return when the treatment stops, and so it was with Didi. At a medical she attended in August 1947 she was found to be suffering once more from headaches, a mist in front of her eyes, palpitations, oppressive sensations in her chest, and a feeling that the walls of her bedroom were both receding and closing in on her. She had become forgetful again and lacked concentration, but she was sleeping better than she had before and she had managed to gain a little weight. She had also moved from Darenth Road and Odile's good care to accommodation in a three-storey Victorian terrace in Dunsmure Road, Stamford Hill, a few hundred metres away.

Despite her poor health, Didi stuck to her art course, although she only managed to attend for about two-thirds of the hours that were available to her. Nonetheless she did what she could and one of her instructors, Mr Holger, was of the opinion that although she followed her own inclinations rather too much, she worked hard and by the end of the first year had made a slight improvement. Other instructors commented on her occasional interesting work, but it was obvious that although she had artistic talent, her delicate health and the after-effects of life in a concentration camp meant that she was unlikely ever to make a living from art. In many ways this did not matter, as her creative work helped her to come to terms with what she had been through. After she left art school she continued to paint, and produced some vivid and rather strange abstract paintings that some regarded as beautiful but others believed to be disturbing and sinister.

By 1950 Didi had obtained a position as a trainee teleprinter operator for the Post Office and had moved again, this time to St Kilda's Road, Stamford Hill, where she lived with her brother Fred. Her medical condition had not improved and an appointment was arranged with Harley Street psychiatrist Ellis Stungo, a former major in the Royal Army Medical Corps. He examined her and made a very full report, in which he noted:

> She has premonitions which are invariably correct and believes she has second sight. She exhibits psycho motor overactivity. She talks to herself and writes poetry and highly imaginative stories. She identifies herself with characters in books. She has feelings of unreality and detachment. She has ideas of reference and is suspicious. While waiting for interview she [?] some characteristically schizoid representations.
>
> She exhibits many schizoid characteristics, but feels better since commencing training as a teleprinter operator.[16]

Stungo himself was a rather controversial character. The previous year the BBC had broadcast a programme about telepathy in which he was a witness to a supposed demonstration of telepathy between a married couple.

After he surprised the listeners by declaring 'I'm sure there is no possibility of a fake,' his unexpected evidence was reported in newspaper articles in places as far away as Australia. Six months after examining Didi he was again in the news, this time because of a court case in which he was accused by a former patient of having fathered her child after he had taken her to live in his own home. Although it was said that there was evidence that the patient had lived with him as his mistress, the case was thrown out. Eight years later Ellis Stungo found himself in court again, this time at the Old Bailey, where he was accused of counselling a Dr Newman to perform an abortion on one of his patients. Newman did as he had been advised but the patient died, and the doctor was convicted of criminal abortion and manslaughter, and sentenced to five years in prison. Stungo was not convicted because the judge found that the prosecution's evidence against him was insufficient to put to the jury. The adverse publicity about one of her doctors can have done nothing to boost Didi's confidence about the treatment she had received but she quietly got on with her life, continuing to work as a trainee teleprinter operator and receiving her disability pension, although the amount had gradually been reduced from 100 to 80 and then 50 per cent.

Then, in December 1950, Mariquita Nearne, Didi's mother, died at her home in France. Her death was a blow to everyone. Although she had not been well for much of the year and had had several weeks of bed rest while being treated by her doctor, her death had not been expected. She was only 63 years old. Didi packed her bags and made arrangements to go to Grenoble immediately. Whether or not she (or indeed Jacqueline) had been to see her parents after the war is uncertain. The precarious state of her health would suggest that she had probably remained in England, but she and her parents kept up a regular correspondence. After her mother's untimely death Didi remained in Grenoble for several months, helping her father come to terms with his loss. Although Jack had been keen to go back to Boulogne (in 1949, he commissioned an architect to draw up plans to renovate the family home there[17]), without his wife at his side it no longer seemed a priority and he remained in Grenoble until 1962, when he died at the age of 72.

Fred had also gone to Grenoble for his mother's funeral, so the accommodation in St Kilda's Road that he and Didi had shared was vacated, as neither knew when they would be returning to England. Didi wrote to the Ministry of Pensions on 20 December from France, explaining why she was away and that she would be away for several more weeks or months, and giving her temporary address as care of her father in Grenoble. She asked if her pension could be sent to her in France via the British Consulate in Lyons and also mentioned that she no longer had any pension cheques, the last one having expired on 30 November. A reply was sent to her at her father's address, telling her that as she was only going to be in Grenoble for a temporary stay, her pension could not be transferred there but that it would be paid, as usual, in England when she returned. This did not seem to be a problem for her during her stay in France, but Didi forgot to tell the Ministry of Pensions that when she returned to England it would not be to her previous address in St Kilda's Road, Stamford Hill.

Throughout 1951 and well into 1952 the people at the Ministry of Pensions tried to get in touch with Didi to sort out where she was living so that she could continue to receive her pension, but letters sent to St Kilda's Road were returned with 'Not known at this address' written on the envelope. Someone was eventually sent to the address to find out where Didi was and spoke to the new tenant, who said that she had moved at least a year before without leaving a forwarding address. In the end they stopped trying to find her and her pension was cancelled, with a note being placed on the file that said it could be reinstated if Didi contacted the office again.

When she finally returned from France several months after her mother's death Didi found a place to rent at 33 Hampstead Hill Gardens. Without her pension life was more difficult but she received help from her family. It didn't seem to have occurred to her to contact the Ministry of Pensions again until 1954, when she reapplied for the pension. Her letter reached the Ministry, its arrival being noted in Didi's records, but she received no reply to her request.[18]

At the end of 1951 Fred Nearne married a girl called Marjorie Collins and the couple also lived in Hampstead for a time. Their only child, a daughter whom they named Odile, was born in 1954, by which time they had moved to Essex. As a consequence of this move Odile has only a few childhood memories of her aunts, but she clearly recalled one visit by Jacqueline while she was on home leave from the United Nations. Remembering that her small niece was not a fan of dolls, Jacqueline brought her a bright-red toy car, which Odile loved. She recalled that whenever she was back in England Jacqueline always brought some little gift for her young niece and Odile never forgot her gentle, elegant aunt who was always so kind to her.

Her early memories of Didi were not so happy, as Didi was still very troubled by her experiences. She vividly remembered visiting Didi one day with her parents and, when her aunt heard the doorbell, she poked her head out of the window and yelled at them to go away as she did not feel well.

Didi remained in Hampstead for several years and liked the area. When she decided to move again she found herself another bedsit in Hampstead Hill Gardens and lived there for six years. The man who owned the building had been told something of Didi's background and he mentioned it to a lady named Jenny who lived next door to Didi, asking her to 'be nice' to her new neighbour. It was now the beginning of the 1960s and the two women soon became good friends. Jenny was a nursing sister at the nearby Royal Free Hospital, and when she heard that there was a vacancy for a nursing auxiliary she thought of Didi and recommended her for the position. Didi got the job, working on a permanent night shift at the hospital, and it seemed that, at last, she had found something that she really enjoyed. Jenny remembered that Didi hated bugs and insects, so she did not tell her that there were thousands of cockroaches in the hospital. Then one night Didi found a cockroach in a patient's bed and was so disgusted that she handed in her notice immediately. It reminded her of the filthy conditions in the camps.

But she liked taking care of people, so she found a similar position, this time as a care assistant at Branch Hill home for the elderly in Camden, where she again worked on a permanent night shift. She enjoyed her work, and was appreciated by patients and staff alike. Now less troubled by the problems she had suffered after returning from

Germany, she settled down to the pleasant life she so richly deserved with a job she enjoyed and friends with whom she spent her free time.[19]

In 1970 Fred Nearne was taken ill. After visits to doctors and specialists he received the news that he was suffering from cancer of the stomach. Having moved back to the Hampstead area he spent the last few weeks of his life in St Columba's Hospital, where Didi used to go after her night shift had finished to keep him company and help him in any way she could during the final days of his life. He died on 21 December 1970, exactly a month before his 52nd birthday. His elder brother Francis had died prematurely, too. Resuming his old job after he managed to return to France at the end of 1945, he was once again able to look after his family and was content to be back in their home near Grenoble, wanting nothing more than to be with his wife and son. For nearly 20 years he was perfectly happy with the quiet life he led but, tragically, the domestic bliss did not last. He died on 21 April 1965, just before his 51st birthday, it is believed from cancer. His son Jack was also diagnosed with cancer and died in 1983 at the age of just 43, while Thérèse Nearne outlived both her husband and her son.

By the mid-1970s Didi had decided that she wanted a change of scenery and made up her mind to move again. She found a studio flat in Belsize Square on the borders of Hampstead and Swiss Cottage, just a mile or so from her work. Jacqueline was worried that she would not be able to afford it and suggested that she ask if there was another smaller room that might be less expensive, but Didi was confident there would not be a problem. Jacqueline, who had been helping Didi with a cheque each month, wrote in reply to a letter telling her about the new flat:

I received your letter this morning – I was very shocked that you haven't received your cheque for April – because the cheque was sent by the bank on the 18th of March and you should have received it for the end of the month, verified by the bank. Perhaps they will deposit the cheque in your account without notifying you …

I'm glad you're happy in your apartment … the main thing is that you like the area and that you're comfortable and peaceful – and if you can afford it – stay there for now and look leisurely for something better. Have you bought a little trunk? I would if I were you so you can get rid of all the boxes. Do you have closet space in your room? Are you close enough to your work?

It's very important to have a nice place to live, it greatly influences morale.[20]

Jacqueline understood that everyone needed somewhere to go, where one could shut out the world when the difficulties of life became too much; somewhere to feel safe, a place in which to relax, alone or with friends. It was what she had always had during the years she had lived in New York and it was what she wanted for Didi. While she was in America there was not much she could do except send Didi money each month to help with her bills. But all that changed after she retired and returned to England. After finding herself somewhere comfortable to live in London she suddenly realized that there was something that she might be able to do for her sister after all.

CHAPTER 23

The Ultimate Secret Agent

When Jacqueline retired and returned to London in 1978 she decided to buy a flat and eventually found one that she liked at 14 Chesham Place, Belgravia. It was only 5 or 6 miles from where Didi was living and they were able to enjoy time together again in London, as they had when they first came to England in 1942. But despite the many things they had both done since those days, the SOE just wouldn't go away.

Shortly after her arrival in New York as a new liaison officer, Jacqueline had been the subject of an article written by journalist and war correspondent Charles Lanius that was published in *Woman's Day* magazine in January 1947. It described the life she had led in occupied France as an agent of the SOE and told how she would be helping the nascent United Nations Organisation to ensure that wars would not happen again. Shortly before she left New York to retire to England she was asked to appear in a show on the listener-funded radio station Pacifica Radio, and again was asked about her life as an agent.

The quest for more information about the SOE and what had happened during the Second World War did not diminish, and two years after she returned to England Jacqueline was invited to help make a documentary about the work of the SOE in France. She was reunited with Harry Rée, with whom she had starred in the film *Now It Can Be Told*, and admitted that many of the scenes in that film had been over-dramatized. She also thought that most of the television programmes about the organization were inaccurate and cited *A Man Called Intrepid* as being one of the worst, saying that 'not one of those agents would have lasted a day in occupied France'. Despite having spent almost half her entire life – 32 years in fact – working for the United Nations, it was the 15 months she spent as an agent in France that were to be her lasting legacy.

Her well-earned retirement was tragically short. She had only been back in England for four years when she became ill and was diagnosed with cancer. Didi moved to her flat to care for her in the final few months of her life, and on 15 August 1982 Jacqueline died, aged 66 years. Didi, who had suffered so much and for whom Jacqueline had been a lifeline, was devastated.

Messages of condolence for Didi, along with stories of her sister's kindness, her humour and her friendship, poured in from Jacqueline's friends and colleagues from across the world. At her funeral, Harry Rée delivered a eulogy, in which he said:

Jacqueline radiated friendship and at the same time attracted friendship. And while her magnetism, her generosity and her extrovert energy were surely felt deeply by all who came into contact with her, she remained always composed – in control, keeping those of us who could claim friendship with her, not so much at a respectful distance, as at a respectful closeness; she shunned effusion at any time. This makes it difficult to speak of her now since she certainly wouldn't want an emotional eulogy from me or any of us.

You can hear her, can't you? 'Dis, Henri – pas de comédie, pas de tragédie, non plus.' And she'd pout a little, then smile and toss her head back and utter her infectious characteristic laugh, and then look at you, waiting for you to say something ... so – no comedy, no tragedy.

... It was a great joy to have her back in England when she retired – she really enjoyed these last few short years, and when a year ago her suffering started, increasingly disagreeable pain in her teeth and lower jaw, she bore it so lightly; and as it got worse – with typical stoicism. She was of course lucky, in the last month or so, when things got really bad, to have her sister, whom we know as Didi, to look after her day and night. We, her friends, can also count ourselves fortunate that Didi was there, and [are] grateful to her for all she did for Jacqueline during those last sad weeks.

... Jacqueline [has] a very special and permanent place in our hearts, and memories, and we can continue to be grateful to her because even now she exerts her influence. We are, and will be, better people for having known and loved her.[1]

She was also greatly missed by her friends and former colleagues in America. A service of remembrance was held for her on 19 October 1982 in New York, at the Catholic Church attached to the United Nations, which she used to attend. Didi did not attend that service but received letters from many of her sister's friends there telling her about it, and about how much they loved and missed Jacqueline.

During the service Jacqueline's boss, the Chief of Protocol, Sinan Korle, gave a moving tribute to her. He, like Harry Rée, managed to highlight many of the lesser-known facets of Jacqueline's character:

It is very hard for me to use the past tense while speaking about Jacqueline. I have known her for many years but the last 14 years she was part of my daily life, at least from nine to five every day. I used to work with her, chat with her, argue with her and joke with her.

... She was interested in everything which was beautiful, good and inspiring ... to Jacqueline her work was her sublime responsibility, she would give herself wholly to it. She had joined the UN on the eve of its creation and was the pillar of the Office of Protocol.

She was a true friend; a friend you could depend on, a friend you could confide in. She would always try to help you and be useful. In short, to know Jacqueline was to love her.

... Jacqueline could communicate with anybody, even if there was a language barrier. A few years ago when she was visiting us in Turkey during her summer vacation, she not only made friends with all members of my family and friends she met there, but conquered the heart of my sister's old maid. Jacqueline did not speak Turkish and the maid could not understand English yet they could understand each other. The day Jacqueline was leaving to return to New York the maid said: 'If angels really exist this lady must be one of them.'

Jacqueline was at ease with everybody; diplomats used to invite her to official functions. She would also be the guest in their private parties. Many dignitaries used to come and visit her in her small office at the UN. She was a friend and the confidante of old and young, rich and poor. The Italian grocer next to her building used to call her Signorita Nearney; for the drug store man she was Miss United Nations. In short she was loved and respected by everybody. We have lost a friend who has lived her life the way she wanted and quietly faded away.

Thank you Jacqueline for what you have been.

After Jacqueline's death Didi discovered that her sister had left her the flat in Belgravia. After all the rooms, bedsits and studio apartments that Didi had lived in since she had returned from Germany Jacqueline wanted her to have her own 'good place to live'. The flat was her final gift to her much-loved sister.

Didi remained on the night shift at Branch Hill care home for the rest of her working life, travelling the five miles from her new flat in Belgravia to her work by public transport each evening. She retired in 1986 and, at her farewell party, was presented with a diploma, detailing her many years of service at the home, by the mayor of the Borough of Camden.

Although she had enjoyed her time looking after the elderly residents in Branch Hill, she sometimes thought back to the days she had spent as an agent in Paris. It had been a dangerous but exhilarating time for her and, despite what had happened to her after her arrest, she still missed it sometimes and said that everything that followed had been very tame by comparison.

With the passing of time the troubles that life had dealt her no longer had the power to defeat her and she accepted her lot, not as before with a feeling of depression that she had found hard to shake off but with a hope for what the next part of her life might bring. But despite her newfound strength and stability, she couldn't help looking back over her life and wondering what might have been.

Being a part of the SOE had changed the lives of Didi and Jacqueline for ever. While women were cautioned to tread carefully when broaching the subject of what their menfolk had been through during the war, there was little thought for what the women who had served in the military or other related services might have seen or done, largely because women were never frontline military troops; although their input in the conflict was invaluable, freeing as it did the men for the actual fighting, there were relatively few who saw the real horror of war at first hand during their wartime careers. The female SOE agents were different. Almost without exception they had seen that horror and, having done so, would never be the same again.

For Didi and Jacqueline the war had intervened at a time when, like many girls of their age at that time, they would have been looking forward to marriage and a family of their own. Didi was fond of children and it is likely that if she had remained at home, rather than going to war, she would have settled down to marriage and motherhood. But after the mental problems that her protracted exposure to Nazi atrocities had induced, that way of life eluded her; by the time she had recovered, her chance of marriage and children had disappeared.

While Didi lost her exuberant, carefree attitude and shrank into her own isolated world, Jacqueline gained from her war service a confidence she had lacked at the start of the war. Her success as a courier and the trust that Maurice Southgate and the other members of the Stationer circuit had placed in her had given her a belief in her own ability. With this, she was able to continue to make her life one of service through her work at the United Nations, which she truly believed would help to bring people of different cultures and beliefs together so that a lasting peace could be achieved.

Didi did not regret joining in the fight for freedom against Nazi oppression, and she knew that her sister was glad to have served as well, but she also knew that by doing so, both she and Jacqueline had sacrificed so much.

Didi felt the loss of her sister keenly. Having looked forward for so many years to the time when they could be together again, it was a cruel twist of fate that parted them so soon after Jacqueline's return to England. Didi had looked up to her kind, beautiful and exceptional sister for as long as she could remember, and had tried to be like her. Her love and admiration for her had never changed, and when she found that Jacqueline had left her the flat in Belgravia, she realized that it was so much more than a place in which she could live; it was the final expression of the care and consideration that Jacqueline had always shown her throughout her life. Like Jacqueline's many friends, Didi also felt that she had become a better person for having known her and, although she was no longer with her in this life, the influence of her very special sister would remain with Didi to the end of her days.

*   *   *

With the death of her beloved sister and her own retirement, Didi's life changed yet again. But in her remaining years Didi was not the recluse she was portrayed as being in the articles written at the time of her death in 2010. She simply did not court publicity, and saw no need to disclose the minutiae of her life to all and sundry.

The flat she had inherited in Belgravia was much bigger than her previous rented accommodation, and she was able to hold several dinner parties there for friends she and Jacqueline had known from the SOE, and for her own friends whom she had met after starting work at the Royal Free Hospital. Jenny, who had secured the job for her at the hospital, remembers that Didi engaged someone to cook for her at these dinner parties, which she thought was a good thing, as although Didi could cook, she was rather heavy handed with the garlic. Letters from the friends who attended Didi's parties speak of a generous hostess, good food and wine, and very enjoyable evenings.

On Jacqueline's death, Didi began corresponding with several of her sister's friends, and one of the SOE women who sometimes visited Didi when she was in England was Jacqueline's good friend Lise de Baissac. Their friendship seems to have begun in earnest after Jacqueline's death, and among the papers found in Didi's flat in 2010 were many of the letters that Lise sent to her from her home in Marseilles, where she lived with her husband Gustave Villameur, whom she had married in 1950. Lise died on 28 March 2004, just six weeks short of her 99th birthday.[2]

Didi also kept letters from Vera Atkins, Maurice Buckmaster, Brian Stonehouse and Pearl Cornioley. But among some of her most prized letters were some from just after the war: two from Jean Savy, the chief of the

Wizard circuit to which she had belonged when she first went to France as an agent; one or two from Louise, her first contact in France; and one from Louise's mother. These also give an interesting insight into how affectionately Didi was regarded by the people with whom she worked.

Although Savy had been back in England when Didi was arrested and had, by then, been transferred to another circuit, when he returned to France he made extensive enquiries about what had happened to her. This was a dangerous thing for him to do, for had the Germans got wind of his interest in Didi he might also have been arrested. Although very few details were available, he passed what he knew to London so that her family could be informed. In December 1946 he wrote to her on his own headed notepaper but signed himself with his code name, *Regis*. In his brief letter he said:

> My dear Eileen,
>   I'm sorry we missed each other. I was in Park Lane
> from five to six and then at the club. On my next trip to
> London I'll telephone you again and we'll go to the
> club together. Maybe in the interim, if you came to
> Paris before I return to London, our friend would be
> very happy to see you.
>   See you soon dear Eileen and as always, warmest
> wishes to you.
>   Regis

The club to which Savy referred was the Special Forces Club, which was founded in 1945 on the initiative of the Chief of the SOE, Major-General Sir Colin Gubbins,

KCMG, DSO, MC. Unlike most of the other London clubs, whose membership was only open to men, the Special Forces Club was open to both men and women on equal terms and took members from other Resistance organizations with whom the SOE had worked, and also from the SAS, SBS and the FANY. Didi eventually became a club member herself and remained one for many years. The cryptic reference to 'our friend' remains a mystery, although Savy might have been referring to René Dumont-Guillemet, the chief of the Spiritualist circuit, for whom Didi had worked after Savy went back to London, and who was known to them both. Savy followed up his first letter with another short note, on New Year's Day 1947, in which he expressed his 'most sincere and cordial wishes for 1947' and added: 'I hope you have started the New Year well and that it will allow me the pleasure of seeing you soon.'

One of the messages from Louise was written, in July 1951, on a postcard showing the Pont Neuf. She wrote:

I'm sending you this card to show you that I never cross the Pont Neuf without thinking of how I met you there for the first time and, as in this picture, it was snowing as we met each other in front of the statue of Henri IV. No doubt you remember all that – you like France like a second home ...

... I hope you still have good news of Jacqueline. We thought of her when the ONU was signed again in Paris. It would make us really happy to see you both ... Mum, my sister and I give you a hug and await a letter from you.

Louise

Le Pont neuf

Louise's mother was also clearly very fond of Didi. In May 1952 she sent an affectionate letter to her, which began:

Dear Eileen,
But you will always be my very lovely Marie ...
From my daughters who are away from Paris and from me, our thanks for your lovely present. How kind to associate us, through this, with the good times you'll have, knowing from the press the magnificence one is preparing for the festival of the coronation.
... Alas, I cannot write to them [her daughters], not knowing how to get in touch and I'll have to wait until their return, which I think will be the end of June, to tell them about things and give them your present. Please be sure that once Louise is here it will give her great pleasure to write to you and thank you for your kindness.

I'll go now dear ..., assuring you of my affectionate friendship.
Madame C. Gredt
6 place Saint Michel
Paris IV

The reference to Marie at the start of the letter indicates that Madame Gredt must have known Didi by the 'documentary name' on her file, Marie Louise Tournier. The letter itself is plainly not just a polite message of thanks for a gift; it shows real affection which, given the short time that Didi was allowed to visit the household in the Place Saint-Michel, reveals the immediate, favourable impression that she must have made on the family.

Didi sometimes received letters asking for information about the war from people writing books or making television programmes. At times she agreed to speak about what she had been through; more often she refused to talk about it at all. Occasionally she would ask the advice of Vera Atkins or Maurice Buckmaster. Whether or not she was aware of Buckmaster's disparaging remarks about her during the war is not clear. He certainly wrote friendly notes to her in later years and when Didi sought advice he was always ready with an answer. In reply to one query from Didi about whether he thought she should speak about her work to a particular author he said: 'I don't see any objection to your meeting this lady and giving her general information about your work in the SOE. You could suggest that she contacts me if she wishes to do so and I will try to give her the general background.' He then suggested that Didi should 'talk briefly about the training in Wanborough Manor and the careful briefing you received before going into the field'. Had he considered this a little more carefully he might have advised her differently, as Didi had not been trained at Wanborough Manor so would only have known very little, if anything at all, about it.

When the lady author got in touch with Buckmaster, he told Didi that he had agreed to see her 'for a more general revision, so we will do our best for her'. He went on to complain about the people at the BBC and ITV, saying that he was concerned about the way they portrayed the girls of the SOE and that when he tried to explain how things really were, his comments were totally disregarded. Both television companies refused to accept the truth because it was not exciting enough, he said; he was of the opinion that 'They don't care a damn about the facts – they just make up what they think are romantic stories to attract viewers who have no recollection or knowledge of World War II.' Buckmaster appeared in television programmes and argued vociferously against presenters who accused the SOE of incompetence, which had caused the deaths of some agents. Despite his denials, there clearly had been situations that had led to the deaths of agents, but whether these were because of genuine mistakes or deliberate sacrifice is debatable. In both scenarios these mistakes were inexcusable, so his righteous indignation was rather misplaced. It must have been difficult for agents such as Didi, who obviously respected Buckmaster, to accept what he told them when they themselves knew that certain of his 'facts' were untrue. In the 1950s he had written two books about the SOE that were littered with errors, and it could even have been these books that accounted for the television people's scepticism when Buckmaster tried to set them straight. Didi couldn't bear to be thought of as a liar, so eventually, rather than upset her former boss, she just stopped asking for his advice and made the decisions herself about whether or not to talk to authors or appear on television programmes.

Strangely, in view of Vera Atkins's reputation for being rather cold and aloof, she and Didi developed quite a close friendship. They not only kept up a long correspondence but also sometimes visited each other, usually when Vera came to London. Vera proved to be a good friend and Didi found that she could get better advice from her than from Buckmaster. After all the years that had passed since the end of the war, Vera still saw herself as the guardian of the SOE girls and she proved to be a great help to Didi in many ways. Despite her still busy life she remembered to contact Didi on the first anniversary of Jacqueline's death. She sent her a card on which she wrote: 'You are in my thoughts on this sad anniversary as I gratefully remember Jacqueline and the lovely person that she was. You have been wonderful, dear Didi, in getting through this difficult year with so much courage, sense and style. I hope that you will find it all a little easier as time goes on.'

By the 1980s Didi's friend Jenny had left London and moved to Llandovery in Carmarthenshire, where Didi sometimes visited her. Jenny was still unable to cope with her friend's love of garlic, so when it was free she rented the holiday cottage next door to her own home so that Didi could stay there and cook for herself the sort of food she loved. Even after all the years she had been back in England Didi still spoke with a slight French accent, and sometimes when she and Jenny went out for a meal she would speak to the restaurant staff with a very strong accent. When

Jenny asked her why, she smiled and, with a twinkle in her eye, said that it was because she had found that she received much better service if the staff knew she was foreign.[3] It was her own private joke. She enjoyed role playing and was obviously good at it. Jenny completely refuted the later claims that Didi was a sad recluse. They were simply not true. Her friend was fun, had a good sense of humour and enjoyed life.

When she stayed with Jenny in Wales, Didi loved to walk. She was very fit and could easily cover long distances, unlike Jenny, who quickly became exhausted by her friend's boundless energy. After one visit to Wales, Didi came home with a dog that Jenny had found for her, a cross between a spaniel and a collie. She loved the little dog, which she named Bobby, and took him everywhere with her. He gave her love, companionship and a reason to take the long walks she so enjoyed, without having to go out on her own. Trouble arose for poor Bobby, however, when Didi tried to take him with her to the Special Forces Club: she received a note from the club officials telling her that dogs were not allowed. She was so annoyed by this that she wrote back to them cancelling her membership. If her Bobby wasn't to be allowed to visit the club, Didi decided that she didn't want to go there again either.

Although Didi enjoyed living in Jacqueline's lovely flat and would forever be grateful to her sister for leaving it to her, when it became clear that she would soon have a hefty bill for maintenance she started to look for other accommodation. The flat was on a short lease anyway and the building required a lot of work to be done, which Didi thought was not a good use of her money. So, by the summer of 1989 she had decided to sell, and she and Bobby began looking for another flat near to the coast. She had never lost her love of the sea and wanted to spend the remainder of her days looking out at its vast expanse.

Didi found a place to rent on the Kent coast, and she and Bobby moved in, but it wasn't long before she decided that it wasn't right for her; nor was the fisherman's loft in Lyme Regis where she went next. Eventually her search took her as far as Torquay and when she arrived she knew she had found the perfect place. For Didi it had the feel of a Continental seaside town and she immediately felt at home. She found a small flat to rent in Lisburne Crescent and moved for the last time. When she had moved out of the Belgravia flat Vera Atkins had offered to help, saying, 'I don't envy you the selling and clearance of the flat. There are so many difficult decisions which only you can make.' But Didi had been unable to part with Jacqueline's possessions – they were all that was left to her of her sister, and she couldn't bear to sell them or throw them away – so they had moved with her, and now they took up a large amount of space in her tiny new home.

It was around the time that Didi moved to Torquay that she began in earnest to try to recover her family's property in Nice that they had had to leave after the fall of France and that Didi's parents had been unable to reclaim after the war. During the war the tenant had paid them a very small rent. After the war she continued to live in the house but refused to pay any more than the rent she had agreed at the start of her tenancy. Jack and Mariquita tried to have her evicted but had no luck, mainly because they had no idea how to do it and because of Jack's inability to speak French very well. With all their children, except Francis, living abroad and so unable to help, they found it difficult to get through all the legalities involved and although Francis was nearby, getting the tenant evicted was not something that he felt competent to tackle. Over the years that followed, the family made efforts periodically to have the tenant in Nice evicted, always without success, and when she died in 1994 her daughter continued to live in the property, paying the same rent as her mother had done for a further two years. By 1996 she had decided not to pay at all.[4]

With Didi turning her attention to the problem, letters from her sister-in-law, Thérèse, and the French lawyer in Grenoble were copied, translated by Didi and sent to her niece Odile, so that she could also sign the relevant papers to have the tenant evicted and they could repossess the house, which they intended to sell. Month after month letters flew backwards and forwards between France, England and Italy, where Odile lived with her Italian husband, Enore, and their sons, Silvio, Fabio and Giulio. At one point, when it seemed that a stalemate had again been reached, Didi wrote to Odile to tell her that she was thinking of moving back to France to live in the house herself. But despite all the efforts that were made to evict the woman and reclaim the house, they didn't manage to achieve anything, and Didi became very tired with the whole situation and decided to put it on hold for a while and 'go back to business'. To this day Odile, the only member of the Nearne family left, is still fighting to get back the house her family loved.

The 'business' to which Didi referred was her self-appointed role as fundraiser for a local charity, Animals in Distress. She was particularly busy with this work in the summer, when she spent every day walking along the beaches collecting from holiday makers. Sometimes, although it was not strictly legal, she would also visit the town's pubs during the evening and collect from people having a drink or something to eat. She never worried about going into a bar by herself or asking for donations for the animals and, as her friend Jenny said, this was not the behaviour of a sad recluse. She liked people and loved animals, and collecting was a way of making herself useful to a cause she believed to be worthwhile.

In 1993 Didi bravely agreed to return to Ravensbrück to attend a ceremony in which a plaque was unveiled and dedicated to the memory of those who had not survived their incarceration in the camp. The trip had been arranged by the then SOE adviser at the Foreign and Commonwealth Office, Gervase Cowell, in conjunction with the British Embassy in Berlin and the Ravensbrück Museum, and the party that made the journey included Vera Atkins, code master Leo Marks, agents Francis Cammaerts and Brian Stonehouse, Lilian Rolfe's sister Helen, Violette Szabo's daughter Tania, John de Cunha, who had been a prosecutor at the Nuremberg war crimes trials after the war, representatives from the FANY and the WAAF (now the WRAF), and several members of the French Resistance. Also attending the ceremony was Odette Hallowes, formerly Sansom (she and her husband, Roy Sansom, were divorced after the war and, in 1947, Odette married Peter Churchill, the leader of the Spindle circuit; they too were divorced and, in 1956, she married Geoffrey Hallowes). On the morning of 10 June 1993 Odette, Yvonne Baseden and Didi, the only SOE survivors of the camp, unveiled the plaque. Didi wore a white suit with a red blouse, and her MBE and the Croix de Guerre pinned to her jacket. She was photographed standing next to Odette Hallowes, whose many awards weighed down the front of her outfit.

At the beginning of 1994 Didi's beloved dog Bobby died. It was a huge blow to her. Vera Atkins, sensitive to how Didi would be feeling, sent her a letter saying, 'I know how much you miss Bobby, your friend and companion and am so sorry that the poor fellow died relatively young – at least he seemed youthful.' Didi had certainly benefited from all the exercise she had enjoyed with Bobby. She was still extremely fit, and when she wrote to Odile she commented that she had recently had a check-up and that her doctor had declared her to be in A1 condition.

At regular intervals Odile and her family came over to England and spent time with Didi. They usually stayed in a hotel, as Didi's flat was so small. In fact, although they visited her at Lisburne Crescent, they never actually went inside the flat; Didi always waited for them outside the building, and they would fetch her in their hired car and make day trips to all the sights in the Torquay area and beyond. Odile was very fond of her aunt and had really enjoyed getting to know her properly as an adult after the difficulties that Didi had suffered when Odile was a child. One holiday in particular still stands out in her memory. That year Didi advised Odile to rent a flat, 'which she found for us at Babbacombe, overlooking the gardens and the sea. We had a super time that year, for we used to eat at home and then go on outings together, and then come back to eat at home in the evenings, just like a little family.'

Didi liked Odile's husband, Enore, very much, although they could only speak to each other with Odile's help, as he spoke very few words of English. They enjoyed sharing a bottle of wine, however, and after one of the family's visits

Didi decided it was time to learn Italian, so at the age of 73 she bought herself a cassette player and an Italian Linguaphone course so that she would be to able to speak to Enore properly the next time they were together.

Odile came to regard Didi as a second mother and was particularly grateful to her for the help she gave her when she decided to become a Roman Catholic. Didi herself still attended church each week, although she distanced herself from church-related social events. When she had a fall in the town and broke her wrist, she asked to be taken to the church and a Sister Damian accompanied her to hospital, but when Didi heard that she was trying to find out her name and other personal details from the hospital staff she was annoyed because, although Sister Damian was only trying to help, Didi regarded it as prying. As far as she was concerned her relationship was with God, not the congregation, and only God needed to know anything about her. She felt that she could no longer attend that church, so began going to services at another Roman Catholic church in the town. Her religion was still very important to her and she passed on many things to help Odile:

She left me all her prayer books and many religious pamphlets which have helped me tremendously. There were even little booklets on how to say the Rosary. She must have bought them specially for me.

Didi loved going on pilgrimages too. She went to Chartres, Knock, Fatima, Lourdes, Banneaux, Lough Derg (St Patrick's Purgatory), and of course Medjugorje to which she was very close.

She was very witty and charming to be with, at the same time she was wise and a deep thinker. I used to love looking into her eyes, which were full of compassion and kindness. Being a devout Roman Catholic she talked about her faith a great deal, especially about Medjugorje and any miracles that had taken place. We used to listen to the messages together. I can truly say that she guided me in my religious faith.[5]

As time went by many of the people whom Didi had known from her SOE days died. She had always believed that she would live to a great age and, having been one of the younger agents herself, it was inevitable that she would eventually lose many friends from those days. However, apart from those who had perished during the war, many of the other members of the SOE had long lives too, despite their wartime activities.

Jacqueline's boss, Maurice Southgate, chief of the Stationer circuit, had managed to avoid a mass execution of agents in Buchenwald in September 1944 and, although physically and psychologically weak, had remained in the camp until it was liberated by the Americans in April 1945. He was well enough to give evidence at the war crimes trials in 1947 but he never fully recovered his pre-SOE health. He was awarded a DSO, and when his health had improved enough for him to return to work he resumed his former occupation of furniture designer and manufacturer. He died in France in March 1990 at the age of 77.[6] Maurice Buckmaster died on 17 April 1992 aged 90[7] and Vera Atkins followed him on 24 June 2000 aged 92.[8]

By 1998 Didi had already begun to consider her own mortality. Although she was still cheerful and busy, and had been joined at her flat by a new companion, a stray ginger cat she called Whisky,[9] she spoke to Odile about what she wanted to happen after her death, telling her that she wanted to be cremated and have her ashes scattered at sea. While she was still alive she didn't want anyone to know what she had done during the war and made her niece promise that she would tell no one, saying that if she did talk about it, Odile would not see her again, as she would simply disappear.

Was she a secret agent to the last or had she simply had enough of being asked what she had done in the war, a time that she would much rather have forgotten? It is an interesting question. Being a prisoner had taught Didi what counted most in life. She was her own person, kind, funny, perhaps slightly eccentric, but a devoted sister and aunt, a loyal friend, a devout Catholic and a tireless charity worker. For her these were the things that were important – much more important than anything that had gone before.

Epilogue

After Didi's death the unearthing of the documents, medals and old French banknotes in the tiny flat in Torquay, and the subsequent discovery of the role that Didi had played for the SOE during the war, led to a change of plans for her funeral. It was no longer sufficient to have a quiet, anonymous ceremony; the people of Torquay felt that they had lost a heroine they had not known was living amongst them and, although they no longer had the chance to speak to her, they wanted to ensure that her passing was marked in an appropriate way.

On 21 September 2010 a Requiem Mass was held at the Church of Our Lady Help of Christians and St Denis in St Marychurch, Torquay. Hundreds of people lined the streets to watch as the cortège made its way to the church, led by two Scottish pipers. The coffin, draped in British and French flags, was carried into the church while members of the local British Legion lowered their own flags.

The church was full and there were television cameras filming the whole event. The film would be shown on the news bulletins later that day. The priest who conducted the Mass, Father Shaddock, spoke of Didi as being 'a humble, brave and quiet lady'. The chairman of the Special Forces

Club, Adrian Stones, delivered a eulogy. His closing words were: 'I believe Eileen's modest heroism was an inspiration to those around her in 1944. That heroism has remained an inspiration down the years. Her photograph hangs in a very special place in the club. It will stay there.'[1]

Then the congregation heard Odile talk about her aunt: 'She had a very strong character and was determined in her patriotic views. It is because of people like her that we can live peacefully today and have a good life. She was polite. She never wanted to speak about what she had done in the war. In fact, she did not want to be famous. People like her just want to forget and not relive their suffering.'[2]

As Didi's coffin was carried from the church, buglers from Britain and France played the Last Post while French Consul General Edouard Braine told reporters, 'Personally I owe her the freedom of my country ... all my compatriots think the same way.'[3]

Some days later, following Didi's cremation, Odile and her family were taken out to sea in a Royal Navy boat, followed by French Marines. After a short ceremony conducted by a Roman Catholic priest, Odile scattered her aunt's ashes on the sea she had loved, just as Didi had requested.

One of the papers found in Didi's flat after her death is what appears to be a draft of an unfinished letter. Written in English and dated 25 October 1999, it is addressed to a man she simply calls 'Sir'. From the contents it seems that she was annoyed at the number of people who kept contacting her to talk about her time in the SOE. The English is somewhat disjointed, giving the impression that Didi was exasperated, and the last words that she had written were, 'Can you continue please not to give my address and phone number to anyone else who have access to the book.'⁴ She doesn't say to which book she was referring, but the letter seems to show that she was being hounded by this person and that she had reached the end of her tether.

When one morning in September 2010 I listened to a radio news bulletin about the death of Didi, I heard the newsreader say that no one had ever known what Eileen Nearne had done during the war, as she had never spoken about her role with the SOE. I knew that statement was untrue, as she had spoken about her undercover work to a handful of people, and I was lucky enough to have been one of them.

I had contacted her in 2001 to ask for help concerning a book I was writing about SOE agent Violette Szabo, as I knew that they had known each other and had been incarcerated in Ravensbrück concentration camp together for a short while. Having had no idea that Didi was so upset at being pursued, when I contacted her my only worry was that I might stir up memories that she would rather have forgotten. Had I known about her annoyance at being constantly contacted I would never have called her. When she spoke to me, however, she gave no hint of being irritated or upset. I found her to be a delightful lady, friendly, polite, very helpful and patient in answering my questions.

I hope that she spoke to me because she felt she could trust me. She told me that she didn't want her contact details to be given to anyone else and I assured her that I wouldn't dream of passing them on without first seeking her permission. With the protection of her anonymity in mind, she made one more condition. If I wanted to mention her in my book, or quote anything she had told me, I would have to give her another name. I, of course, agreed to this condition and we settled on the name Hélène. Our conversation continued long after she had finished telling me about Violette Szabo, and she began to talk about her own experiences at the hands of the Nazis and as an inmate of a concentration camp. Although many of the details that she told me were harrowing, I felt very privileged to be speaking to such a brave lady. I knew then that it would be wonderful to be able to write a book about her life but had no intention of breaking my promise to her.

I didn't tell anyone who Hélène was until after her death. By then her name was becoming very well known and several newspaper reports about her were giving incorrect details about what she and her sister had done during and after the Second World War. Apart from wishing to set the record straight, I felt it was tragic that, because of the modesty of Didi and Jacqueline Nearne, their sacrifices, courage and heroic deeds would not be remembered. I was therefore delighted when I discovered that their niece Odile believed, as I did, that their stories should be told. Thanks to her invaluable help and support, I was able to tell them. I hope that with this book the true story of these two exceptionally brave sisters will not be forgotten.

Notes

All information about Eileen (Didi) and Jacqueline Nearne that has not been attributed in the following notes came from their niece, Odile Nearne, or from conversations between the author and Eileen Nearne.

Prologue
1. ITV news film following the death of Eileen Nearne.
2. Email from Iain Douglas to the author in reply to a request for information, 16 January 2012.
3. Reported in the *Guardian*, 13 September 2010.
4. BBC News interview, 14 September 2010.

Chapter 1: Exile
1. John and Mariquita Nearne's marriage certificate.
2. Information about the children's grandmother from Odile Nearne.
3. Information from Jenny Campbell-Davys.
4. French newspaper *Boulogne*, date unknown, but after the death of Jacqueline Nearne in 1982.
5. Francis Nearne's personal file, HS9/1089/3.
6. Information from Odile Nearne.
7. Ibid.
8. Francis disclosed in his personal file, HS9/1089/3, that his father was known as Jack.

9. RAF records for Aircraftman 2nd Class Frederick John Nearne (1270875).
10. Information from Odile Nearne.
11. Jacqueline Nearne's records from the FANY.
12. Letter from Claire Wrench to Jacqueline Nearne, 16 November 1980.

Chapter 2: Secrets and Lies

1. Letter from Jimmie to Jacqueline Nearne, 27 June 1942.
2. Letter from Jimmie to Jacqueline Nearne, 17 August 1942.
3. Selwyn Jepson's personal file, HS9/796.
4. Interview at the Imperial War Museum, 1986.
5. STS 54, which came under the Signals Section of the SOE, had two locations: Fawley Court, Henley-on-Thames, Oxfordshire, and Belhaven School, Dunbar, in East Lothian, Scotland. Didi's personal file does not say at which of these two schools she received her wireless training.
6. Since Didi was believed to have worked in Oxfordshire, this was likely to have been at the radio listening and transmission station of Poundon House near Bicester, Oxfordshire, although her personal file does not give details of the actual location.
7. According to Patrick Yarnold, on p.70 of his book *Wanborough Manor: School for Secret Agents*, the ladies of Party 27.OB 'were sent direct to the finishing course at Beaulieu ... [and] did not pass through Wanborough'. Wanborough Manor was one of the preliminary training centres for recruits to the SOE.
8. Reported in Foot, *SOE in France*.
9. Reported in Escott, *The Heroines of SOE*.
10. Jacqueline Nearne's personal file, HS9/1089/4

Chapter 3: A Shaky Start

1. Noreen Riols, who worked for the SOE, in conversation with the author, 27 June 2012.
2. Aonghais Fyffe, Security Liaison Officer, Special Training Schools, Scotland, reporting what he had been told by

various people who knew Buckmaster, in conversation with
the author on 11 June 2001.

3. Helm, *A Life in Secrets*, p.40.
4. Vera Atkins's personal file, HS9/59/2.
5. Jacqueline Nearne's personal file, HS9/1089/4.
6. Buckmaster, *Specially Employed*.
7. Ibid., and photo of Jacqueline's fake ID card.
8. Yvonne Rudellat's personal file, HS9/1289/7.
9. www.paradeantiques.co.uk.
10. Jacqueline Nearne's personal file, HS9/1089/4.
11. Ibid.
12. Maurice Southgate's personal file, HS9/1395/3.

Chapter 4: Escape

1. Maurice Southgate's personal file, HS9/1395/3.
2. Text of a broadcast made after the war for the French
    Service of the BBC World Service.
3. Maurice Southgate's personal file, HS9/1395/3.
4. Jacqueline Nearne's personal file, HS9/1089/4.
5. The money that came to Francis via the Swiss consulate in
    Lyons is documented in his personal file at the National
    Archives. Although there is no explanation of the origin of
    the funds, they may have been from Swiss banks that held
    accounts for his parents or maternal grandparents who had
    given him a small allowance.
6. Francis Nearne's personal file, HS9/1089/3.
7. Ibid.
8. Ibid.

Chapter 5: Broken Promises

1. According to Yarnold, op. cit., p.70, the ladies of Party
    27.OB 'were sent direct to the finishing course at Beaulieu ...
    [and] did not pass through Wanborough'. Wanborough
    Manor was one of the preliminary training centres for
    recruits to the SOE but not all prospective agents had any
    preliminary training; Didi's personal file does not give details
    of any preliminary training at all. There is no reference in

her personal file either to Didi receiving the paramilitary training, which was conducted at several schools in Inverness-shire, the main one used by F Section being Arisaig. Although by this stage in the war many of the women agents had done this training, it is possible that wireless operators did not do it. Shrabani Basu in her book *Spy Princess*, about the life of Noor Inayat Khan, also an SOE wireless operator, says, 'There is no evidence from Noor's training files that she went to Arisaig. As a radio operator, it was probably thought better to concentrate her training in her specialized field.'

2. Recounted in Cunningham, *Beaulieu: The Finishing School for Secret Agents*, p.66.

Chapter 6: Betrayal

1. Jean Overton-Fuller, *The German Penetration of SOE*, p.111.
2. Foot, op. cit., pp.300–2; Helm, op. cit., p.50.
3. Nicholas, *Death Be Not Proud*, pp.126–7; Foot, op. cit., p.296.
4. Francis Nearne's personal file, HS9/1089/3.
5. Ibid.
6. Conversation on 26 June 2012 between the author and Noreen Riols, who worked at SOE HQ and at the finishing schools in Beaulieu, and who knew Buckmaster.
7. Francis Nearne's personal file, HS9/1089/3.
8. Ibid.

Chapter 7: Buckmaster Passes the Buck

1. http://france.usembassy.gov/whm2.html; http://www.parisvoice.com.
2. Ibid.
3. Maurice Southgate's personal file, HS9/1395/3.
4. McCue, *Behind Enemy Lines with the SAS*, p.70.
5. Maurice Southgate's personal file, HS9/1395/3.
6. Copy of note to Jepson from Atkins on Francis Nearne's personal file, HS9/1089/3.

Chapter 8: Coming Home

1. Eileen Nearne's personal file, HS9/1089/2.

Chapter 9: Monumental Errors

1. Marks, *Between Silk and Cyanide*, p.399; Basu, op. cit., p.199.
2. Various sources including Marks, op. cit., Basu, op. cit. and Helm, op. cit.
3. Maurice Southgate's personal file, HS9/1395/3.
4. Ibid.

Chapter 10: An Uncomfortable Journey

1. Jones, *A Quiet Courage*, p.233.
2. BBC Radio Devon report, 21 September 2010.

Chapter 11: The Deadly Discovery

1. Dufour was the agent with whom Violette Szabo was travelling when they came across German troops and a firefight ensued. While Szabo kept shooting, Dufour was able to escape.
2. Maurice Southgate's personal file, HS9/1395/3.
3. Ibid.
4. Ibid.
5. Pierre Mattei's citation for MiD, WO/373/102.
6. Maurice Southgate's personal file, HS9/1395/3.
7. www.metpolicehistory.co.uk.

Chapter 12: A Bad Decision

1. Maurice Southgate's personal file, HS9/1395/3.
2. Ibid.
3. Jacqueline Nearne's personal file, HS9/1089/4.
4. See Nicholas, op. cit., p.272, and Ottaway, *Violette Szabo*, p.156.

Chapter 13: A Brilliant Actress

1. Eileen Nearne, speaking as *Rose*, in a television interview in 1997.

2. Evidence of Mme Dubois, which was passed on to Jean Savy and is recounted in Eileen Nearne's personal file, HS9/1089/2.
3. Conversation between Eileen Nearne and the author in 2001.
4. Ibid.
5. Ibid.

Chapter 14: Torture

1. Jacqueline Nearne's personal file, HS9/1089/4.
2. Ibid.
3. Conversation between Eileen Nearne and the author in 2001.
4. Jones, op. cit., p.280.
5. Conversation between Eileen Nearne and the author in 2001.
6. Eileen Nearne's personal file, HS9/1089/2, and Circuit and mission reports and interrogations, HS6/576.
7. Eileen Nearne, speaking as *Rose*, in a television interview, 1997.

Chapter 15: Didi Vanishes

1. Maurice Southgate's personal file, HS9/1395/3.
2. Ibid.
3. Ibid.
4. Ibid.
5. Ibid.
6. Despite a post-war MI5 investigation into Starr's behaviour, it was decided that no grounds existed for his prosecution. His story, and a justification for his strange behaviour in the hands of the Germans, were given in Jean Overton Fuller's book, *The Starr Affair*.
7. Francis Nearne's personal file, HS9/1089/3.
8. Ibid.
9. Ibid.
10. Ibid.
11. Details of the transportation of the French prisoners from Fresnes on 15 August 1944 taken from a conversation with

Eileen Nearne and an account by Monique Corblet de
Fallerans, née Level, in her book *Voyage nocturne au bout
du parc.*

Chapter 16: The End of the Line

1. Maurice Southgate's personal file, HS9/1395/3.
2. Cecile Pearl Witherington's personal file, HS/9/355/2.
3. It has been said that Pearl Witherington pushed for
   Jacqueline's return to England so that she could take over
   her role on D-Day. In Maurice Southgate's personal file,
   HS9/1395/3, there is a record of a message that he sent for
   Jacqueline soon after she had arrived in London in which he
   wished her well and said, 'Tell her also that *Marie* [Pearl
   Witherington] will take over the Maquis on D-Day. If
   Jacqueline wants to do the same, let her think of her
   uniform.' This perhaps suggests that the rumour may have
   had some basis in fact.
4. Francis Nearne's personal file, HS9/1089/3.
5. Ibid.
6. Ibid.

Chapter 17: Lost Opportunity

1. Tillion, *Ravensbrück*, pp.238–9.
2. Anthonioz, *God Remained Outside*, p.34.
3. Morrison, *Ravensbrück*, pp.24–5, and Tillion, op. cit., p.69.
4. After she left Ravensbrück in 1943 Grese was sent to
   Auschwitz and ended her career in 1945 at Belsen
   concentration camp, where she was known as both the
   'Bitch' and the 'Beast' of Belsen. Details of atrocities
   committed by her were found in the transcripts of
   the Belsen War Crimes trials, which took place in
   Lüneburg, Germany, between 17 September and 17
   November 1945.
5. Tillion, op. cit., pp.68–9.
6. Eileen Nearne in conversation with the author, 2001.
7. Professor M. R. D. Foot disputed the location of this
   particular camp, claiming it was Königsberg on the river

Oder. However, Marie Lecomte, who was a prisoner in Königsberg with the 'little paratroopers', says it was in eastern Prussia and it has been confirmed in Morrison, op. cit., p.209, that there was a camp at Königsberg in the eastern Baltic (eastern Prussia) where women prisoners worked on airstrips.

8. Eileen Nearne in conversation with the author, 2001.

Chapter 18: The Getaway

1. Stessel, *Snow Flowers*, p.28.
2. Official records of prisoner movements. Table shown in Stessel, op. cit., p.39.
3. Eileen Nearne in conversation with the author, 2001.
4. Stessel, op. cit., p.211.
5. Ibid.
6. Stessel, op. cit., p.212.
7. Stessel, op. cit., p.214.
8. Eileen Nearne in conversation with the author, 2001.
9. Corblet de Fallerans, op. cit.
10. In a document obtained by the author from the National Archives in 2001 (HS6/576 Circuit and mission reports and interrogations) and dated 15 May 1945, Didi mentioned having met Suzanne at Torgau. She also gave the name and full address of Yvette Landais. This document was added to Didi's personal file when it was released after her death but the names of the two French girls had been removed. Didi's friendship with Mlle Landais was confirmed to the author in 2012 by Pierre Landais, Yvette's brother. M. Landais named Monique Level as a friend of both his sister and Didi, and says that Yvette told him that Monique escaped from the Germans during the march from which she and Didi also escaped. He also told the author that Yvette knew Didi by the name of Jacqueline du Tertre.
11. Information received by the author from Pierre Landais about his sister Yvette.

Chapter 19: A Narrow Escape

1. Letter from Pierre Landais to the author, July 2012.
2. Ibid.
3. Corblet de Fallerans, op. cit.
4. Ibid.
5. Ibid.
6. Letter from Pierre Landais to the author, July 2012.
7. Eileen Nearne's personal file, HS9/1089/2.
8. Ibid.
9. Ibid.
10. Ibid.

Chapter 20: Allies or Enemies

1. Mercer (ed.), *Chronicle of the Second World War*, p.622.
2. Eisenhower, *Crusade in Europe*, p.446.
3. Eileen Nearne's personal file, HS9/1089/2.
4. Corblet de Fallerans, op. cit.
5. Ibid.
6. Eileen Nearne's personal file, HS9/1089/2.
7. Ibid.
8. Letter from Major Rollo Young to the author, 14 May 2012.
9. Eileen Nearne's personal file, HS9/1089/2.
10. Ibid.

Chapter 21: Thoughtless Demands

1. Judex Mission records, HS7/134.
2. Ibid.
3. Ibid.
4. M. Nerault died in Buchenwald in March 1945. Colette and her mother were sent to Ravensbrück, where Mme Nerault died in late 1944. Colette was rescued by the Red Army at the end of April 1945 and put in the care of the Swedish Red Cross. She returned to France, and her young brother, Jean, in the summer of 1945. McCue, op. cit.
5. Judex Mission records, HS7/134.
6. Ibid.
7. Ibid.

8. Cutting from the *News Chronicle* found in Eileen Nearne's personal file, HS9/1089/2.
9. Copy of a letter from Paulette to Didi that was sent to the author by Odile Nearne.
10. Eileen Nearne's personal file, HS9/1089/2.
11. Helm, op. cit., p.358.
12. Jacqueline Nearne's personal file, HS9/1089/4.
13. Eileen Nearne's personal file, HS9/1089/2.
14. Dame Irene Ward, in Helm, op. cit., p.365.
15. Aonghais Fyffe in conversation with the author, 2001.
16. Helm, op. cit.

Chapter 22: Adventures, Problems and Losses

1. Records of the Ministry of Pensions, PIN93/2.
2. Jacqueline Nearne's records from the FANY.
3. www.aviewoncities.com/nyc/unitednations.htm.
4. Shipping records at www.ancestry.com.
5. Records of the Ministry of Pensions, PIN93/2.
6. Ibid.
7. Ibid.
8. Letter to Jacqueline from her friend Odile.
9. Records of the Ministry of Pensions, PIN93/2.
10. Records of the Protocol and Liaison department at the United Nations archive in New York.
11. Ibid.
12. Jacqueline Nearne, quoted by Charles Lanius in *Woman's Day* magazine, January 1947.
13. Memo to all liaison officers from the UN Chief of Protocol, Captain Johan de Noue, in the records of the Protocol and Liaison department at the United Nations archive in New York, 1946.
14. Brian Stonehouse's obituary, *Independent*, 20 January 1999.
15. Letter from Freddy (surname unknown), found in Eileen Nearne's flat after her death.
16. Records of the Ministry of Pensions, PIN93/2. file PIN93/2.
17. Letter from Jack Nearne to Didi.
18. Records of the Ministry of Pensions, PIN93/2.

19. Conversation between Jenny Campbell-Davys and the author.
20. Letter from Jacqueline to Didi, a copy of which was sent to the author by Odile Nearne.

Chapter 23: The Ultimate Secret Agent

1. Copy of the eulogy sent to the author by Odile Nearne, who also supplied copies of all other material quoted in this chapter that is not otherwise attributed.
2. Obituary in *The Times*, 14 April 2004.
3. Conversation between Jenny Campbell-Davys and the author.
4. Information from Odile Nearne.
5. Information from Odile Nearne.
6. www.nigelperrin.com/mauricesouthgate.htm.
7. Obituary in *The Times*, 20 April 1992.
8. Obituary in the *Guardian*, 6 July 2000.
9. Details on a postcard sent by Eileen Nearne to her niece, Odile.

Epilogue

1. Eulogy given by Adrian Stone and shown on the website of the Special Forces Club at the time of the funeral. Some of his words were also quoted in various newspaper articles.
2. Odile Nearne's address at Eileen Nearne's funeral, reported on BBC News.
3. BBC television news report on 22 September 2010.
4. Copy of a letter discovered after Eileen Nearne's death and sent to the author by Odile Nearne.

Bibliography

Anderson, Murray, *Saint Praftu*, Grosvenor House Publishing
    Limited, 2009
Anthonioz, Geneviève de Gaulle, *God Remained Outside*,
    Souvenir Press, 1998
Aubrac, Lucie, *Outwitting the Gestapo*, University of Nebraska
    Press, 1993
Bailey, Robin, *Forgotten Voices of the Secret War*, Ebury Press,
    2009
Basu, Shrabani, *Spy Princess*, The History Press, 2008
Binney, Marcus, *The Women Who Lived for Danger*, Hodder &
    Stoughton, 2002
Buckmaster, Maurice, *Specially Employed*, The Batchworth Press,
    1952
—, *They Fought Alone*, Odhams Press Limited, 1958
Bull, Dr Stephen (Introduction), *The Secret Agent's Pocket
    Manual*, Conway, 2009
Burney, Christopher, *Solitary Confinement* and *The Dungeon
    Democracy*, Macmillan, 1984
Clark, Freddie, *Agents by Moonlight*, Tempus, 1999
Cookridge, E. H., *Inside S.O.E.*, Arthur Barker Limited, 1966
Corblet de Fallerans, Monique, *Voyage nocturne au bout du
    parc*, Editions Heimdal, 1992
Crowdy, Terry, *SOE Agent: Churchill's Secret Warriors*, Osprey
    Publishing, 2008
Cunningham, Cyril, *Beaulieu: The Finishing School for Secret
    Agents*, Leo Cooper, 1998

Eisenhower, General Dwight D., *Crusade in Europe*, William Heinemann Ltd, 1948

Escott, Squadron Leader Beryl E., *The Heroines of SOE*, The History Press, 2011

Foot, M. R. D., *SOE in France*, HMSO, 1966

Fuller, Jean Overton, *The Starr Affair*, Gollancz, 1954

—, *The German Penetration of SOE*, William Kimber, 1975

Gleeson, James, *They Feared No Evil*, Corgi Books, 1978

Helm, Sarah, *A Life in Secrets*, Abacus, 2005

Hudson, Sydney, *Undercover Operator*, Leo Cooper, 2003

Humbert, Agnes, *Resistance: Memoirs of Occupied France*, Bloomsbury, 2008

Jones, Liane, *A Quiet Courage*, Bantam Press, 1990

Mackenzie, William, *The Secret History of S.O.E.*, St Ermin's Press, 2002

McCue, Paul, *Behind Enemy Lines with the SAS*, Pen & Sword Military, 2007

Marks, Leo, *Between Silk and Cyanide*, HarperCollins, 1998

Marrus, Michael R., and Robert O. Paxton, *Vichy France and the Jews*, Schocken Books, 1983

Maurel, Micheline, *Ravensbrück* (translated by Margaret S. Summers), Anthony Blond, 1959

Mercer, Derrik (ed.), *Chronicle of the Second World War*, Chronicle Communications Ltd & Longman Group UK Ltd, 1990

Miller, Russell, *Behind the Lines*, Secker & Warburg, 2002

Morrison, Jack G., *Ravensbrück: Everyday Life in a Women's Concentration Camp 1939–45*, Markus Wiener Publishers, 2000

Nicholas, Elizabeth, *Death Be Not Proud*, Cresset Press, 1958

Oliver, David, *Airborne Espionage*, Sutton Publishing, 2005

Ottaway, Susan, *Violette Szabo: The Life That I Have*, Leo Cooper, 2002

Rigden, Denis (Introduction), *SOE Syllabus*, Public Record Office, nd

Schoenbrun, David, *Maquis: Soldiers of the Night*, Robert Hale, 1980

Stessel, Zahava Szász, *Snow Flowers*, Farleigh Dickinson University Press, 2009

Tickell, Jerrard, *Odette*, Pan, 1976

Tillion, Germaine, *Ravensbrück*, Anchor Books, 1975

West, Nigel, *Secret War: The Story of SOE*, Hodder & Stoughton, 1992

Wilkinson, Peter, and Joan Bright Astley, *Gubbins & SOE*, Leo Cooper, 1997

Yarnold, Patrick, *Wanborough Manor: School for Secret Agents*, Hopfield Publications, 2009

Index